Institutional Incentives
and Sustainable Development

Theoretical Lenses on Public Policy

Series Editor, Paul A. Sabatier

Institutional Incentives and Sustainable Development:
Infrastructure Policies in Perspective,
Elinor Ostrom, Larry Schroeder, and Susan Wynne

FORTHCOMING

Policy Change and Learning: An Advocacy Coalition Approach,
Paul A. Sabatier and Hank Jenkins-Smith

Government, Business, and American Politics,
Richard A. Harris and Jay A. Sigler

Institutional Incentives and Sustainable Development

Infrastructure Policies in Perspective

Elinor Ostrom
Workshop in Political Theory and Policy Analysis
Indiana University, Bloomington

Larry Schroeder
Metropolitan Studies Program
Syracuse University

Susan Wynne
Workshop in Political Theory and Policy Analysis
Indiana University, Bloomington

Westview Press
BOULDER • SAN FRANCISCO • OXFORD

Theoretical Lenses on Public Policy

Copyright © 1993 by Westview Press, Inc.

Published in 1993 in the United States of America by Westview Press, Inc., 5500 Central Avenue, Boulder, Colorado 80301-2877, and in the United Kingdom by Westview Press, 36 Lonsdale Road, Summertown, Oxford OX2 7EW

Library of Congress Cataloging-in-Publication Data
Ostrom, Elinor.
 Institutional incentives and sustainable development : Infrastructure policies in perspective / Elinor Ostrom, Larry Schroeder, Susan Wynne.
  p. cm. — (Theoretical lenses on public policy)
 Includes bibliographical references and index.
  ISBN 0-8133-1618-9 (alk. paper). — ISBN 0-8133-1619-7 (pbk. : alk. paper)
  1. Infrastructure (Economics)—Developing countries.
2. Sustainable development—Developing countries. I. Schroeder, Larry D. II. Wynne, Susan G. III Title. IV. Series.
HC59.72.C3085 1993
338.9'009172'4—dc20
                                                                        92-42521
                                                                        CIP

Printed and bound in the United States of America

10 9 8 7 6 5 4 3 2 1

To Our Parents
for nurturing a spirit of inquiry in each of us

Leah Hopkins Awan and Adrian Awan
Freda Volk Schroeder and Carl Schroeder
Geraldine Hunt Wynne and Hal C. Wynne, Jr.

Contents

List of Illustrations   xiii
Preface   xv
Acknowledgments   xvii
Introduction, Paul A. Sabatier, Series Editor   xix

1   **The Role of Infrastructure in Development**   1

Postwar Development Initiatives, 2
   Foreign Assistance Strategies, 3
   The Role of Social Infrastructure, 6
An Institutional Approach to Explaining
      Development Outcomes, 8
The Importance of Physical Infrastructure, 10
What Do We Mean by Infrastructure Sustainability? 13
   A Definition, 13
   Evaluative Criteria, 16
An Overview of Our Approach, 18
Conclusion, 21
Notes, 22

2   **The Problem of Sustainable Infrastructure**   25

Infrastructure Maintenance and Its Finance, 25
Phases of Infrastructure Development, 29
   Design, 29
   Finance, 32
   Construction, 32
   Operation and Maintenance, 33
   Use, 33
Factors Influencing Maintenance Decisions of a
      Single Owner-User of Private Capital, 34
Conclusion, 40
Notes, 41

3   **Individuals, Incentives, and Transaction Costs**   43

Assumptions About the Individual, 44
Problems of Contractual Uncertainty and
     Transaction Costs, 46
Information Asymmetries as Sources of
     Contractual Uncertainty, 49
   Time and Place Information and Scientific
        Knowledge, 49
   Other Types of Information Asymmetries, 55
Kinship Networks as Counteracting Institutions, 62
Nepotism and Corruption, 65
Conclusion, 68
Notes, 71

4   **Provision and Production of Rural Infrastructure**   73

Distinction Between Provision and Production, 74
Attributes of Rural Infrastructure Primarily
     Affecting Provision, 76
   Nonexcludability and the Free-Rider Problem, 77
   Problems of Joint Use, 84
   Problems of Measurement, 90
   Problems of Rent Seeking, 96
Attributes of Rural Infrastructure Primarily
     Affecting Production, 97
   Economies of Scale, 97
   Asset Specificity, 102
   Rate of Deterioration, 103
   Public-Private Industry Structure, 104
Conclusion, 105
Notes, 108

5   **Evaluating Institutional Performance**   111

Overall Performance Criteria, 112
   Economic Efficiency, 112
   Equity, 113
   Accountability, 115
   Adaptability, 116
   Trade-offs Among Criteria, 116

Intermediate Performance Criteria, 118
    Costs of Provision, 119
    Costs of Production, 122
Conclusion, 124
Notes, 125

6   Analyzing Institutional Arrangements   127

Institutional Arrangements for Private Infrastructure
    Development, 128
    A Simple Market, 128
    A Differentiated Market for Infrastructure
        Development, 129
    Comparative Evaluation, 131
Institutional Arrangements for Public Infrastructure
    Development, 134
    User Groups, 134
    Comparative Performance, 135
Conclusion, 139
Notes, 139

7   Centralized Institutional Arrangements   141

Centralized Infrastructure Development, 142
    Anticipated Performance on the Production Side, 143
    Anticipated Performance on the Provision Side, 148
    Anticipated Overall Performance, 151
The Problem of Truncated Analyses, 154
The Role of Donor Agencies, 156
Conclusion, 159
Notes, 161

8   Decentralized Institutional Arrangements   163

Decentralization Efforts, 164
    The Evolving Meaning of Decentralization, 165
    Multiple Dimensions of Decentralization, 166
Does Administrative Decentralization Improve the
    Performance of Centralized National
        Governments? 168
Conclusion, 175
Notes, 175

9   Polycentric Institutional Arrangements   177

The Concept of Polycentricity, 178
    Economic Rationale for Polycentricity, 181
The Possibility of Polycentricity in Developing
        Countries, 184
    Sources of Polycentricity, 185
    Principles Versus Blueprints, 191
Some Common Concerns About Polycentric
        Arrangements, 192
    Governance Issues, 193
    Finance Issues, 202
Privatization as a Form of Decentralization, 206
    Public Concessions as a Buttress for Centralization, 207
    Monopolies Versus Competitive Markets, 208
    Privatization Is Not a Panacea, 208
Conclusion, 209
Notes, 210

10   Implications of an Institutional Approach to   213
        Sustainable Development

The Proposed Analytical Approach, 215
General Policy Implications of Our Approach, 218
Immediate Policy Implications of Our Approach, 223
    Sustaining Small-scale Infrastructure, 224
    Sustaining Large-scale Infrastructure, 227
Conclusion, 230
Notes, 231

References   235
About the Book and Authors   256
Index   257

Illustrations

Tables

5.1   Criteria to Be Used in Judging the Comparative
      Performance of Alternative Institutional
      Arrangements   124

6.1   Comparative Performance of Institutional Arrangements
      Related to the Provision and Production of a
      Private Infrastructure   133
6.2   Comparative Performance of Institutional Arrangements
      Related to the Provision and Production of Small-scale
      Irrigation Systems   137

7.1   Performance of a Centralized National Government
      Bureau Related to the Construction and O&M of
      a Large-scale Irrigation System   144
7.2   A Truncated Analysis of Institutional Performance
      Related to the Design and Construction of
      Large-scale Infrastructure   155

Figures

5.1   Components of Information Costs   122

6.1   A Simple Market for Infrastructure Development   129
6.2   A Differentiated Market for Infrastructure Development 130
6.3   User Group Organization for Infrastructure Development 134

7.1   A Centralized National Government for Infrastructure
      Development   142

9.1   A Polycentric Arrangement for Infrastructure
      Development   179

Boxes

1.1   The Debt Burden of the Jamaica Feeder Roads Project   5
1.2   The Sustainability of World Bank Projects   15

2.1   The Recurrent Cost Problem   27
2.2   Recurrent Costs of Irrigation   30
2.3   Jamaica Rural Feeder Road Improvement Project   35

3.1   Hayek's Discussion of Time and Place Knowledge   51
3.2   An Experimental Irrigation System Rehabilitation
         Project in the Philippines   56
3.3   Using Primordial Ties to Reduce Transaction Costs   64
3.4   Banglung Suspended Bridges Project   69

4.1   The Importance of Being a Government (Rather Than
         a Voluntary Organization)   79
4.2   Self-Governing Philippine Irrigation Community   87
4.3   Ascertaining Willingness to Pay for Water   91
4.4   Malawi Village Water Supply Systems   99

7.1   The Mahaweli Development Program   152
7.2   The Capital-intensive Bias in Development Projects   158

8.1   The Bicol River Basin Development Program   171
8.2   The Provincial Development Assistance Program in
         the Philippines   173

9.1   Informal Judicial Authority in Peru   186
9.2   Chhattis Mauja: A Large-scale, Farmer-managed
         Irrigation System   188
9.3   Many Problems, Many Publics, but Not Enough
         Governments   199

Preface

As indicated by our subtitle, this volume addresses a practical, yet extremely complex, public policy issue confronting nearly all developing countries—the problem of insufficient maintenance of rural infrastructure facilities. Where maintenance is inadequate, public investments deteriorate long before their expected useful lives are completed. This premature deterioration in capital assets results in a further drain on the already scarce resources of low-income countries. Countries that choose to mine their stock of natural resources to cope with their financial crises threaten the survival of whole ecosystems and further reduce their own prospects of sustaining long-term economic development.

Although the subject of this book is a narrow one, the mode of analysis we develop here will be of interest to a broad group of persons engaged in the study of methods of public policy analysis. Drawing on heretofore poorly integrated literature from institutional economics, public finance economics, and institutional analysis, we demonstrate how important concepts from these fields can be woven together to produce a method for comparing alternative policy reform proposals. This method of analysis is based on the assumption that there are no perfect institutions and demonstrates the trade-offs that are necessarily involved when one moves from one type of institutional arrangement to another. This mode of analysis also reflects a broader view of the maintenance problem than is taken by many analysts. In an effort to explain successful and unsuccessful efforts to develop sustainable facilities, we consider the institutional arrangements within which rural infrastructure facilities are designed, financed, constructed, operated, maintained, and used. All of these arrangements, as they operate with regard to a specific type of facility in a particular physical and social environment, shape the incentives of individuals responsible for developing and maintaining that facility. In order to increase the likelihood that infrastructure investment will be sustained, institutional changes must be made to alter these incentives.

The bulk of the volume is devoted to developing our theoretical argument and illustrating a mode of analysis. We have also included descriptions of several infrastructure development efforts and brief summaries of important theoretical discussions, which are presented in the form of "boxes." The development efforts described in the boxes are not cases and do not represent a random sample of development efforts; rather, they are amplified examples purposefully chosen because they buttress our arguments and illustrate important conceptual ideas. We have, however, attempted to draw lessons from both successful and unsuccessful efforts throughout the developing world and from several rural infrastructure sectors. These examples illustrate centralized, decentralized, and polycentric institutional arrangements, some of which are firmly rooted in long-standing indigenous traditions of self-governance. Readers should realize that a one-to-two-page extract obviously cannot do justice to the complexity of any of these examples.

This book was written for both practitioners and students of development administration and economic development. It is appropriate for use in a variety of upper division and graduate university courses. Although the mode of analysis introduced in this book is applied to only one particularly difficult policy problem, we feel it is applicable to a wide variety of policy problems in urban as well as rural settings in developed as well as less developed countries. It is our hope that all those engaged in analyzing public policy problems, particularly those wrestling with the challenging task of developing and maintaining successful infrastructure investments, will find our work informative and helpful.

Elinor Ostrom
Larry Schroeder
Susan Wynne

Acknowledgments

During the preparation of this text, our efforts have been greatly assisted by many individuals who have taken the time to read the results of our work and to talk or correspond with us. Their helpful insights have proven invaluable during this long process.

We are particularly indebted to James Wunsch of Creighton University, who produced considerable background material that was especially useful in preparing our initial draft and who made valuable comments on all of our drafts. Others critiqued our work throughout the writing process and have provided us with insights that appear in this volume, often without sufficient attribution. Among those offering particularly useful assistance are Edwin Connerley, David Greytak, Kenneth Kornher, Jerry Miner, Ronald Oakerson, Vincent Ostrom, Louis Siegel, James Thomson, and Tjip Walker.

Another set of reviewers read a completed draft of this work and provided extensive, detailed comments on which we relied heavily in preparing the final draft. These helpful colleagues include Elizabeth Anderson, Robert Bish, Kenneth Davey, William Fox, Christine Glaser, Shiro Gnanaselvam, Goran Hyden, Timur Kuran, Edella Schlager, William Siffin, and Norman Uphoff. Paul A. Sabatier, our series editor, has given us extremely useful guidance throughout the revision process. Although these colleagues are likely to find that not all of their comments were ultimately incorporated into what we present here, they should know that their insights were considered and stimulated much thought. We certainly are indebted to them.

We also acknowledge the fine help of the support staffs at each of our institutions. Patty Dalecki at Indiana University's Workshop in Political Theory and Policy Analysis has suffered with us through all drafts and has painstakingly taken us all the way through the pageproofs of the book; she has literally typeset this volume and done all page layouts. Gayle Higgins and Angela Dortch at the Workshop and Esther Gray at the Metropolitan Studies Program at Syracuse University helped on earlier versions. Our collaborative efforts have also been facilitated by the School of Public and Environmental Affairs at Indiana University, which provided Larry Schroeder with a visiting professorship during the 1989–1990 academic year, allowing us to carry out one of the major drafting efforts in the same geographic location. Finally, the staff of Associates in Rural Development (ARD) was extremely helpful in overseeing production of an earlier report. The help of Project Manager Louis Siegel has been indispensable throughout the project. We were blessed by having the assistance of two able and dedicated editors: Sue Jaynes at an early juncture and Joan W. Sherman, who greatly improved the manuscript for this book. Any errors that remain in the volume despite the tremendous assistance provided by so many are our responsibility. Portions of several chapters have appeared as "Analyzing the Performance of Alternative Institutional Arrangements for Sustaining Rural Infrastructure in Developing Countries," *Journal of Public Administration Research and Theory* (3)1 (January 1993).

We also wish to thank Series Editor Paul Sabatier, and Project Editor Deborah Lynes and Acquisitions Editor Jennifer Knerr of Westview Press for all of their help and encouragement.

This research has been supported by the Decentralization: Finance and Management (DFM) Project that is sponsored by the Office of Rural and Institutional Development of the Bureau for Science and Technology (S&T/RD) of the U.S. Agency for International Development (USAID) under USAID contract number DHR-5446-Z-00-7033-00. The positions expressed are ours alone and do not represent the official views of the sponsoring agency.

EO

LS

SW

Introduction

Paul A. Sabatier, Series Editor

The field of policy studies—at least for political scientists—is currently in disarray. Much of the problem can be attributed to the absence of a limited set of clearly articulated theoretical lenses through which policy scholars view their field (Sabatier 1991). True, the subfield in policy evaluation shares a framework grounded in welfare economics and benefit-cost analysis. But much of the work in public policy consists of descriptive and prescriptive analyses of a substantive policy area—education, welfare, pollution control—guided by no explicit theory and of little interest to scholars outside that policy area. The best work by scholars in this field during the 1970s and early 1980s concentrated on certain aspects of the policy process, notably implementation and agenda-setting. Unfortunately, the work has not been cumulative across policy stages because it is based on a conceptual framework—the stages heuristic of Jones (1970) and Anderson (1974)—that is not really a causal theory at all. It simply divides the policy process into a set of stages (agenda-setting, policy formulation, implementation, and evaluation/reformulation), but it offers no unifying theory of the factors affecting policy decisions and their societal impacts across stages.

The Westview Press series "Theoretical Lenses on Public Policy" seeks to fill this void. It welcomes volumes that develop one or multiple explicit theoretical frameworks or that apply such frameworks to specific policy problems (for example, housing, health care, transportation regulation, or water pollution control). In all case studies, however, the material must be of sufficient theoretical merit to appeal to students and scholars who have no special interest in the specific policy area discussed.

I take great pleasure in introducing the first volume in the series, *Institutional Incentives and Sustainable Development: Infrastructure Policies in Perspective* by Elinor Ostrom, Larry Schroeder, and Susan Wynne. This book builds upon Lin Ostrom's award-winning *Governing the Commons* (Cambridge University Press 1990). Whereas that volume dealt with the development of self-governing institutions to manage a variety of common pool resources—including fisheries, groundwater basins, and water supply systems—this book looks in greater detail at the difficulties in maintaining irrigation systems, road networks, and other critical rural infrastructures in developing countries.

Both books develop and then apply what I would term an "institutional rational choice" (IRC) approach to the problem. This approach combines two critical elements. First, it views actors as "intendedly rational," that is, as seeking to maximize a few largely material goals in a world where they have only imperfect information concerning the consequences of alternative behaviors. Actors are usually assumed to be self-interested—concerned only with their own welfare and that of their families. The second critical feature of an IRC approach is the recognition that the same individual will behave differently in different decision situations and that institutional rules play a critical role in defining those decision situations.

In the case of rural infrastructure, for example, why should a rational individual contribute substantial amounts of labor annually to help repair and maintain a local irrigation system? In many decision situations, individuals face an enormous temptation to "free ride"— to let others perform the work while they share in whatever benefits are produced—because it is very unlikely that the individuals' contributions will bring them benefits that exceed their costs. One possible solution has been to let central government authorities be responsible for infrastructure construction and maintenance, but Ostrom, Schroeder, and Wynne argue that central government officials are much more interested in building new systems than in maintaining existing ones. The end result is that many such systems are poorly maintained—as anyone who has traveled in a developing country can amply attest.

A more promising solution, according to *Institutional Incentives and Sustainable Development,* is to alter individuals' decision situations by developing self-governing institutions. These are basically contracts involving a contingent commitment: A rational individual agrees to provide labor or other services as long as other similarly situated individuals do the same. This usually requires that local individuals play critical roles in designing the institutional rules, in monitoring compliance, and in enforcing sanctions. Individuals who do not provide their fair share of services must also be excluded from access to the resource. These sorts of self-governing institutions have been quite successful in maintaining irrigation systems, although maintaining road networks has proven more difficult because of higher information, transaction, and enforcement costs.

The basic logic of the institutional rational choice approach has been applied to a wide variety of policy problems in addition to the management of common pool resources and the maintenance of rural infrastructure. For example, Chubb and Moe (1990) argued that public school systems in the United States are academically inferior to most private schools in the same area because citywide school boards seek to impose their decisions on individual schools and teachers by developing an extensive corpus of rules that inhibit educational innovation and responsiveness to parents. Public school systems have, however, been responsive to teachers' unions and their preoccupation with the job security and salary of their members. Chubb and Moe contended that improving student academic performance requires changing the fundamental rules by which schools are governed: to wit, the use of educational vouchers that will encourage local school officials to please parents and children—rather than school boards and unions—if they are to survive.

Institutional Incentives and Sustainable Development makes several important contributions to the expanding literature applying an institutional rational choice approach to the policy process and to policy design. First, it extends an approach firmly rooted in Western culture to countries with very different cultural traditions, thus building upon the work of Popkin (1979) and others seeking to develop a universal theory of human behavior. Second, it deals with one of the world's most pressing policy problems: the development of institutional arrangements that will enable developing countries to efficiently utilize their scarce resources for the long-term benefit of their populations. Third, the discussion of polycentric institutional arrangements in Chapter 9 is part of a concerted effort to wean political elites in developing countries from their overreliance on centralized bureaucratic regimes. And Chapter 3 strikes me as a particularly excellent review of the difficulties that information asymmetries create for effective institutional design.

The central goal of the Westview series "Theoretical Lenses on Public Policy" is to encourage the development of causal theories of the policy process (including guides to policy design) that are superior to the stages heuristic. Institutional rational choice is the most utilized and the best developed of these alternatives. Although it is a superb vehicle for policy design, other approaches may provide a better understanding of the policy process over considerable periods of time (Jenkins-Smith 1991). The series particularly encourages the application of several theories to the same problem, for that is likely to be the best strategy for assessing their relative strengths and weaknesses for understanding different aspects of the policy process.

1

The Role of Infrastructure in Development

For more than half a century, the United States has been engaged in ambitious and self-conscious efforts to orchestrate accelerated economic development in other countries. The earliest efforts were undertaken in Western and Southern Europe. Later, attention shifted to the predominantly agricultural economies of Africa, Asia, and Latin America. A central feature of the development strategies pursued by the United States, other donors, and host governments during this period has been massive investments in physical infrastructure. This emphasis on improving infrastructure has been based on the presumption that it will serve as the foundation for a more productive and differentiated economy, which, in turn, is a prerequisite for economic growth.

Development efforts in these two phases have produced strikingly different results. Investments in Western Europe expedited a remarkable rebirth of economic vitality. In many cases, however, large infrastructure investments in what have been called the less-developed countries (LDCs) produced grossly inappropriate facilities that failed to serve as catalysts for growth. Economic stagnation has made it especially difficult for these countries to finance the maintenance of even those structures that have the potential to play a productive role in economic development. Thus, one finds that the problem of rusting, crumbling infrastructure is particularly severe in countries where economic growth has been anemic or has failed altogether. Because of the key role it plays in supporting economic growth, sustainable infrastructure is a necessary condition for sustainable development.

In this book, we explain the unexpected and undesirable results of the efforts to develop physical infrastructure in rural areas of LDCs. We address two fundamental questions:

Why has so much rural infrastructure been unsustainable? What can be done about it?

The first question is sufficiently difficult that we devote most of this volume to it. To address the question of why such perverse results have occurred requires us to draw on an analytical literature developed by institutional theorists in several disciplines, including economics, political science, public administration, game theory, and organizational science. We conclude that the current structure of governance arrangements in many parts of the world creates the wrong kind of incentives for most participants engaged in infrastructure development. Although our focus is primarily on rural infrastructure, we presume that many of our conclusions are relevant to problems with sustaining urban infrastructure as well. Once perverse incentives permeate all aspects of infrastructure development, changing these incentives is difficult because many well-placed individuals benefit from the current system. When we address the question of how to alter these incentives, we do so recognizing that this is an extraordinarily difficult task.

Before we begin to lay out our institutional analysis of the problem of unsustainable infrastructure, it is important to explain how an institutionalist would approach an explanation of nonsustainable infrastructure development, how the failure of rural infrastructure development is related to the larger problem of sustainable development, and what we mean by sustainability. Following a brief introductory discussion of postwar development initiatives and their outcomes, we devote this chapter to discussing these topics.

POSTWAR DEVELOPMENT INITIATIVES

Modern international development efforts were initiated at the Bretton Woods Conference in July 1944. The International Bank for Reconstruction and Development, better known as the World Bank, and the International Monetary Fund (IMF) were created at that time. Early reconstruction efforts focused largely on providing scarce foreign exchange to import capital goods that were used for many war-related infrastructure development projects, including the rural electrification of Southern Italy, the repairs of Holland's dikes, and the reconstruction of Japan's railroads (Yudelman 1985:2). It was not until after Harry S Truman promulgated his Point Four Program in January 1949 that the United States and its Western European allies turned their attention to the development challenge in the Third World.

Foreign Assistance Strategies

Those who were asked to put the Point Four ideas into practice regarded "development as a process in which 'modernization,' industrialization, and GNP [gross national product] growth, achieved largely by means of public investments and comprehensive national planning, would lead to increasingly prosperous and contented free societies" (Stone 1992:36). In a review of the twentieth century's economic development initiatives, P. T. Bauer provided a concise summary of one of the key theories that served as the basis for the development policies of Western donor countries:

> The advance of LDCs depends on ample supplies of *capital to provide for infrastructure*, for the rapid growth of manufacturing industry, and for the modernization of their economies and societies.
>
> The capital required cannot be generated in the LDCs themselves because of the inflexible and inexorable constraint of low incomes (the vicious circle of poverty and stagnation), reinforced by the international demonstration effect, and by the lack of privately profitable investment opportunities in poor countries with their inherently limited local markets.
>
> General backwardness, economic unresponsiveness, and lack of enterprise are well-nigh universal within the less developed world. Therefore, if significant economic advance is to be achieved, governments have an indispensable as well as a comprehensive role in carrying through the critical and large-scale changes necessary to break down the formidable obstacles to growth and to initiate and sustain the growth process. (Bauer 1984:27; our emphasis)

Most applied theories of development used in the immediate post–World War II era identified industrialization as the central building block of economic development.[1] The agricultural sector was considered to be of secondary importance—providing the necessary labor (because there was excess labor in the countryside) and the surpluses needed for investment in industrialization. Strategists believed that the development of infrastructure of all kinds—roads, bridges, dams, power stations and networks, telephone systems, irrigation systems, airports, railways—was a crucial prerequisite for building an industrial sector and for enhancing the productivity of the agricultural sector. For this reason, a major proportion of the massive transfer of resources that followed was invested in infrastructure projects.

During the 1950s and 1960s, the development strategy adopted by the U.S. and Western European countries and multilateral agencies had strong parallels in the strategy being used by the Soviet Union to promote the industrialization of its own economy and the economies of Eastern Europe and China.[2] The foreign assistance strategies adopted by the First and Second Worlds were both influenced by the first postwar relief, reconstruction, and development effort undertaken in Western Europe under the Marshall Plan. The remarkable recovery of Germany and the rest of Western Europe encouraged planners to believe that economic development could be orchestrated—that, with external infusions of capital and technology, the economies of the Third World could be industrialized in a relatively short period of time. But, as a World Bank "insider" reflected two decades later, experience was to reveal that "successful projects in most developing economies required far more than the bare provision of finance for capital imports" (Yudelman 1985:2). Thus, when the bank tried to apply its earlier experience to new settings, "it had a lot to learn" (Yudelman 1985:2). Aid and loans were usually extended on a government-to-government basis and frequently linked to the use of donor-country exports.

The outcomes in the LDCs and in Eastern Europe and the Soviet Union have radically diverged from those anticipated. With the exception of the four Asian "tigers" (South Korea, Hong Kong, Taiwan, and Singapore), which are now highly competitive players in world markets, few developing countries have been able to shake off their Third World status. Protected import substitution industries have generally not grown competitive with age. Massive capital investments in inappropriate infrastructure have neither enhanced productivity nor served as a foundation for economic differentiation. Agricultural output has stagnated or declined in response to perverse pricing incentives for both inputs—fertilizers, seeds, machinery—and agricultural products. Cyclical changes in the prices of commodities such as copper, coffee, cocoa, and sugar continue to devastate the economies of the same countries so affected in the 1950s. The social inequalities characteristic of developing countries remain serious. Even the modest successes realized in education and health care have exacerbated political instability by raising the expectations of a growing population that must now share a stagnant or declining national product.

The debt accumulated over time by many developing countries has now become a serious burden on their economies. Infrastructure development projects, in particular, have frequently been funded by public and private loans as well as by grants. Projects originally intended to improve productivity and raise income levels in LDCs have, perhaps, been more successful in increasing debt burdens than improving productivity (see Box 1.1). Indeed, debt repayment levels are so high in some countries that insufficient foreign exchange remains to purchase imports necessary to maintain even the more productive

BOX 1.1   The Debt Burden of the Jamaica Feeder
Roads Project

Evaluators assessing the impact of USAID's Jamaica Feeder Roads Project (also see Box 2.3) three years after its completion in 1977 concluded that the Ministry of Works and Communications had done a good job of carrying out the project, but improving rural feeder roads had had no positive impact on project objectives, which were to increase rural employment, reduce rural-urban migration, reduce urban crime, promote tourism, increase agricultural production, and improve rural social services (Berg et al. 1980). The tragedy, however, extended beyond the failure to achieve project goals. Of the $18.8 million spent on the project, $10 million was lent to Jamaica by the United States, and $8.8 million was provided directly by the government of Jamaica. In this case, the $10 million contributed by U.S. taxpayers was spent to no effect. More lamentable, the $8.8-million contribution Jamaica made to the project represented an opportunity cost of vast size for such a small country. The mistakes made in the economic and political analyses underpinning the project also increased the country's debt burden by $10 million plus interest at a time when Jamaica's economy was already in serious decline.

The extent of the Jamaican contribution to this project was addressed in the evaluation.

It is worth noting for American readers the magnitude of the mistake. In terms of absolute amounts the project funding was small for Americans: the U.S. loan amounted to about $0.05 per capita of which (in real terms) about $0.02 is to be repaid. This net cost of $0.03 per capita can be compared with the per capita cost to Jamaicans: the immediate outlay amounted to $4.50 per capita and an additional $5.00 (plus interest) per capita will need to be repaid to the United States. To Jamaicans the cost per capita is 317 [9.50/0.03] times the U.S. per capita costs. When the fact that the Jamaican standard of living is well less than a fifth the U.S. standard, the relative impact on Jamaicans was about 1600 times that borne by Americans. (Berg et al. 1980:15)

Thus, those who were the poorest were left with the largest burden. In many instances like this, instead of yielding economic growth, development efforts have exacerbated a country's debt problem.

manufacturing enterprises. Facing difficulties in organizing to produce new wealth, the leaders of some countries have mined existing wealth in the form of natural resources in order to service the national debt. But coping with debt burdens by cutting down forests is necessarily unsustainable in its own right when few efforts are made to replenish renewable resources.[3] The foreboding tone of much of the sustainable development literature reflects the concern that an already bad economic situation will be rendered even more desperate by the strategies political leaders may find most convenient. To many observers, LDCs "appear locked into a vicious cycle of economic decline, increasing poverty, and environmental degradation; and the world as a whole now seems to be facing both financial and ecological problems unprecedented in scope and seriousness" (Arnold 1989:21).

The Role of Social Infrastructure

Knowing that a complete accounting of all the sources of development policy failures in the LDCs would be a very complex task, how would institutionalists begin to approach the question of what went wrong? A first step would be to compare the institutional endowments of aid recipients and donors' evaluations of these endowments.

Although Europe's physical infrastructure was in ruins by the end of World War II, most of its social infrastructure was still intact. Social infrastructure consists of *institutions*—the people and the patterns of regular, repetitive interactions among them that transform inputs into outputs. Institutions include such things as families, private firms, government agencies, local communities, churches, and garden clubs. Those designing the European reconstruction and development effort not only assumed that the region's social infrastructure was intact but, for the most part, they also understood it, valued it, and quite consciously built upon it. Because most of the social infrastructure for a modern economy already existed, infusions of external capital could be utilized in a relatively quick and effective manner to construct that modern economy. In fact, social infrastructure was itself a form of capital—social capital—that made it possible for Europe to use external infusions of physical capital in productive ways (Schultz 1981).

When the foreign assistance effort aimed at developing countries began in the 1950s, no one doubted the fact that the LDCs had social infrastructure—orderly life is impossible without it. But those designing development policies did not consider this institutional infrastructure to be a useful base upon which to build a modern economy. Indeed, the principal objectives of the development efforts of policymakers in Western Europe and the United States, as well as in the Soviet Union, were to strip authoritarian traditional leaders of their authority, to suppress tribal affinities, to end nepotistic practices, and to reduce extreme social inequalities. In fact, existing institutions had evolved to support subsistence agricultural economies, and different institutions would be needed in the future. Indigenous institutions might, however, have been recognized as an important foundation upon which to construct a social infrastructure that was consistent with a modern democratic political economy.

Instead, with varying degrees of success, donors from the Eastern and Western blocs proceeded, or as was the case with the former imperial powers, continued to support the destruction of indigenous institutional infrastructure in LDCs and the replacement of this social infrastructure with institutional arrangements that were familiar to the donors. They found willing accomplices in the new national leaders of LDCs who hoped to suppress any organizational activity outside their control in order to prevent the emergence of viable political competitors. We now see that development efforts have succeeded in reducing the influence of traditional leaders, but, in other regards, they appear to have reinforced the social inequality, ethnic hostility, and nepotism that they were designed to destroy. At the same time, development efforts have undoubtedly destroyed social infrastructure that was crucial to a productive social order.

The one institutional feature of LDCs that all donors found potentially useful as a foundation for development was the highly centralized national governments, which were primarily the legacy of the colonial period. National governments were viewed as the instruments through which change and economic development would be accomplished. They were considered so crucial, in fact, that development efforts were specially fashioned, for most of the past half century, to enhance the capacity and authority of these national governments at the expense of subnational public agencies and private sector institutions. In the most recent "structural adjustment" phase, this tendency to reinforce national institutions has been accelerated. Major policy reforms have been devised by small teams composed almost exclusively of representatives from ministries of finance and central banks working with consultants engaged by the World Bank and IMF. The donors' penchant for encouraging ever-more-centralized governments in developing countries contrasts sharply with the thrust of reconstruction efforts in Europe and Japan, which sought to increase the accountability of national governments and reduce their authoritarian tendencies.

AN INSTITUTIONAL APPROACH TO
EXPLAINING DEVELOPMENT OUTCOMES

Identifying the reasons for the failure to maintain many capital investments and proposing remedies to reduce the squandering of resources in impoverished settings are demanding tasks. Where capital is invested in physical facilities, the cause of failure could occur at any or all of the stages of the development process; there is no solitary, easily identifiable cause. One cannot point to poor design, lack of resources, inadequate training, lack of coordination, opportunistic behavior, or overly centralized institutions as the single source of the problem, even though some of these factors are most likely involved whenever a particular facility is inadequately maintained or completely abandoned.

On the other hand, we argue that there *is* one underlying analytic cause for the failure to sustain investments in facilities. That cause is the set or sets of perverse incentives facing participants in the design, finance, construction, operation, maintenance, and use of facilities. In other words, when we find major investments in facilities, including rural infrastructure facilities, abandoned or deteriorating rapidly soon after construction, we presume that some of the actors involved in the development process confronted a set of incentives that rewarded them (or did not sanction them) for actions that yielded an unsustainable investment.

Incentives are more than just financial rewards and penalties. They are the positive and negative changes in outcomes that individuals perceive as likely to result from particular actions taken within a set of rules in a particular physical and social context. Other types of inducements include (1) opportunities for distinction, prestige, and personal power; (2) desirable physical conditions in the workplace, including clean, quiet surroundings or a private office; (3) pride in workmanship, service for family or others, patriotism, or religious feeling; (4) personal comfort and satisfaction in social relationships; (5) conformity to habitual practices and attitudes; and (6) a feeling of participation in large and important events (Simon, Smithburg, and Thompson 1958:62). Incentives stem from many sources. The internal values of an individual or the cultural values he or she shares with a community can act as a strong motivation. The existing science and technology and perceptions of the costs of breaking rules also affect the likelihood that an individual will follow a particular course of action.

The design and funding of any development project involve human actors. These same people or others handle construction. Still others are involved in the day-to-day decisions about whether and how to operate, maintain, and use a particular facility. And when facilities are poorly designed or inappropriately sited or when the resources required to build and/or maintain them exceed the resources available, the consequences are the result of human choice.

Rather than presume that the individuals involved planned to produce an unsustainable facility, we prefer to assume that they are intendedly rational decisionmakers trying to generate net benefits in a given situation. We base our analysis on this simple assumption:

> Individuals, who are expected to invest resources (including their own time and labor) in sustaining rural infrastructure, must perceive that the benefits they obtain (including the benefits they share with others) exceed the costs of the resources they devote to this effort.

In other words, we assume that there are reasons why individuals involved in the development, maintenance, and use of a facility do what they do. Because decisionmakers and members of their communities are interdependent, the choices individuals make regarding the development of a facility purposely or inadvertently benefit or harm others. When incentives are well matched to the situation, individuals make decisions that produce outcomes that are both personally and socially rewarding. In such cases, the advantage that one individual derives also produces benefits for others. In an optimal institutional arrangement, the incentives motivate the individual to generate net benefits, rather than net costs, for all. Few operational institutions, however, approach such optimality, and many generate incentives that lead to grossly suboptimal outcomes.

Nothing about the process of designing, financing, constructing, operating, maintaining, and using public facilities makes it impossible for humans to create systems of incentives that lead to relatively efficient and equitable outcomes. Indeed, many facilities have proved valuable enough that members of a community regularly invest resources to sustain their continued operation. Although it is not impossible to design incentive systems that motivate individuals to develop sustainable rural infrastructure facilities, this is more difficult than designing physical structures within which many other goods and services can be efficiently produced. The additional difficulty derives from the special characteristics of public facilities. This analysis carefully considers these characteristics and identifies those principles that, when applied to institutional reform, might improve the incentives to produce sustainable infrastructure.

THE IMPORTANCE OF PHYSICAL INFRASTRUCTURE

The central role that physical infrastructure can play in improving economic productivity is a tenet of all theories of economic development. *Webster's Third International Dictionary* defines infrastructure as "the underlying foundation or basic framework of a system." Even the existing level of productivity in an economy—let alone growth—cannot be sustained unless it is supported by a maintainable physical infrastructure.[4] It is understandable, then, that a recent concern has focused on the problems of environmental externalities generated by poorly planned and executed design, construction, operation, and use of physical infrastructure.

Many early investments in infrastructure turned out to be not only economic failures but environmental disasters as well. Thayer Scudder (1972) documented the results of the construction of a dam on Zimbabwe's Zambezi River in the early 1960s that uprooted 57,000 people, the propagation of aquatic plants that threatened the viability of commercial fisheries, and the construction of irrigation works that led to reduced soil productivity rather than increased economic gains. Similarly, Robert Repetto cogently described the environmental destruction caused by many large-scale irrigation systems constructed in recent years:

> Between 1965 and 1980, the total world acreage under irrigation increased 2.2 percent per year, reaching 15 percent of all cropland. . . . The costs of irrigating additional acreage have risen, while yields on large tracts of already irrigated land are declining due to salinization and waterlogging.
>
> High water tables markedly concentrate salts in the root zones. In many irrigation areas without adequate drainage, in India and Pakistan for example, water tables have risen to within a few meters of the surface. Providing needed drainage can add substantially to water resource project costs and has frequently been deferred or neglected. Inefficient water use in large irrigation projects—due to poor operation and maintenance, as well as to the absence of incentives for water conservation—have also exacerbated serious waterlogging and salinization problems. . . . Many aquifers underlying irrigated areas have become so brackish that their usefulness has been impaired or destroyed. (Repetto 1987:21)

The mountainous areas of Nepal provide what are perhaps the best examples of environmental devastation resulting from inappropriate road-building techniques, including indiscriminate dynamiting, mass wasting, and inadequate drainage (for a description of the Dhading Development Project, which is a road-construction project specifically designed to reduce these environmental costs, see GTZ 1991). Increased rates of hillside erosion in northern Nepal have accelerated siltation and flooding downstream in the terai and in Bangladesh, which have further complicated the already difficult task of constructing and maintaining appropriate irrigation and transportation infrastructure facilities there.

Much of the burgeoning literature on sustainable development that has been written since the report of the influential Brutland Commission has defined this concept as "development that meets the needs of current generations without compromising the ability of future generations to meet their own needs" (World Commission on Environment and Development 1987:43).[5] Some proponents of sustainable development argue that to achieve it, project evaluations need to be based on a very low discount rate to reflect more concern for the future. We agree with Lawrence H. Summers, the chief economist for the World Bank, that the appropriate way to avoid future economic and environmental disasters lies not in routinely lowering the discount rate used in analysis of future infrastructure projects but rather "in properly incorporating environmental costs into the appraisal of projects. The world's problem is not too much cost-benefit analysis, but too little that is done well" (Summers 1992:65).

Investments in appropriate infrastructure that can be maintained result in a flow of benefits to communities of users that exceed the costs of constructing, operating, and maintaining the facilities, as well as the costs of environmental externalities. Improved rural roads lower the costs of transporting agricultural inputs and outputs which, in turn, can raise farmgate prices of agricultural products and stimulate production. In much the same way, irrigation facilities can increase the productive output of land by increasing crop yields and by making double or even triple cropping feasible. And improvements to local water supply facilities can lower the costs of obtaining drinking water and reduce the incidence of waterborne diseases.

Rural infrastructure investments may also have a positive indirect impact on local employment and income. Evidence suggests that significant additional multiplier effects on rural nonfarm employment and income result from linkages between rural farm and nonfarm activities (see Mellor and Johnston 1984). As farm production and income rise, perhaps in response to improved infrastructure, increased demand is created for locally produced goods (such as farm equipment) and services (such as those provided by transporters and blacksmiths). The production of many of these goods and services is likely to be labor intensive thereby creating additional opportunities for local employment. Furthermore, as emphasized by Mellor (1976), Mellor and Lele (1973), and Hazell and Roell (1983), middle-income farmers purchase locally produced consumer goods and services, which are also produced with labor-intensive technologies. A paper by Haggblade, Hazell, and Brown (1989) cited studies showing that for each additional unit of agricultural income generated, from 0.5 to 0.8 additional units of local nonfarm incomes are produced. The authors suggested that one infrastructure-related reason for the smaller multiplier effects in Africa (1.5) as compared to those in Asia (1.8) is the limited feasibility of irrigation in Africa, which in turn, limits the demand for locally produced pumps and other irrigation equipment (Haggblade, Hazell, and Brown 1989: 1185).

Public infrastructure facilities are obviously not the sole cause of increased farm incomes in the rural areas of developing countries, but they constitute an important component of the growth process even in countries with extremely low incomes.[6] The implication of this is that increasing the long-term productivity of capital infrastructure in rural areas can promote regional economic development and help to create local off-farm employment opportunities.[7] Increasing the availability of productive rural infrastructure and ensuring that it is sustained is, therefore, a sensible objective.

Decisions about rural infrastructure development usually involve long-term commitments; hence, time is an important factor in all such decisions. When investment decisions are made in a static environment, it is possible to project future flows of benefits and costs and calculate them in terms of present value. Uncertainty about the future will necessarily produce some specific investments that will over- or underestimate actual benefits and/or costs. Thus, some projects will be constructed that generate lower net benefits than presumed, and some projects that would have produced net benefits will not be undertaken. Some degree of error is unavoidable. And the likelihood of errors in projecting benefits and costs is further increased by the fact that infrastructure investments are made in a constantly changing environment.

Rural infrastructure investments are intended to stimulate economic growth—growth that, in itself, can produce changes in the patterns of demands for and uses of rural infrastructure (whether or not the growth was the result of past infrastructure investments). Consequently, the structure of the situation may evolve over time. An infrastructure investment that makes economic sense at one juncture may not be economically viable at another. Predicting an evolving structure of demands is a risky enterprise. We do not argue that all infrastructure investments that are later abandoned are the result of previous erroneous calculations, but we do recognize that making fixed commitments in an evolving economy may constrain capabilities for corrective adaptations in the future.

WHAT DO WE MEAN BY INFRASTRUCTURE SUSTAINABILITY?

The issue of sustainability has been salient to a greater or lesser degree since the international development effort began. Indeed, a critical but largely unexamined assumption underlying the Western industrial nations' decisions to offer development assistance was that a carefully orchestrated succession of investments in preindustrial countries could be sustained. It was presumed that, for example, the infrastructure network required by a modern economy could be gradually constructed by adding a new road or power station each year to compliment improvements completed in earlier years.

A Definition

Various international institutions define sustainability differently, but many use the term to evaluate projects that have received external financial support. Hence, the concern of these institutions is whether, once external support has ended, the supported activity continues through to the end of the expected useful life of the project. For example, a review of USAID's interventions in health programs defines sustainability as a program's capacity to continue to deliver services or sustain benefits after the donor's technical, managerial, and financial support has ended (Buzzard 1987:2). This definition does not consider the size of the benefits relative to the costs of sustaining them, although it might be presumed that if actors were willing to incur the costs necessary to keep benefits flowing, such incremental benefits would exceed the incremental costs. Nevertheless, decisionmakers who concern themselves only with the continuation of a project risk forgetting that the creation of net positive benefits is the principal objective of any investment.

The World Bank avoids this risk by defining sustainability strictly in terms of an investment's outcome. It considers a project sustainable if the economic rate of return it generates is at least equal to, if not greater than, the opportunity cost of capital (see Box 1.2). This conceptualization is compatible with the objective of maximizing net social welfare because it requires a project to yield net benefits that exceed the total costs of the undertaking. Total costs include capital as well as operation and maintenance costs and, as stated previously, they should also include all external costs. Projects might continue to operate after a donor has left the scene but still not be considered sustainable in this sense if the project has failed to yield benefits in excess of total costs.

We use the World Bank definition of sustainability in this volume because it focuses attention on the principal objective of infrastructure development—indeed, of all development: the creation of net benefits through the utilization of scarce resources. This definition has the added advantage of applying equally well to both infrastructure activities that are undertaken without the support of externally supplied funds and those that rely on donor support.

In this definition, it is also possible that an infrastructure investment may be sustainable under one set of circumstances but not under another set. Consider, for example, the construction of a road embankment x kilometers in length. In the midst of this embankment is an unbridged gap that makes the road impassable during several months of monsoon floods. Investment in such a project would likely be undertaken only if ex ante estimates suggest that the road will yield positive net benefits during nine months of dry-season use. It could easily be the case that ex post evaluations show that the road is not maintained simply because nine months of usage is inadequate to yield benefits that exceed the costs of required maintenance. However, it is also possible that building a bridge that would allow the road to be used throughout the year would result in benefits far outweighing the costs of the bridge, thereby achieving the objective of sustainability. In fact, an evaluation of efficiency should ignore the original costs of building the road because, once incurred, they are sunk costs and ought to play no role in subsequent decisions on whether to invest in the bridge. Interestingly, in an instance like this, the incremental investment in the bridge, which is sustainable under our definition, can also result in ex post evaluations that show the entire investment in the road plus the bridge was sustainable.

It is also quite possible that a facility's benefits are considerably larger than the recurrent costs of operating and maintaining it but the facility is still not maintained. If an appropriate set of institutional arrangements is not in place, including methods of mobilizing resources from beneficiaries, a facility that should generate net benefits may

BOX 1.2 The Sustainability of World Bank Projects

Michael Cernea, a World Bank sociologist, used the results of twenty-five in-depth evaluation reports to identify those factors making an important contribution to the long-term sustainability of past bank projects. The definition of sustainability he used was an economic one: Project sustainability over time was defined as "the maintenance of an acceptable net flow of benefits from the project's investments after its completion, that is, after the project ceased to receive World Bank financial and technical support" (Cernea 1987:3). An economic rate of return on the investment was calculated at the time each evaluation study was carried out. The standard for determining economic sustainability was whether or not the rate of return was equal to, or greater than, the current opportunity cost of the capital invested in each project. Cernea's analysis found a high correlation between the involvement of appropriate, local community institutional arrangements and the long-term sustainability of bank investments.

Data for Cernea's analysis was supplied by the impact evaluation studies (IESs) of twenty-five agricultural projects—a group of projects that had been previously selected by the bank for an in-depth IES, not a representative sample of World Bank–financed projects. Nevertheless, the resulting set was quite diverse in terms of sectors covered, geographical areas, design, and results. IESs are detailed impact studies of selected projects, timed at intervals of four to ten years after project completion. This type of evaluation study is particularly appropriate for infrastructure projects because full development in such projects should, by design, be expected years after completion, not immediately following construction. The IESs analyzed by Cernea were carried out by sociologists, social anthropologists, economists, and other researchers between 1980 and 1984, on projects completed between 1969 and 1980.

Each of the twenty-five projects originally selected for an IES was judged to be successful in an audit at project completion and considered to have good prospects for long-term sustainability. Typically, the prognosis for long-term, postcompletion success is based on qualitative and quantitative indicators gathered at the time of the audit. The audit report for each of these bank projects projected that the physical assets created by the project's investments would be maintained and used efficiently; that the new technologies introduced by the project would continue to be applied and renewed over time; that the institutional arrangements would remain effective; and that the overall policy environment would remain significantly unchanged and be propitious for the development promoted by the project.

(continues)

BOX 1.2   (continued)

Cernea's analysis of IESs found that only twelve of the twenty-five projects appeared to have successfully achieved long-term sustainability. In five of the twelve successful projects, the flow of benefits at the time of the IES was even significantly higher than the level of returns at completion time as measured by the audit; in the other seven projects, the level remained constant. The highest success durability rate was in East Asia (six projects) and Latin America (four projects), and the lowest rate was in East and West Africa, with only two of fifteen projects able to sustain their initial good results.

The analysis showed that five sets of factors had a decisive impact on the sustainability of the projects analyzed. These factors were identified by comparing the experiences of projects that performed above the predicted economic rate of return at the time of the project audit with those that performed below. They included (1) provisions for institutional development and participation by beneficiaries, (2) technological improvements, (3) socioeconomic compatibility, (4) a favorable policy environment, and (5) provisions for recurrent cost financing. The study established empirically that all the successful projects involved, at the design stage, specific efforts to enhance institutional capacity in some way; in the projects that failed to achieve sustainability, institutional development objectives were absent.

be allowed to deteriorate even though the infrastructure facility is potentially sustainable.

Thus, although the recommendations we offer are intended to increase the probability that investments in rural infrastructure will be sustainable, we stress that maintaining a facility simply for the sake of maintaining it is not an appropriate objective. Maintaining past investments is justified only if the benefits of doing so exceed the costs, regardless of the amount of resources previously invested.

Evaluative Criteria

Although infrastructure maintenance is often a necessary condition for sustainability, identifying means of maintaining existing facilities is not the principal objective of this analysis. Instead, the objectives of this analysis are to clarify the causes of unsustainable infrastructure investment and to specify the institutional design prerequisites for maintaining facilities whose operation is or promises to be economically efficient. As we have noted, facilities operate efficiently if the long-term benefits to users exceed the overall costs of operating and maintaining them. When the resources necessary to operate and maintain a facility exceed the benefits to be gained from such activity, any community would be better off allowing that structure to deteriorate.

Economic efficiency, however, is not always the sole concern of efforts to sustain capital infrastructure. Equitable treatment of all people within a community of users is often of equal concern, and policies that redistribute resources to poorer individuals are of considerable importance in developing countries where distributions of wealth are highly skewed. Thus, though efficiency would dictate that scarce resources be used where they produce the greatest net benefit, equity goals may temper this objective, resulting in the development of facilities that benefit particularly needy groups.

We do not dispute the crucial importance of redistribution in some contexts, but the primary focus here is on an efficient allocation of resources. This does not necessarily conflict with distributional goals. Even if infrastructure investments are targeted toward particular segments of society, such as the poorest of the poor, these facilities should still be operated in a way that maximizes their outputs, so that the target groups can derive the largest benefits possible from the investment. Although any ultimate decision regarding trade-offs between equity and efficiency must be made by policymakers in the developing world, maximizing returns from targeted investments is still preferable to a total lack of concern for the efficiency of investments of scarce resources.

We also recognize that officials must be accountable to citizens concerning a facility's use. This may be especially true in the case of donor-financed facilities where effective resource utilization (meaning reasonably efficient use of resources consistent with equity goals) is of great concern to those underwriting the project. This need not conflict greatly with efficiency and equity goals because, as we will argue in subsequent chapters, efficiency, like accountability, commonly requires that information about the preferences of citizens be available to decisionmakers. Institutional arrangements that aggregate this information will help to increase efficiency at the same time that they increase accountability and promote the achievement of redistributional objectives.

Finally, public investments in developing and maintaining infrastructure are intended to provide a community of users with structures that increase the productivity of public and private economic activity. As the nature of this activity changes in response to an ever-changing natural and social environment, so must infrastructure be adapted to facilitate these changes. Sets of institutions fostering infrastructure-related decisions that are appropriate responses to external change demonstrate the crucial characteristic of adaptability. We will return to these objectives and discuss them in greater detail in Chapter 5.

AN OVERVIEW OF OUR APPROACH

With this definition of sustainability and these criteria in mind, we develop a theory of human behavior within institutions that better explains the failure to sustain infrastructure and suggests policy reforms. In Chapter 2, we will focus on the problem of sustainable infrastructure and the types of choices facing single individuals making decisions about infrastructure investments.

This volume builds on a rapidly expanding literature variously referred to as the new institutional economics or as institutional analysis. Within this literature, theoretical work on transaction costs and collective action is particularly relevant to the problem of infrastructure sustenance. In Chapter 3, we will apply transaction-cost analysis to situations in which multiple actors must make complex decisions about infrastructure development. Rural infrastructure facilities are frequently used jointly by many individuals whose preferences, stakes, and use patterns vary dramatically. These individuals may differentially obtain the benefits and pay the costs of rural infrastructure development. Further complicating the issue is the fact that many of the infrastructure investments of interest here are made by public officials acting as agents for a poorly specified public. This often means an even less direct link between the ultimate beneficiaries of development and maintenance efforts and those individuals who are responsible for undertaking such efforts.

Because many actors and considerable sums of money are involved in infrastructure development, a large set of complex contracts among the actors is required. The people involved in contracting require substantial information both prior to the signing of a contract and during its implementation. As emphasized in Chapter 3, the difficulties in obtaining, processing, and controlling such information impose costs and provide opportunities for strategic behavior that may produce unintended results. Institutional arrangements that are able to counteract these incentives effectively are essential.

The characteristics of rural infrastructure facilities that require collective action by prospective users add complexity beyond that explored in Chapter 3. The problems of contracting among multiple actors who attempt to limit the costs they incur due to the opportunism of others have been analyzed principally in the context of markets for private goods (see Williamson 1979, 1985). In Chapter 4, we will begin to consider these same problems in the context of developing and maintaining such public facilities as rural roads, irrigation systems, and village water supply systems. Excluding nonpayers from enjoying the services provided by rural infrastructure is often difficult or inappropriate. In such cases, public provision for development activities is necessary, but public provision poses several difficulties. For one, it creates opportunities for special interests to seek preferential treatment. Furthermore, public authorities may not know whether maintaining a facility is worthwhile because of the difficulties of measuring the benefits it generates within the technological constraints faced in most developing countries. Determining just which public authority should develop and maintain a facility may also be difficult. Substantial economies of scale can sometimes be gained from constructing large infrastructure facilities that will provide services most effectively operated and maintained by smaller communities of users.

Having discussed a variety of intermediate costs associated with the provision and production of rural infrastructure, we will return to the question of evaluating institutional performance in Chapter 5. There, we will define in more detail how we intend to measure the concepts of economic efficiency, equity, accountability, and adaptability.

Given that the processes of infrastructure development and maintenance involve diverse individuals, all with their own preferences and perceptions of benefits and costs relating to complex goods in uncertain and, at times, evolving environments, it is little wonder that sustaining infrastructure has proven to be so difficult throughout the world. The design of institutional arrangements to change the structure of incentives facing individuals who make decisions about infrastructure is obviously a crucial place to intervene in a policy process. Redesigning existing institutional arrangements to enhance their performance is a challenge.

Much current institutional analysis relies on crude categories that identify institutional arrangements as either public or private—that is, as part of "the state" or of "the market." This leads to simple diagnoses of *market failure*—and the need for government intervention—or of *state failure*—and the need for privatization. As explained in Chapter 6, the institutional arrangements involved in infrastructure development frequently defy any attempt to classify them as either public or private sector institutions. And though many institutional failures occur, they are not simply the result of market or state failures.

Although recommendations favoring highly centralized provision and/ or production of infrastructure facilities are rarely questioned, they are often supported by analyses that are truncated—based on only a partial consideration of the costs and benefits of such arrangements. In Chapter 7, we will suggest that policy reforms often focus solely on the problems of limiting free riding, capturing economies of scale, and utilizing technical expertise in developing and maintaining infrastructure. Such truncated analyses fail to consider the problems of limiting rent-seeking behavior and shirking, as well as the difficulty of capturing the relevant local time and place information that is necessary in the design of all infrastructure projects. We will then use the intermediate performance criteria that are implied by this broader conceptualization of the sustainability problem to evaluate alternative institutional arrangements to provide (plan and finance) and produce (construct) infrastructure.

We conclude that no institutional arrangement will perform better than all others in regard to all performance criteria; trade-offs are always necessary. No perfect institutions exist, but it is possible to alter the rules in particular institutional settings and thereby improve the behavioral incentives that these rules create for all involved, including external donors.

Given the numerous unintended and/or undesirable consequences of overly centralized institutional arrangements, decentralization provides a logical alternative. Chapter 8, therefore, will first address the diverse meanings that have been attributed to the term *decentralization*. The difficulty of sustaining improvements in the performance of those involved in infrastructure development, which have been experienced by many decentralization programs, points to insufficiencies in the theories informing the design of these programs.

Performance depends on the quality of the fit achieved between institutional arrangements and the attributes of the goods and services being produced in a particular social and physical environment. Therefore, the most important policy implication of our entire analysis is that the complexity of sustaining rural infrastructure precludes any simple blueprint solution. Instead, analysis of the particular situation with a variety of interrelated institutional arrangements, coupled with an imperative that the analysis recognize the incentives each arrangement provides, is much more likely to lead to better institutional reform proposals. In Chapter 9, we will explore the concept of polycentric institutional arrangements and its applicability in the context of a developing country.

But just as some previous analyses have oversimplified the choice between state versus market arrangements, the assumption that the only choice is between centralization and decentralization is also a gross oversimplification, as we will contend in Chapter 9. Instead, a more reasonable, albeit complex, approach to institutional arrangements features noncentral or polycentric arrangements. The problems of developing sustainable rural infrastructure, including maintaining and regulating patterns of use, are simply too complicated for a simple arrangement to address adequately. Rather, multiple, nested institutions are needed. These complex institutional arrangements must be created if the constraints to achieving sustainable infrastructure investments are to be overcome; alternative arrangements must be analyzed if policy changes designed to relax some of these constraints are to be implemented.

The final chapter recaps the arguments made in the volume and suggests types of strategies that national governments and donor agencies might adopt to enhance the likelihood that infrastructure facilities, once constructed, will be maintained. We feel strongly that the development of polycentric governance systems is a particularly desirable long-term goal, but there are other interim strategies that can and should be pursued.

CONCLUSION

Conscientious postwar efforts to accelerate the development process everywhere in the world have involved considerable investments in physical infrastructure. The results of these efforts have, however, varied tremendously from place to place. In some cases, development assistance helped build a sound, increasingly sophisticated infrastructural base that has contributed substantially to sustained economic growth. In others, public and private donors and lenders have generated infrastructure whose costs have outstripped the benefits they have produced. Some of these structures were inappropriate and attempting to maintain them would have been an irrational use of investment capital. Even where facilities have been appropriate and capable of generating substantial contributions to the productivity of the wider economy, arranging to adequately maintain these structures over time has proven to be beyond the capability of many countries. For practitioners and academics concerned about development, the "sustainability problem" is not new. What is new is the alarm generated by the unsustainability of many capital investments in LDCs and Eastern Europe. This alarm reflects the perception, and, in many cases, the fact that many inappropriate investments can no longer be considered simply a waste of resources; some have done real harm and, in the aggregate, the consequences of this harm may be global in their impact.

The purpose of this chapter has been to introduce our institutional approach to explaining sustainable and unsustainable development initiatives. This approach considers the nature of the incentives facing the various actors involved in the wider process of developing, operating, and using rural infrastructure to be the principal explanation for the sustainability of these facilities. Incentives, in turn, are generated by institutions operating in a particular social and physical environment. Because most aspects of the social and physical environments are fixed in the shorter term, changes in these arrangements constitute the principal policy tools available to citizens and public officials who want to alter incentives in order to improve the sustainability of public investments. The remainder of this book is devoted to describing a method of conducting a systematic comparison of alternative institutional arrangements for the development of rural infrastructure facilities in developing countries. Much of the analysis is, however, equally relevant to the comparative analysis of the institutional arrangements associated with the development and maintenance of social forms of infrastructure for rural areas, such as training centers and agricultural extensions services, and public investments in urban areas in both developed and less developed countries.

NOTES

1. The specific theories used by development scholars in the 1950s and 1960s to justify the importance of infrastructure development varied from one development school to another. In this volume, we do not review the differences among the early development theories but rather stress their commonalities. Almost all theories of development that informed the activities of major donor countries considered large-scale investments in infrastructure as an essential prerequisite for development. The reader who wishes to explore these early theories should consult Huntington and Weiner 1987; Morss and Morss 1982; Prebisch 1970; Rostow 1960; and Uphoff and Ilchman 1972.
2. The similarity of approaches is illustrated by the reaction of students invited to an informal gathering in Managua, Nicaragua, hosted by the Jesuit economist Peter Marchetti, to discuss economic problems. After an evening in which a foreigner had dominated discussions with "suggestions of expensive, highly centralized, high-tech approaches that the young Nicaraguans viewed as absurdly inappropriate," they asked Marchetti why he had invited "that American businessman." Marchetti replied, "that was no American businessman; that was a Soviet technical adviser" (recounted in Black [1991:6]).
3. Roger Stone (1992:254) has documented the way in which Nigeria became a textbook example of coping with external debts through a structural adjustment program that depended in part, on the unsustainable mining of renewable

resources. After the oil revenue collapse, the devaluation program encouraged by the World Bank had many positive results. "But thanks to what the Bank termed the revitalization of the tree-crop sector, Nigeria's annual deforestation rate also became the world's second highest, far surpassing sustainable limits and heralding no more than vestigial forest cover by the year 2000." See also Chapter 5 in Pearce, Barbier, and Markandya (1990), describing the policies of the Indonesian government that have encouraged unsustainable levels of timber harvesting in that country.

4. The role that inadequate public infrastructure investments have played in the decline of the productivity and growth of the U.S. economy has recently received considerable attention by economists (see, for example, the papers in Munnell 1990). Aschauer (1990:1) concluded that lower public infrastructure spending accounts for more than one-half of the decline in productivity growth during the past two decades. Although there is not unanimous agreement with the validity of these numerical estimates (Aaron 1990), most studies have concluded that public sector investments in infrastructure do contribute importantly to economic growth.

5. Recent articles that provide a good overview of the different approaches being taken to the subject of sustainable development include Barbier (1987), Brinkerhoff and Goldsmith (1990), Honadle and VanSant (1985), D. Korten (1991), Lele (1991), Redclift (1987), and Tisdell (1988).

6. For example, Ahmed and Hossain (1988) found significantly higher levels of local economic activity in Bangladesh communities that had better-developed rural infrastructure facilities than in localities where such facilities either were nonexistent or had deteriorated. Their findings also suggested that the poor shared in these benefits primarily because of the increased demand for labor services.

7. This can occur in developed countries, as well; for example, Eberts (1989) showed how public infrastructure and economic development are positively related across regions in the United States.

2

The Problem of Sustainable Infrastructure

A principal message of the previous chapter is that infrastructure can and does play an extremely important role in the development process. Unfortunately, as we also suggested there, many past investments in public infrastructure in developing countries have not been sustained. Throughout this volume, we will argue that a variety of complex reasons make it highly probable that an infrastructure facility built in a developing country will not operate long enough to generate sufficient economic returns to offset the total costs of its development and maintenance. It is useful, however, to begin our discussion of the sustainability problem by examining in greater detail the narrower but particularly troublesome problem of maintenance. The purpose of such an examination is to explain the special difficulties of organizing an effective maintenance regime and introduce the other stages of infrastructure development during which decisions are made that may doom an investment to rapid deterioration.

After a brief review of the magnitude of maintenance problems in developing countries today, we will broaden our discussion of the causes of infrastructure deterioration beyond the paucity of maintenance: The long-term viability of infrastructure investments also depends on design, construction, operation, and use. We will close the chapter by illustrating how, even for a single owner-user of capital, the infrastructure investment and maintenance decisions are complex. Chapters 3 and 4 will then illustrate how these decisions are further complicated when the capital investment decisions are made jointly and the facilities are provided in the public sector.

INFRASTRUCTURE MAINTENANCE AND ITS FINANCE

Investments in infrastructure facilities such as roads and bridges, irrigation systems, and water systems have played a major role in efforts to develop rural areas. A recent review of the World Bank's investments in rural development concluded that "overall, expenditures on infrastructure account for nearly half the project costs for all RD [rural development] projects" (World Bank 1988:18). When such facilities are permitted to deteriorate and be abandoned prior to the end of their expected useful life, it is tempting to blame this on a lack of sufficient maintenance. Because maintenance is often most conveniently measured in terms of currency units—for example, dollars—much of the literature on the problem of deteriorating public capital facilities in developing countries has focused on shortfalls in maintenance expenditures. Naturally related to this is the problem of mobilizing and spending additional resources to operate and maintain the facilities that have been built. This subject has also been of considerable interest to development analysts (see Box 2.1).

When sufficient resources are not available or are not allocated to operation and maintenance, infrastructure facilities deteriorate over time. And because the initial investments are not sustained, the facilities gradually fall into disuse. Summary USAID evaluations of irrigation and road projects have all reached similar conclusions regarding the significance of inadequate maintenance. In a 1983 comprehensive evaluation of irrigation projects, for instance, the authors concluded:

> The effective productive life of irrigation infrastructure is limited—often by more than the internal rates of return in project papers might indicate—but the deterioration and ultimate death of such systems can be hastened through poor design, environmental degradation, a lack of operational skills and inadequate preventive maintenance. Thus, gross inefficiencies in the system result, and transfiguration through rehabilitation is required if production or income targets are to be met. (USAID 1983:83)

Similarly, the authors of a summary report on eight evaluations of USAID-supported rural roads projects noted: "Except in a few countries, maintenance of roads has been woefully neglected, as confirmed by six of the eight rural road impact evaluations. The deterioration of a road results in high political, social, economic, and environmental costs and may result in a complete loss of the original investment" (Anderson and Vandervoort 1982:46). The problem is not, of course, unique to USAID-funded projects. A recent review of the road maintenance crisis by the World Bank concluded that

> more than one-quarter of paved and one-third of the unpaved roads in 85 countries receiving roadway assistance from the World Bank already are in such poor shape as to require partial or complete

BOX 2.1   The Recurrent Cost Problem

Development analysts addressing the problem of sustaining infrastructure have devoted considerable attention to the problem of financing recurrent costs, a problem that has yet to be resolved. In an analysis of the recurrent cost problem in Kenya, for example, Heller (1974) argued that efforts to launch large-scale public investment programs in many developing countries have a myopic quality due to the assumption that projects will actually realize their full productivity. Many of the projects do not achieve the benefits anticipated from the investment. He asserted that

> this loss in productivity arises from a neglect of the dynamic fiscal commitments engendered by public investments within the overall budgetary constraints in the public sector. It is perhaps obvious that, in order for any investment project to be fully productive, there must be future expenditure outlays for operations and maintenance. Yet unlike private investments there is no guarantee that a public sector project's social productivity will be reflected in its operating revenues. (Heller 1974:251)

One important contribution of Heller's work in Kenya and elsewhere has been his technique for estimating ratios that reflect net recurrent expenditure requirements relative to initial investment expenditures. These so-called *r* coefficients, when multiplied by the initial capital investment, estimate the flow of resources that must be forthcoming for an investment to reach its full productivity, that is, to be sustainable. In his 1979 work, for example, Heller found that *r* coefficients for feeder roads range from 6 to 14 percent and that those for trunk roads vary from 3 to 7 percent. This implies that an investment of $1 million in construction for feeder roads requires an annual investment of $60,000 to $140,000 over the life of the roads to cover the upkeep and repair that will enable users to realize the maximum possible benefits. Ramakrishnan (1985:118) found that *r* coefficients for water development activities in Kenya ranged from 16 to 44 percent between 1976 and 1983. Other *r* coefficients for various types of development projects are shown in the following table. The entries show the crucial importance of recurrent spending for such inputs as labor, medicine, and supplies for rural health centers or for teachers, books, and other educational supplies for elementary schools.

The important lesson to be drawn from such data is that the construction of a new infrastructure facility brings with it continuing resource requirements for operation and maintenance that must somehow be met if infrastructure investments are to be sustained. Moreover,

(continues)

BOX 2.1   (continued)

not only must the necessary resources be mobilized, they also must
be allocated for that purpose.

TABLE: Examples of *r* Coefficients for Different Types of Projects

Type of Project	r Value
Forestry	0.04
Livestock	0.14
Rural development	0.08–0.43
Primary schools	0.06–7.00
Secondary schools	0.08–0.72
Universities	0.02–0.22
District hospital	0.11–0.30
General hospital	0.18
Rural health centers	0.27–0.71
Feeder roads	0.06–0.14
Trunk roads	0.03–0.07

Source: Heller 1979.

---

reconstruction. Over 40 percent of currently passable paved roads are
at the critical stage where strengthening is necessary to prevent structural
failure which would necessitate reconstruction. An additional US$4–
5 billion is estimated to be necessary every year to slow future deterioration
in the roads and highways of developing countries. (Harral 1987:1)

Most sobering is the recognition that a principal cause of today's
road maintenance crisis is the failure to maintain these roads in the
past. If about $12 billion had been spent on preventive road maintenance
in the 85 countries, the $40- to $45-billion costs now required to
reconstruct deteriorated roads could have been avoided (Harral 1987:1).
One characteristic of maintenance, especially routine maintenance,
makes it particularly easy for public officials to defer it or to forget
it entirely—the fact that maintenance often produces no immediate
or noticeable improvement in the operation of a facility. Indeed, most
capital facilities will operate for quite some time without much investment
in maintenance. Routine maintenance primarily affects how a facility
will operate in the more distant future, rather than today or tomorrow.[1]
Filling small cracks in the surface of a road has no immediate impact
on the ride enjoyed by persons driving across that road; likewise,

painting the metal gates of an irrigation system does little to improve their immediate performance.

The future benefits of reduced rates of capital deterioration are also likely to be very difficult to measure. To perceive a change in a deterioration rate requires considerable localized information and knowledge about how fast a facility deteriorates with or without various types of maintenance activities. Individuals, particularly public officials, must be strongly motivated if they are to invest scarce resources in efforts to reduce an imperceptible rate of deterioration, rather than in other activities producing more obvious and immediate returns.[2]

For maintenance expenditures to be made, there must be both sufficient resources available for this activity *and* a willingness on the part of decisionmakers to allocate funds for that purpose. At the same time, however, it would be a mistake to attribute all public infrastructure failures to a lack of maintenance spending. For example, not all infrastructures generate sufficient benefits to their users to fully meet capital, operation, and maintenance costs (see Box 2.2). Creating sustainable infrastructure involves more than simply solving the maintenance problem. To better appreciate this, it is useful to consider the several phases involved in developing an infrastructure facility.

PHASES OF INFRASTRUCTURE DEVELOPMENT

Although maintenance (and its financing) is a key determinant of long-term sustainability, it cannot be adequately considered apart from the other activities involved in infrastructure development. The type and level of maintenance required is intimately related to how a project is designed, financed, constructed, operated, and used (see Uphoff 1986b:63–70).[3]

Design

The *design* stage of infrastructure development generally occurs prior to construction and is integral to sustainability because a facility can fail to generate benefits in excess of costs unless it is properly designed for its particular setting and specific use. Failures can take many forms. There may be an overly rapid deterioration of the facility in spite of maintenance or an outright collapse of the infrastructure; the structures may be too costly for the outputs generated or simply inappropriate for the use to which it is to be put.

BOX 2.2   Recurrent Costs of Irrigation

Insufficient funding is a major cause of inadequate levels of maintenance, but it is by no means the only cause. Solving sustenance problems involves more than simply finding the resources needed to cover operation and maintenance (O&M) costs, as a recent study of the performance of large-scale, government-owned irrigation systems in five Asian countries illustrated. Scholars from the International Irrigation Management Institute (IIMI) found that irrigation fees paid by farmers varied substantially, from a low in Thailand of $8 per hectare (ha) to a high in Korea of $192 per ha. As shown in the following table, O&M costs also varied substantially, from a low in the Philippines of $14 per ha to a high in Korea of $210 per ha. Only in the Philippines did the farmers contribute sufficient revenue to cover the annual costs of maintaining these large-scale irrigation works.

TABLE: Revenue Collected, O&M Costs, and Estimated Benefits

Country	(1)[a] Revenue from Farmers ($)	(2)[a] O&M Costs ($)	(3)[b] Revenue as a Percentage of O&M	(4)[c] Benefits as a Percentage of O&M	(5)[d] Benefits as a Percentage of Capital plus O&M
Indonesia	26	92	79	370–1000	32–178
Korea	192	210	91	278–370	38–71
Nepal	9	16	56	135	82
Philippines	17	14	121	233	102
Thailand	8	30	27	64	36

[a]The entries in columns 1 and 2 are in $US/hectare converted from local prices at official exchange rates in June 1985.
[b]The entries in column 3 represent column 1 as a percentage of column 2.
[c]The entries in column 4 are estimated benefits of irrigation as a percentage of column 2 (the range for Indonesia and Korea are based on low and high estimates for benefits).
[d]The entries in column 5 are estimated benefits of irrigation as a percentage of estimated capital costs (the range for Indonesia and Korea are based on low and high estimates for benefits and for costs).

Source: Small, Adriano, and Martin (1986:35, 37), as cited in Repetto (1986:5, 8).

BOX 2.2 (continued)

Even more sobering, IIMI scholars found that the estimated benefits to be derived from these projects were disappointingly low relative to the capital and recurrent costs associated with them. Only in the Philippines is it clear that farmers could actually have afforded to bear the full capital and operating costs of these projects without being left worse off than they were before the projects were constructed. Unfortunately, these findings are not at all unusual. Recent studies in Mexico, Bangladesh, and Pakistan have also found that irrigation fees do not cover recurrent costs and that estimated benefits from newly constructed, large-scale irrigation projects are not high enough to enable farmers to pay the full costs of these projects from increased income (Repetto 1986). Such projects are not economically sustainable.

Design is frequently thought of as the product of technically trained engineers. This is an accurate image for many new, large-scale infrastructure projects, but it does not occur in all cases. This image implies that the design of an infrastructure facility is based almost entirely on scientific and technical knowledge, but in fact, as we will argue in the following chapter, effective design involves both technical knowledge and knowledge of the characteristics of a specific location. The importance of technical knowledge to the construction of a facility varies from one project to the next. Local time and place information, however, is always needed to design sustainable infrastructure facilities because it ensures that the facilities will be well fitted to the problems a specific group of people face at a particular time and place.

Designs based exclusively on statistical summaries available to engineers who live in the capital city and/or who are unwilling to involve local users in the design process will not incorporate sufficient time and place information. Uphoff (1986b:63) described three well-documented cases in which farmers in the Philippines, in Nepal, and in Mexico told engineers who were designing dams across rivers with high seasonal crests that these dams would not last. The engineers refused to alter their plans, and, in all three cases, the dams were washed out (see D. Korten 1980; Shrestha 1980; Cernea 1984). Evaluations of facilities that have been effectively maintained substantiate the important role the ultimate users played in the design process (see Haratani, Viveros-Long, and Becerra Marzano de Gonzales 1981; World Bank 1976).

Finance

Because scarce resources are necessary inputs to each phase of the infrastructure development process, *financing* these inputs is crucial to sustainability. Sufficient funds must be available for both the construction and the operation and maintenance (O&M) costs of the project. Note, too, that the availability of funds is necessary but not sufficient: Those involved in the budgeting process must also be willing to allocate those funds to maintenance.

Finance, like design, is frequently thought of as a one-shot activity. Indeed, some of the problems associated with infrastructure maintenance may stem from the presumption that the only major problem in financing infrastructure is the aggregation of the funds required to pay for design and construction. This view ignores the problem of obtaining adequate resources to operate and maintain a structure, as explored by Heller (see Box 2.1). The question of how to efficiently and equitably mobilize resources—monetary as well as nonmonetary— for infrastructure development and maintenance is a crucial determinant of sustainability.

Construction

Physical infrastructures must be *constructed*; the task may, however, be undertaken by any of a wide variety of public or private enterprises. Construction activities may require the use of capital-intensive modes of production, such as those involved in building a major road network or a large-scale irrigation project. But many construction activities are not necessarily capital intensive and may be tackled by enterprises that rely on relatively untrained laborers. In fact, many small-scale, rural infrastructure facilities have been built by those who will use them, relying on local materials and simple technology. An extensive literature on labor-intensive approaches to road building also exists (International Labour Organization 1979, 1982; National Research Council 1981; Beenhakker 1987).

Regardless of the methods used or the entity involved, construction can significantly affect the sustainability of the facility. Even if an infrastructure is well designed, the quality of the finished facility may be jeopardized if the design is not followed in the construction process or if substandard materials or improper construction techniques are used. For example, if building contractors try to earn additional profits by using too few reinforcing rods in a concrete building, the entire structure will be weakened, and no amount of routine maintenance will correct this deficiency.

Operation and Maintenance

The design and construction of infrastructure facilities, including the activities involved in financing these phases, can be completed in relatively short periods of time. Efforts to organize and finance operation, maintenance, and use, on the other hand, require a long-term perspective.[4] Infrastructure facilities vary in terms of how much and what type of labor is required for their *operation*. A rural road, for example, requires little, if any, additional labor to operate, but the distribution of water to the subsections of an irrigation system may require daily attention by highly trained personnel. And a school does not operate at all without teachers.

No infrastructure facility can continue to operate efficiently for its expected life without some level of routine and emergency maintenance. Generally speaking, *maintenance* is any activity that slows the deterioration of a facility, whether caused by use or aging. The most important maintenance tasks are routine activities, which are performed throughout the life of a facility, and periodic activities, which are undertaken at specified intervals. With its emphasis on retarding deterioration, maintenance should, therefore, be distinguished from emergency repairs or reconstruction and improvement activities. Repairs are those activities carried out in response to unexpected failures in a structure; reconstruction is designed to return the usefulness of a facility to its original level; and improvements increase the quality or quantity of services available from a facility. For some rural infrastructure facilities, such as rural roads, it is not always easy to distinguish these various types of activities.

Use

How much and what type of maintenance activity is needed depends not only on the infrastructure design and local factors (such as the weather) but also, to a great extent, on the facility's level and type of *use*. Thus, the appropriate maintenance activities for a rural road depend on the number and weight of vehicles using it, as well as on the road type and the quality of its construction. Rules limiting access to roads, particularly when they are most vulnerable to use-based damage (for example, when used by overweight vehicles or during extremely wet seasons) can be as effective as maintenance at slowing deterioration of the roadway. Similarly, the cost of maintaining the walls of irrigation canals is affected by the nature and effectiveness of the rules regulating animal and vehicular traffic across the canals.

Because maintenance requirements are determined by all the other phases of infrastructure development, any effort to analyze failures to maintain a facility must also consider the design, construction, operation, and use of that infrastructure. The multiple factors affecting infrastructure outcomes is well documented in the case of a Jamaica rural roads project (see Box 2.3). Furthermore, as will be emphasized in subsequent chapters, the incentives facing participants in each phase of infrastructure development are crucial in determining what decisions they make and, hence, the overall sustainability of a facility. In later chapters we will discuss these incentives and choices in the context of the development, operation, and use of *public* infrastructure facilities. But first, it is useful to consider the complexity of even those decisions facing individuals developing a *private* facility that they alone will own and use.

FACTORS INFLUENCING MAINTENANCE DECISIONS OF A SINGLE OWNER-USER OF PRIVATE CAPITAL

To understand better why the inadequate maintenance of rural infrastructure is such a common problem in developing countries, we begin with a simple model of capital maintenance that pinpoints the economic variables that enter into maintenance decisions.[5] An owner of capital (that is, any durable or long-lasting input that yields services over a period of time) recognizes that the quantity and quality of services that capital delivers deteriorate over time due to the twin forces of aging and use. The rate of deterioration can, however, be slowed through maintenance. Because it can increase the productivity of capital and/or prolong its useful life, maintenance itself is an investment. The basic economic model of investment suggests that maintenance will be performed only if it yields a rate of return greater than that resulting from alternative uses of the resources so invested.

Several factors are likely to influence a decision to invest in maintenance. One is the expected benefits from maintenance activities— in the form of additional benefits during each year of the life of the capital facility or as an extension of that facility's useful life. A second factor is the cost of maintenance. Higher maintenance costs are less

BOX 2.3   Jamaica Rural Feeder Road Improvement Project

This road improvement project was intended to assist a badly ailing economy. The implicit model underlying the project was that road improvements would lead to more intensive cultivation of existing farms and bring into production new acreage, thereby increasing farmer income and improving social services. Project planners even argued that this would eventually slow rural-urban migration and lessen urban crime, which, in turn, could boost tourism. Unfortunately, the project failed to meet these extremely lofty goals.

Roots of this failure can be traced to the project design. The project called for the production of low-technology road improvements consisting primarily of gravel surfaces, except where the road gradient was so steep that such surfaces would be washed away by heavy rainfall. (In those places, a double bituminous surface treatment was to be used.) But the design standards were then altered to require that all project roads be upgraded sufficiently to handle an average daily traffic level of 100 vehicles. This significantly decreased the number of miles of road that could be improved (from a planned 325 miles to only 181 miles completed) and meant that considerably fewer unskilled jobs were created through the project than had been planned (1,262 person-years realized, compared to 5,250 planned).

Ex post analysis revealed that few of the roads carried sufficient traffic to justify the new investments in them. Average traffic on the busiest roads was estimated to be only about 25 vehicles per day. As the evaluators noted, "While some roads appear marginally worthwhile (if the economy had grown), many do not. They are high-cost improvements with low traffic use" (Berg et al. 1980:D-1–D-2).

Even then, there was considerable road surface deterioration. Nearly half of the 84 miles inspected were found to require either a large amount of pothole repair or major reconstruction and/or resurfacing (Berg et al. 1980:H-3). This was attributed to two factors: poor design of drainage structures and little or no road maintenance (which, given the uneconomic levels of traffic, was probably not an irrational policy).

The centralized Ministry of Works was chosen to carry out the project. Although this decision probably expedited the rate of progress on the project, it ignored the fact that the Ministry had experience mainly in primary and secondary roads and had "little experience in and sympathy for low technology roads" (Berg et al. 1980:2). The decision to rely on a single design standard may also have been due to reliance on a single ministry.

The final choice of project roads by a special task force consisting of employees of the four national government ministries was also quite

(continues)

BOX 2.3   (continued)

centralized. The project roads (actually 68 road segments, averaging
less than 3 miles in length) were scattered throughout the island in
areas whose economic characteristics varied markedly. This probably
reflected primarily a greater concern for spreading improvements across
the country rather than locating them where they might have had
the greatest economic impact.

The failed Jamaica rural roads project shows the crucial importance
of project design in infrastructure sustainability and indicates the potential
problems associated with using a single, centralized agency to oversee
such an undertaking. Though it was hoped that high-quality pavement
would lessen the need for maintenance, even that trade-off was not
realized. Furthermore, the optimistic projections for increased traffic were
not forthcoming on the bulk of these short road segments. The net
result was an unsustainable investment.

likely to bring positive returns and, hence, should lead to lower
maintenance efforts. If the capital facility is capable of yielding a
positive return even without maintenance, maximization of returns
will mean that the facility will be replaced when its useful life is
ended. Because maintenance can extend this useful life, the costs of
replacing the facility will also enter into the decision; higher replacement
costs will, ceteris paribus, make maintenance a more attractive alternative.
Finally, because these costs and benefits all occur over time and
affect the future, the rate at which the future is discounted will
also influence the maintenance decision. A high discount rate means
that costs (and benefits) to be incurred in the future have little weight
in the decision; thus, if the rate of discount is sufficiently great,
a decisionmaker may forego maintenance (and the costs it requires)
today even though this may mean that the capital must be replaced
sooner in the future.

The discussion thus far has implied that maintenance is a simple,
binary, yes/no choice. In actuality, for many capital facilities, different
types and levels of maintenance are possible. A complete model of
maintenance must consider alternative maintenance regimes and the
costs and benefits of each. Moreover, routine and emergency maintenance
programs involve different sets of activities. Routine maintenance activities
are supposed to be done on a regular basis. If undertaken properly,
they may allow the capital owner to reduce the need to carry out

emergency maintenance, which is necessary only when the flow of services from the capital structure is threatened or impaired. Again, the choice between routine and emergency maintenance is expected to depend on the perceived relative benefits of the two sets of activities and their relative costs and availability. In addition, however, the two types of maintenance and the demand for each may depend on the capital owner's perception of the risk involved. If routine maintenance is expected to lower the likelihood of a breakdown and the need for emergency maintenance, a capital owner who finds emergency shutdowns to be very costly is more likely to engage in routine maintenance than is an owner who would not be adversely affected by such shutdowns.

To this point, the discussion has assumed that decisions about investing in maintenance are made independently of the initial decision about investing in the capital facility. Of course, for existing facilities, the original capital cost as well as the cost of past maintenance are irrelevant to decisions about how the facility should be maintained now and in the future. In some cases, however, the maintenance decision is an integral part of the initial capital investment decision. Different types of capital that produce the same output may require different types and levels of maintenance. In that case, the initial planning decision concerning which type of capital yields the greatest return will depend on the expected flow of net benefits from the maintained facility. Hence, one individual may opt for a capital investment that has low initial costs but is expected to require considerable upkeep (purchasing a "handyman's special" house, for example), whereas another may choose a more costly initial investment that may require less maintenance effort (such as purchasing a new or nearly new house). In a similar vein, the anticipated use of a capital investment may influence the initial choice. Some activities can use up capital more rapidly than others and therefore may require a higher level of maintenance effort if the useful life of the investment is to remain unaltered.

To illustrate these concepts, consider the hypothetical case of an owner-user of a truck. With "normal" maintenance, the vehicle may be expected to travel 150,000 miles during its useful life. With more than normal maintenance, perhaps this mileage can be increased to 200,000 miles of travel, and with less than normal maintenance, the truck may last for only 100,000 miles. Maintenance is not, of course, the only determinant of the useful life of this or any vehicle. The way the truck is driven will also affect its longevity and the cost of its operation. Furthermore, it could be that even without use, the metal in the truck will deteriorate in twenty years if maintenance, in the form of protection from the weather, is not provided.

Concern for protecting the truck raises another set of interesting investment decisions for our hypothetical trucker, and again, there are a variety of solutions to this problem. Simply purchasing a canvas tarp that can be thrown over the vehicle may stem the deterioration due to weathering (but the tarp itself may have to be replaced after several years). Renting garage space could constitute another alternative. Or the truck owner may opt to build his or her own garage in which to store the vehicle. Even then, the owner faces the choice of building the garage alone, contracting with others for the entire task, or doing all the carpentry work and purchasing contractor services for a portion of the effort—for example, hiring someone with a backhoe to dig trenches for the building's foundation and a professional electrician to ensure that the building is properly wired.

It is expected that, other things being the same, higher replacement costs, lower maintenance costs, and less discounting of the future would each lead to higher levels of investment in maintaining the truck and securing its protection. Furthermore, a truck owner-operator who fears being stranded late at night with a faulty transmission may be more likely to engage in routine preventive maintenance than an owner who does not fear such an eventuality. Of course, as with most economic models, this assumes that the trucker is cognizant of the costs and benefits of maintenance activities and that the necessary inputs are available at some price.

As he or she shops for a new truck, a buyer is also likely to take into account the uses to which it will be put and the levels of maintenance these uses might require. Therefore, the potential truck buyer who expects to travel mainly on superhighways or city streets may opt for a different vehicle than he or she would if the vehicle will be used on unimproved tracks in open pit mines. The dust the vehicle would be exposed to in a mine would require either considerably more maintenance or an engine designed to be used in such an environment. And at some point, as most vehicle owners also recognize, additional maintenance will yield such small incremental benefits that it must be deemed uneconomical; replacing the vehicle then becomes the only sensible alternative.

To summarize this argument, the level of maintenance undertaken by any single owner of private capital is likely to be affected by a variety of factors. Although each decisionmaker may weigh these factors differently, one would generally expect that

- greater expected benefits from maintenance should increase maintenance,

- higher capital replacement costs, including the cost of credit, should increase maintenance,
- greater risk aversion should increase maintenance,
- greater availability of related inputs to maintain and use capital effectively should increase maintenance,
- higher costs of maintenance should decrease maintenance, and
- higher discount rates should decrease maintenance.

Furthermore, the choice of investment type will also depend on the anticipated use of the capital and the maintenance requirements that such use entails (together with the factors included in this list). After some point, no maintenance, routine or emergency, may be deemed economical in light of these factors.

An additional factor that complicates decisionmaking about maintaining private capital investments is the fact that the purchaser of a private capital facility—such as a truck—does not know the full performance characteristics of the investment at the time of purchase. When purchasing a ten-year-old truck, for example, the level of future maintenance that may be needed is heavily dependant upon how the previous owner operated and maintained the truck. When the investment decision was made, the new owner may have calculated estimated benefits and costs assuming one level of maintenance. But on discovering that the used truck breaks down more frequently and requires more routine maintenance than predicted, the new owner faces some tough decisions. He or she may decide that the truck is a "lemon" and not worth further investment: Operating it without maintenance until it stops or selling it to someone else may be a better option than continued repair and maintenance.

One important lesson to be learned from this discussion of the maintenance decision process in the simplest case of a single-owner, privately owned capital good is that each of the relevant variables may be perceived differently by different decisionmakers, thereby leading to different levels of maintenance in different circumstances. A second important lesson is that even the simple case is extremely complex because maintenance is not a one-time-only act but is, instead, a process. Maintenance decisions made at one point affect the need for subsequent maintenance and can alter the useful life of the investment. Consequently, an "optimizing" model of maintenance is necessarily complicated even when only a single decisionmaker is involved.[6]

Although the same factors are called into play in any environment, the determination of optimal maintenance is more complex in public sector cases. In part, this is because the services provided by most rural infrastructure facilities are *jointly* used by two or more people. For example, a rural road will be used by many people, each of whom may have quite different road-use needs; in the case of an irrigation system, one farmer's use of water means that less is available for others. Secondly, multiple decisionmakers, many of them employed in the public sector, are generally involved, rather than a single owner-user. These decisionmakers may perceive the costs and benefits of maintenance decisions differently and may also discount the future differently. Moreover, a direct link among those making maintenance decisions, those benefiting from these decisions, and those bearing the costs of maintenance rarely exists in the public sector. Finally, in the resource-poor environment of most developing countries, the availability of funds may result in a level of maintenance considerably below that which an engineer might deem optimal.[7]

Still, investments in maintenance are not determined solely by the availability or lack of funds. Casual observation, particularly of privately owned capital in many developing countries, suggests that owners (no matter how poor) realize the benefits of maintaining such varied capital as draft animals, rickshas, and houses. Considerable efforts are made to keep these capital stocks operating and yielding benefits. At the same time, though, there is little doubt that, in these countries, many public sector capital investments are not maintained.

CONCLUSION

This chapter has illustrated how potentially costly the problem of infrastructure deterioration is for developing countries. Although inadequate maintenance is a particularly common and troublesome cause of such deterioration, addressing only the problem of maintenance and its finance may still not ensure sustainability. Development of an infrastructure facility that does not deteriorate prematurely requires appropriate design, construction, and patterns of use, in addition to adequate resources to be devoted to its operation and maintenance.

Capital investment decisions are not, however, particularly simple ones, as illustrated by our example of the private owner-user of a truck. Many decisions are faced by such an individual, and in all instances, these decisions are made in an environment of some (or, perhaps, considerable) uncertainty. As we will demonstrate in the following two chapters, these decisions are even more complicated when they are made by numerous individuals who face different incentives and when they involve facilities that are used jointly.

NOTES

1. As we will discuss later, infrastructure facilities vary in regard to how fast they deteriorate without routine maintenance. Some never totally break down and stop operating; they just keep on deteriorating. Others break down often when not maintained and thus provide rapid feedback about their condition. We appreciate several conversations with Ron Oakerson, who has stressed the problems of time-delay and subtleness of infrastructure deterioration.

2. When it comes to funding road maintenance, U.S. public officials are subject to some of the same incentives facing officials in developing countries. Reflecting on how unglamorous road maintenance is, New York's Sen. Daniel Patrick Moynihan captured well the problem this fact poses for local politicians in the United States when he noted that "nobody ever had a ribbon-cutting ceremony for fixing cracks." There is no political capital to be won as a result of directing scarce public funds to preventative maintenance. Moynihan also blamed the existing provision arrangements for discouraging mainten-ance efforts. The U.S. federal government, for example, subsidizes new construc-tion or major reconstruction at 90 cents to the dollar but awards no subsidies at all for maintenance work. It is not difficult to understand, then, why the attitude of local officials toward a deteriorating road is, as Moynihan expressed it, "the faster it crumbles, the faster we get brand-new" (Van Voorst 1992:65).

3. Uphoff (1986b) identified the first four of these stages of infrastructure development. We add use to this list because, as will become apparent in the discussion to follow, alternative use modes can significantly affect the speed at which a capital asset deteriorates.

4. A recognition of this marked difference in the time perspectives of design and construction as contrasted to operation, maintenance, and use leads one to question the dominance of projects or schemes in the budgets of many developing countries. Project budgets are well suited to the initial design and construction phases, but they appear ill suited as mechanisms of support for continued operation and maintenance.

5. The discussion here is intended to be nontechnical in order to provide the flavor of decisionmaking about maintenance. For a more complex modeling of optimal maintenance policies under a variety of conditions in the private sector, see Jorgenson, McCall, and Radner (1967).

6. Housing is a good example of a long-lasting private asset whose service levels and useful life can be significantly affected by maintenance. For an example of a mathematically complex optimal-control model of housing main-tenance, see Dildine and Massey (1974).

7. Indeed, empirical work by Bumgarner, Martinez-Vazquez, and Sjoquist (1989) has suggested that even in the United States, those cities deemed to be "fiscally stressed" undertake less maintenance than fiscally healthy cities.

3

Individuals, Incentives, and Transaction Costs

When a capital investment is owned by a single user as we described in Chapter 2 and when that individual derives the benefits and bears the costs of replacement and maintenance, we can expect that the individual will continue to invest in maintenance as long as the expected returns from this investment are greater than the expected costs.[1] The maintenance of public infrastructure, however, depends upon decisions made by many actors, none of whom bears the full cost of replacement and maintenance or derives all the benefits. Those who design or finance rural infrastructure facilities are frequently not the individuals who construct, operate, maintain, and/or use them.

People who use or maintain the facilities are seldom motivated to contribute as many resources to maintenance as they would if they were the sole contributors and beneficiaries. And the incentives facing the various participants who design infrastructure may differ from those of the people involved in operating or maintaining it later. Furthermore, some individuals act as agents for others, and the interests of agents may differ from those of principals. Coordinating the actions of diverse actors requires that considerable time and other resources be devoted to the process of gaining agreement, monitoring activities, and evaluating performance. Thus, situations relevant to understanding infrastructure maintenance problems are far more complex and uncertain than that depicted in the initial model of capital investment.

Similar problems resulting from the uncertainty of the environment, the costliness of securing pertinent information, and the diverse interests of participants have been analyzed by scholars working in a tradition referred to as the new institutional economics.[2] These scholars have challenged the validity and usefulness of assumptions about human behavior and the lack of attention to institutional arrangements that characterize neoclassical economic theory. Most of the work in the new institutional economics has analyzed factors that affect the type of contract or agreement that participants will select when they attempt to achieve long-term, joint benefits in an uncertain environment, while keeping total costs (including transaction costs) low.[3]

Institutional economists assume that the performance of different institutional arrangements depends on the particular types of problems to be solved. We share this assumption. Incentives are the result of the rules used to reward and constrain the benefits and costs of diverse activities. Prior work in this tradition has emphasized the importance of insufficient information, opportunistic behavior, and uncertainty and highlighted the ways in which these factors affect the performance of diverse organizational forms. This approach has, however, been used primarily to analyze private sector organizations.

Many problems identified by the new institutionalists also characterize rural infrastructure development. Thus, we begin our analysis of the difficulties of achieving sustainable rural infrastructure by concentrating on those problems analyzed by the new institutional economists. In the next chapter, we will identify additional problems that arise in the development and maintenance of infrastructure because of the public nature of these goods and services.

Due to the complexity and uncertainty of the situations analyzed here, we use a model of the individual based on an assumption of bounded, rather than extreme, rationality. Because this and other key working assumptions we make about human behavior differ from those used in many contemporary policy analyses, we will begin with a brief discussion of these assumptions. The remainder of this chapter will then address the problems of information, coordination, and control that stem primarily from the fact that rural infrastructure decisions involve multiple actors with different interests in long-term, complexly interdependent, and uncertain processes.

ASSUMPTIONS ABOUT THE INDIVIDUAL

We accept the classical political economy view that an individual's choice of strategy in any particular situation depends on how he or she perceives and weighs the benefits and costs of various strategies and their likely outcomes (Radnitzky 1987). These perceived costs and benefits include the time and resources devoted to establishing and maintaining relationships (Williamson 1979), as well as the value that individuals attach to establishing a reputation for being reliable and trustworthy (Breton and Wintrobe 1982). Furthermore, we assume that the individuals who calculate benefits and costs are fallible learners who vary in terms of the number of other persons whose perceived benefits and costs are important to them and in terms of their personal commitment to keeping promises and honoring forms of reciprocity extended to them.

Fallible learners can and often do make mistakes, and mistakes are bound to occur in any uncertain setting. Settings differ, however, as to whether the institutional incentives involved encourage people to learn from these mistakes. Fallibility and the capacity to learn can thus be viewed as assumptions of a more general model of the individual. We presume that the various institutional arrangements that individuals use in developing and maintaining infrastructure facilities offer them different incentives and opportunities to learn. In some settings, the incentives lead them to repeat the mistakes of the past. In others, the rate of effective learning about how to sustain infrastructure decisions is rapid. In all cases, the repertoire of institutional design principles known to individuals also affects their capacity to change their institutions in order to improve learning and other outcomes when faced with repeated failures.

When fallible, learning individuals interact in frequently repeated and simple situations, it is possible to model them as if they had complete information about the relevant variables for making choices in those situations. In highly competitive environments, we can make the further assumption that the individuals who survive the selective pressure of the environment act as if they are maximizers (Alchian 1950; Dosi and Egidi 1987). When individuals face a relatively simple decision situation where institutions generate accurate information about the variables relevant to a particular problem, that problem can be adequately represented as a straightforward, constrained maximization problem.

But many of the situations of interest in understanding infrastructure development and maintenance are uncertain and complex and lack the selective pressure and information-generating capabilities of a competitive market. Therefore, we substitute the assumption of bounded rationality— that persons are intendedly rational but only limitedly so—for the assumptions of perfect information and utility maximization used in axiomatic choice theory (see Simon 1965, 1972; Williamson 1985). Information search is costly, and the information-processing capabilities of human beings are limited. Individuals therefore often must make choices based on incomplete knowledge of all possible alternatives and their likely outcomes. With incomplete information and imperfect information-processing capabilities, all individuals may make mistakes in choosing strategies designed to realize a set of goals (V. Ostrom 1986). Over time, however, they can acquire a greater understanding of their situation and adopt strategies that result in higher returns.

All the individuals involved in a transaction do not always have access to the same information. For example, how much any one individual contributes to a joint undertaking is often difficult for others to judge. When joint outcomes depend on multiple actors contributing inputs that are costly and difficult to measure, incentives exist for individuals to behave opportunistically (Williamson 1975). Opportunism—deceitful behavior intended to improve one's own welfare at the expense of others—may take many forms, from inconsequential, perhaps unconscious, shirking to a carefully calculated effort to defraud others with whom one is engaged in ongoing relationships. The opportunism of individuals who may say one thing and do something else further compounds the problem of uncertainty in a given decision situation. Moreover, the level of opportunistic behavior that may occur in any setting is affected by the norms and institutions used to govern relationships in that setting, as well as by attributes of the decision environment itself. Later in this chapter, we will discuss some of the norms found in developing world settings that impinge on the level of opportunistic behavior expressed in various situations.

Decisions are made in environments that differ greatly regarding the availability of unbiased information and the possibility to engage in opportunistic behavior through shirking or failing to meet prior commitments. But the rules individuals use for relating to one another (that is, institutional arrangements) can enhance or exacerbate the quality and type of information they obtain and thus influence the kinds of actions they take. The interaction between the information available and institutional arrangements therefore affects how individuals can achieve their objectives. By overtly assuming bounded rationality and opportunism, we are led to explore the ways in which problems of information, coordination, and control may be reduced.

PROBLEMS OF CONTRACTUAL UNCERTAINTY AND TRANSACTION COSTS

When multiple individuals are involved in environments where complex activities must be coordinated across space and over time, they may attempt to reduce the substantial uncertainties they face through various forms of implicit or explicit agreements. Contracts are simply the arrangements by which individuals agree to directly or indirectly exchange one set of valued activities or objects for another. Contracts are involved in all phases of infrastructure development, from the initial agreement about the design and financing of a project to the various agreements (including tenders and employment contracts) involved in the operation, use, and maintenance of the facilities.

All contracting involves costly activity expended in the processes of achieving agreements *before* and continuing to coordinate activities *after* an initial agreement is reached in an uncertain environment. For individuals contemplating a contractual relationship, these costs are perceived as obstacles to the choice of a particular contract. Oliver Williamson (1985) identified the costs associated with contracting activities as ex ante and ex post transaction costs.[4] Ex ante transaction costs are largely coordination costs that exist to a greater or lesser extent whenever individuals engage in long-term relationships, even when they have the same objectives and refrain from all opportunistic behavior (see Marschak 1972). Ex ante costs consist of the value of the time and resources consumed in such activities as

- obtaining the relevant information needed to plan any long-term undertaking
  EXAMPLE: investigating the technical feasibility of constructing a major capital facility (such as a dam or highway) and obtaining information about potential demands and benefit levels;
- negotiating agreements among participants who may differ substantially in regard to their preferences, resources, and information
  EXAMPLE: negotiating an agreement between a donor and a host government concerning the type and location of an infrastructure facility to be constructed, who will pay what proportion of the construction, operation, and maintenance costs, and how performance will be monitored;
- making side-payments to gain the agreement of those who oppose a particular undertaking
  EXAMPLE: arranging for subsidies to be paid to the supporters of legislators from urban areas to win their backing for infrastructure projects that benefit primarily rural areas; and
- communicating with all relevant parties
  EXAMPLE: publicizing public tenders at the time of contracting for the construction of a facility.

If it were possible for participants to envision all future contingencies, reach prior agreement about how they should be handled, and develop enforceable contracts, all transaction costs involved would be expended prior to agreement. But because these conditions are rarely met, ex post transaction costs are nearly always incurred in long-term relationships

involving multiple actors. Such costs consist of the value of the time
and resources devoted to the following activities:

- monitoring the performance of participants
  EXAMPLE: inspecting the work of contractors, demanding
  replacement of faulty work, auditing financial records, and ensuring that deadlines are met;
- sanctioning and governance costs
  EXAMPLE: litigating disputes about contractor, employer, or
  employee performance or establishing organizations to govern ongoing relationships among participants; and
- renegotiating when an initial agreement does not adequately provide for the resolution of problems that actually arise in practice
  EXAMPLE: amending a new donor-host government agreement
  after an adverse project evaluation report or restructuring an
  operating agency that is not operating and/or maintaining a
  facility effectively.

Some ex ante and ex post obstacles to contracting result from
the potential for opportunistic behavior by participants in environments
characterized by risk. The problems of adverse selection, moral hazard,
shirking, free riding, and corruption (discussed at greater length later)
all result from individuals' efforts to improve their own outcomes
by consciously or unconsciously misleading others. We will refer to
this subset of transaction costs as *strategic costs*, to distinguish them
from those transaction costs derived from the inevitable time and
effort of negotiating, monitoring, and enforcing the terms of a contractual
agreement.

A third type of transaction cost derives from the difficulties participants
incur in acquiring and integrating information used in reaching decisions
in contracting, monitoring, and enforcement processes. Information search
costs are closely related to strategic and coordination costs. The more
information each party has about the characteristics of the other parties
to an agreement and about the time and place context of the activities
to be undertaken, the lower the strategic costs to which they are
likely to be exposed. And if the nature of the potential hazards
for all participants is more transparent, it may be easier to decide
on the terms of a contract, including the necessary monitoring and
enforcement provisions. Therefore, institutional arrangements that help
to generate information or distribute it serve crucial roles in reducing
all types of transaction costs.

Given the importance of information costs in contracting activity,
it is not surprising to find that serious obstacles to the development

and maintenance of appropriate infrastructure facilities are associated with difficulties in acquiring and integrating the necessary information. Information acquisition problems derive both from the characteristics of information itself and from its distribution in the world. In addition to the important differences that exist in the types of information needed for infrastructure-related decisions (with each type posing distinctive difficulties for those who must acquire it), all types of information are also asymmetrically distributed among those who will be involved in the development, operation, use, and maintenance of a given facility. In the following section, we will focus on the difficulties posed by two major information problems. In subsequent sections, we will consider the importance of family and kinship structures for communities in developing countries that typically lack the institutional arrangements that reduce information problems. We will also consider those arrangements for resolving disputes fairly that can be expected to arise in the absence of adequate information among contracting parties.

INFORMATION ASYMMETRIES AS SOURCES OF CONTRACTUAL UNCERTAINTY

The information problems relevant to an understanding of why many rural infrastructure investments are unsustainable extend beyond those of inadequate initial information and insufficient knowledge about particular situations. Decisionmakers concerned with infrastructure development may have different types of information available to them; likewise, the amounts of information available to participants vary. We begin our examination of the problems deriving from information asymmetries with a discussion of the difficulty of acquiring time and place information and integrating it with scientific information in decisionmaking. Because the more highly educated employees of public bureaucracies, in particular, are frequently unaware that they lack time and place information or that the absence of this information constitutes a problem in public decisionmaking, they have often been much less concerned about devising means of coping with this type of information asymmetry.

Time and Place Information and Scientific Knowledge

We assume that two types of information are used by individuals in making choices related to infrastructure development: time and place information and scientific knowledge (von Hayek 1945; see Box 3.1). Both are needed in any effort to develop infrastructure that can be sustained over a long period.

Time and place information is acquired by individuals who come to know the nature of a specific physical and social setting. Examples of time and place information used in infrastructure development include knowledge of (1) local social and physical environmental characteristics, (2) various types of production strategies employed in a region, (3) human or physical capital presently underutilized in an area, and (4) existing institutional arrangements that could be used to construct or maintain infrastructure facilities. Scientific knowledge is acquired by individuals through education and/or experience about the *regularities* of relationships among key variables, rather than the particular state of those variables in a specific context. The scientific knowledge conveyed in engineering schools, for example, is necessary in the design of large-scale capital structures like dams, road networks, or power plants.

The scientific knowledge most donor organizations and ministry officials are eager to bring to bear on development is that generated in Western research facilities. An understanding of regularities—including regularities highly relevant to sophisticated engineering projects—is, of course, also present in local communities (see Brokensha, Warren, and Werner 1980; Chambers 1979; Horton 1967). Paul Richards (1985) argued that field trials carried on by African agriculturalists can be seen as an example of a set of intentional activities designed to identify regularities in the behavior of variable aspects of the natural and physical worlds. Richards cited the case of an officer in Sierra Leone's Department of Agriculture, F. A. Squire, who collected and analyzed Mende rice varieties from farms in three districts of the country in 1942. In Squire's preface to his notes on these varieties, he indicated that he had expected peasant farmers to be "blind to the importance or even the existence of varieties." But he instead concluded that

> nothing could be further from the truth. There are at least fourteen and probably as many as twenty varieties well known to farmers who can recognise them at once and unerringly when shown samples. Moreover, every precaution is taken to keep the varieties pure. Seed rice is reaped from the centre of fields while the borderline between fields of different varieties is eschewed. During the drying process the *padi* is carefully rogued before the seed is put away for the next planting. Almost everybody in the native village appears to be well acquainted with the varieties and the rogueing is generally done by women and even children. . . . All the listed varieties are well liked and widely grown and each farmer may have several fancies. Some

BOX 3.1   Hayek's Discussion of Time and Place Knowledge

Nearly half a century ago, Friedrich A. von Hayek, 1974 Nobel laureate in economics, recognized the importance of local time and place information. He wrote in 1945,

Today it is almost heresy to suggest that scientific knowledge is not the sum of all knowledge. But a little reflection will show that there is beyond question a body of very important but unorganized knowledge which cannot possibly be called scientific in the sense of knowledge of general rules: the knowledge of the particular circumstances of time and place. It is with respect to this that practically every individual has some advantage over all others in that he possesses unique information of which beneficial use might be made, but of which use can be made only if the decisions depending on it are left to him or are made with his active cooperation. We need to remember only how much we have to learn in any occupation after we have completed our theoretical training, how big a part of our working life we spend learning particular jobs, and how valuable an asset in all walks of life is knowledge of people, of local conditions, and special circumstances. To know of and put to use a machine not fully employed or somebody's skill which could be better utilized, or to be aware of a surplus stock which can be drawn upon during an interruption of supplies, is socially quite as useful as the knowledge of better alternative techniques. . . .

This is, perhaps, also the point where I should briefly mention the fact that the sort of knowledge with which I have been concerned is knowledge of the kind which by its nature cannot enter into statistics and therefore cannot be conveyed to any central authority in statistical form. The statistics which such a central authority would have to use would have to be arrived at precisely by abstracting from minor differences between the things, by lumping together, as resources of one kind, items which differ as regards location, quality, and other particulars, in a way which may be very significant for the specific decision. It follows from this that central planning based on statistical information by its nature cannot take direct account of these circumstances of time and place, and that the central planner will have to find some way or other in which the decisions depending on them can be left to the 'man on the spot.' (Hayek 1945: 521–522, 524) are reputedly quick, others heavy yielders; still others most suitable for a certain type of 'bush' according to individual experience. . . . Yet the subject has received but little attention judging by the absence of records and collections. (Squire 1943, as quoted in Richards 1985)

This type of systematic experimentation also takes place with regard to the performance of man-made structures having specific design characteristics. For example, Biggs and Clay (1981) reported that the bamboo tube well, which has been very important to Asian agriculture, was the product of "informal sector R&D [research and development]" (Biggs 1980). One might speculate that the more crucial a structure is to a people's livelihood, the more extensive the experimental engineering activity will be.

It would, however, be misleading to suggest that existing indigenous knowledge is sufficient for rural development. In most instances, local communities can benefit from the application of principles drawn from modern science. Use of local technical and time and place information alone may produce faulty structures that cost more to construct, operate, and maintain than well-designed alternatives. Conversely, reliance solely on scientific knowledge is likely to produce engineering marvels that languish underutilized, consuming more resources than they produce. Combining knowledge of local circumstances with modern science and technology is therefore a crucial prerequisite for developing more efficient, sustainable infrastructure.

Actors have differential access to these kinds of information, and they weigh them differently when making decisions about infrastructure development. Irrigation department engineers will have had formal engineering training and will believe that they know how to design works that will produce the largest possible regular flow of water from a particular water source. They frequently view the waterworks constructed by farmers as unworthy of attention because the channels are not laid out in an optimal pattern. Farmers, on the other hand, know a great deal about the characteristics of local water sources at different times of the year. They also may have developed existing channels and diversion works to reflect property rights in land and water. Indeed, they have been known to replace modern, efficient, cement weirs with their own primitive, inefficient, wooden structures as soon as the engineers have completed a rehabilitation project, if the improved structure did not allocate water to various channels based on established water rights (Coward 1980).

Making these two types of information available to the relevant decisionmakers poses significant problems. The newest scientific information regarding infrastructure design and operation is usually developed by a relatively small number of people; the problem is how to make this available to widely dispersed communities that could make use of it. Time and place information is, by definition, widely dispersed; the problem here is how to aggregate it and make it available to a relatively small number of public officials. Actually, the problem of aggregating time and place information is frequently more difficult than that of dispersing scientific knowledge. Thus, for example, in the Jamaica road project described in Box 2.3, project managers used a single design standard, rather than altering a design to fit particular local circumstances.

When a public official's job depends on pleasing superiors rather than local villagers, he or she has little motivation to acquire extensive and accurate time and place information or local scientific knowledge. John Colmey provided the following example of the information loss that occurred as simple water delivery data were transmitted upward through an agency-managed irrigation system in Indonesia:

> The source rivers in Indonesia are short and relatively fast. . . . The gate keeper is expected to read the gates during the delivery period. . . . However, when I looked at the data in the manager's office and saw that flow rates over a series of issue periods almost exactly equaled the planned rates, I told the manager that it was not possible.
>
> When we followed the feedback from the gate keeper upward, we found the data changed hands three or four times verbally or on slips of paper, and that, by the time it reached the chain of command, it exactly equaled the scheduled flow rates. The system was almost, at least on paper, 100 percent efficient. (Colmey 1988:7)

If officials are rewarded for reporting that work is performed in conformance to the plan or are not sanctioned for inaccurate information, a vicious circle of inaccuracy is reinforced over time. Colmey pointed out that higher-level irrigation officials in Indonesia do not usually refer to field data because they are not considered accurate. But, in a circular fashion, members of the field staff collecting the information do not concern themselves with accuracy because they realize their data are not used (Colmey 1988:7).[5] Large irrigation projects are managed by public officials who are too far from where decisions must be made on a day-to-day basis and who are typically bound by inflexible operating rules to have much motivation to get accurate information.

In contrast to a lack of motivation and biases in transmission, which are the primary problems in aggregating time and place information, illiteracy and inadequate education are the major hindrances to the dispersal of imported science and technology. But, even in a largely illiterate community, dispersing improved technical information may still not be as difficult as aggregating accurate time and place information for nonlocal decisionmakers. Because farmers stand to gain substantially from the acquisition of relevant technical knowledge that increases their control over nature, they can be expected to actively seek out this type of knowledge.

A key task of institutional design is to formulate rules that enhance the likelihood that both types of information will be brought to bear in the various phases of infrastructure development. Levine (1980) described an extremely successful set of irrigation governance institutions in Taiwan that are designed to make officials far more aware of and sensitive to the particular characteristics of each irrigation system's environment. As a regular practice, irrigation officials must meet with intermediaries popularly elected by farmers to discuss broad policies and specific problems, and all these officials are subject to performance ratings by the farmers. Furthermore, the common irrigators who actually open and close the irrigation gates are given technical training by agency personnel but are paid by and are responsible to the farmers.

This type of interaction between agency personnel and farmers has led to specific operating changes that take into account both scientific and time and place information. For example, the design engineers of one Taiwanese system had planned to line the major channels in order to enhance the efficiency of water delivery. They estimated that water losses would be cut by 40 percent, so they recommended that water deliveries to the farmers also be cut by 40 percent. The officials responsible for managing the system objected, and they insisted that field data be collected before water deliveries were reduced. These data substantiated the fears of the local officials. After the channels were lined, the amount of water delivered to the area was reduced. The reduction, however, was based on the field data, rather than on the design projections. The consequent increase in efficiency tended to offset the reduction in water delivered without the adverse affect on the farmers that the originally proposed cutback would have had. Further, because Taiwanese farmers were responsible for maintaining the smaller channels of this system, they noticed that lining the channels had reduced the amount of maintenance required. After obtaining technical information from system personnel, the farmers therefore embarked on their own program of lining the smaller channels (Levine 1980:59).

Institutional arrangements that encourage individuals to acquire both good technical knowledge and good time and place information related to infrastructure development are, unfortunately, rare. It is not possible to provide a single blueprint for a set of institutional arrangements that will accomplish this task. But the Taiwanese irrigation systems and the experimental Philippine irrigation systems described in Box 3.2 demonstrate that it is feasible to develop incentives that enhance the quality, accuracy, and appropriateness of information generated from the regular activities of those who operate, maintain, and use infrastructure facilities.

Other Types of Information Asymmetries

Time and place information and the latest engineering techniques are but two of several types of information that are usually distributed unevenly across a population. And frequently, other kinds of information are also much more difficult for some people to access than for others. These asymmetries can lead to opportunistic behavior, whereby the person who knows something that others do not is able to benefit at their expense.

A very general form of information asymmetry occurs when individuals or goods vary widely in terms of essential quality attributes that are extremely difficult to measure without investing substantial amounts of time or other resources. When the attribute is personal, such as good health or well-developed skills, each individual knows his or her own attributes but finds it difficult to assess those of others. When the attribute concerned is the quality of a good, such as an automobile, the owner of the good acquires information about its reliability through experience. A potential buyer who lacks this experience, however, cannot know whether the automobile is a "peach" (above average in performance for its age) or a "lemon" (below average in performance for its age) (Akerlof 1970).

Unless counteracting institutions have been devised to cope with these information asymmetries, various *adverse selection* and *moral hazard* problems may occur that substantially increase transaction costs. At a minimum, these increased costs can be expected to reduce the volume of beneficial trades or productive activities. In the worst case, when no counteracting institutions have been devised, information asymmetries can eliminate some types of mutually productive activity entirely.

The adverse selection problem was first analyzed extensively in regard to the difficulties facing health and life insurance companies. Without counteracting institutions—such as compulsory insurance—there may be no ex ante incentives for an enterprise to offer insurance to particular categories of people. Health and life insurance for the elderly is one example. As described in an insurance textbook: "Generally speaking policies are not available at ages materially greater than

BOX 3.2   An Experimental Irrigation System Rehabilitation
          Project in the Philippines

The Buhi-Lalo rehabilitation and expansion project was a $10.1-million effort undertaken between 1979 and 1985 as part of the larger, donor-funded Integrated Bicol River Basin Development Program for Luzon Island. The National Irrigation Administration (NIA) adopted the Lalo system as a pilot test area for its participatory approach to irrigation development. Under the project, Lake Buhi was developed into a source of gravity irrigation water for an additional 8,000 hectares by constructing a control structure and regulation facilities. In addition to the rehabilitated and new facilities, the project also supported improved water management, farmer organizations, and farm family training in the Lalo service area.

The irrigators' associations, in return, were required to provide 10 percent of rehabilitation costs in the form of labor, material, cash, and rights of way; furthermore, they had to repay the remaining costs over a number of years, albeit without interest. The policy was based on the presumption that irrigators who pay for system reconstructions will be more likely to operate and maintain them.

In this experimental program, both farmers and engineers worked together in the design and construction phases, rather than relying exclusively on engineers to decide what needed to be done (as was the practice at NIA when it rehabilitated irrigation systems). Rehabilitation was initiated at the request of the farmers, and NIA staff then spent a month collecting data about the system, including the problems to be solved. Once senior NIA officials had approved a proposed rehabilitation project on the basis of the information in the profile, community organizers spent time in the area helping local farmers strengthen their organizational capabilities so they would be able to participate in the design and planning stages.

NIA engineers consulted with farmers about the location of proposed diversion works and field channels. Moreover, farmers were trained to record stream water levels for a period of time prior to the initiation of construction. This "scientific" information was combined with the advice of farmers who had intimate knowledge of the local topography. As a result, engineers found it easier to fit the ditch designs to the area's terrain. This procedure reduced the number and total length of irrigation ditches, thereby lowering construction costs. More importantly, when operations were initiated, all the ditches performed as planned—something the chief engineer said rarely happened in nonparticipatory projects. On several of the channels, farmers' groups began to maintain the ditches (which they had started to refer to as *their* ditches) as soon as these were operational (Illo and Chiong-Javier 1983:233–234).

BOX 3.2 (continued)

One of the innovative administrative procedures adopted was the practice of submitting project cost statements to the irrigators' association every three months during construction, rather than at the end of the project. Farmers were thereby able to monitor the level and appropriateness of charges and to verify the recording of their own contributions to the account. Because they had to repay all construction costs, the farmers insisted that construction materials be fenced and guarded, that employees not use project gasoline for private purposes, and that a minimum number of canals be dug and lined. Finally, efforts were made to change the criteria by which engineers were evaluated by NIA superiors, from those based purely on design expertise to those based on the actual performance of the systems (including whether the farmers actually accepted the reconstructed system) (F. Korten 1982: 21). By the end of 1982, twenty-one rehabilitation projects had been completed under this experimental program, nineteen of which had been successfully turned over to the respective irrigators' associations (Bagadion and Korten 1985:68).

Because it required considerable time and effort to organize the farmers and to alter the incentives of the NIA engineering staff members so that they would work together with farmers, this project was not easy to implement. It demonstrates, however, the advantages of utilizing information from both farmers and engineers. By harnessing the strong interest of the farmers in a successful project, the engineering changes that were made produced a much more effective result than the engineers could have produced on their own.

---

sixty-five. . . . The term premiums are too high for any but the most pessimistic (which is to say the least healthy) insureds to find attractive. Thus there is a severe problem of adverse selection at these ages" (Dickerson 1959:333, cited in Akerlof 1970:493). The very process of increasing the price of insurance to cover the added risk of insuring a particular population leads those in that population with positive attributes (good health) to drop out and those in the population with negative attributes (bad health) to search out insurance opportunities more actively. The positive feedback between price increases and adverse selection processes can lead to a situation where it is no longer feasible to offer particular types of insurance without institutional devices that short-circuit the adverse selection process.

The adverse selection problem can also arise in the production of public services, particularly where production is carried out by private sector contractors. (For further discussion of the distinction between provision and production, see Chapter 4.) If there are substantial differences in the costs of providing services and if contracting arrangements do not recognize these differences, private contractors are likely to engage in adverse selection. For example, if a government were to naively write contracts stating that garbage collection by private contractors would be reimbursed at a flat fee purely on the basis of the number of households or businesses served, contractors would be likely to bid only for service areas with low collection costs. If the flat per household fee had been set on the basis of average costs for the entire service area, the government would likely be obliged to provide garbage collection for only the higher-than-average cost areas, and, as a result, total costs of garbage collection would be increased.

George A. Akerlof (1970) identified the absence of institutional arrangements that substantially reduce information asymmetry about the qualities that different goods (or persons) possess as a fundamental constraint on economic development. His central point was that without various counteracting institutions to help reduce the costs of information asymmetries, many productive activities are not undertaken. Three types of counteracting institutions widely used in industrial economies—brand name goods, chain stores, and licensing—guarantee the reputation of some actors and thereby reduce the risk that others must bear in engaging in long-term relationships (see also the safeguards discussed in Barzel 1982). Akerlof's lemons principle also applies to several phenomena common to developing economies, including the problems of gaining credit and the costs of dishonesty.

To illustrate this argument, Popkin pointed out that it is extremely rare to find peasants sharing a team of plough animals among families (or lending or renting them without a plougher), even though substantial economies could be achieved:

> This is an instance where information problems prevent a form of market from emerging. When plough animals are returned to the owner (or to the collective), it is difficult to determine immediately if they have been overworked, abused, or otherwise damaged. If the water buffalo were overworked or if it has stepped in a hole and cracked a bone, the damage may not show up for several days by which time other persons who had used the animal could therefore have been responsible for the damage. . . . So it is virtually unheard of to see plough animals rented without a driver or plough animals owned cooperatively. There have been, however, times when villagers have owned stud animals cooperatively because the problem of damage caused by overwork or abuse is apparently not so serious. (The amount

of work the stud animal will do is roughly proportional to the number of females in the pen.). (Popkin 1981:68-69)

Even after a contract based on past behavior has been devised, asymmetry of information may make it possible for parties to the contract to alter their future behavior. This phenomenon, known as the *moral hazard problem*, has also been discussed most extensively in connection with insurance. For example, owners of a building who previously took great pains to prevent fires may substantially reduce their efforts after purchasing fire insurance. But, the insurer who knows only about the owners' previous record of vigilance is unlikely to detect a reduction in vigilance without additional investigation.

Moe (1984) contended that moral hazard and adverse selection are potential problems in any contracting and hierarchical relationship. Decentralization, contrary to popular belief, may actually increase the potential for moral hazard. In this case, "tasks and authority are delegated to lower-level units in the expectation that they will use their specialized knowledge and productive capacities to contribute toward organizational ends; but the inevitable information asymmetries create incentive problems" (Moe 1984:755).[6] Lower-level units are in a position to use superior information about local circumstances to their own advantage. The objectives of authorities in higher-level units, however, may not be achieved.

The problem of financing infrastructure maintenance provides some good examples of these dynamics. Higher levels of government commonly provide money to a locality to build a capital facility with the implicit or explicit understanding that the locality will maintain it. Yet, the national government is unlikely to know the extent of the locality's maintenance efforts. And if local leaders think that the facility will be rebuilt once it has deteriorated, they will have little incentive to maintain it (see Connerley et al. 1989a, 1989b).

In an effort to prevent this perverse response, some national governments attach conditions to grant monies provided to local governments, requiring that a portion of the transfer be used for maintenance. Again, asymmetry of information makes it difficult for such mandates to be effective without considerable monitoring. Recipient governments can simply label some types of spending as maintenance when, in fact, the activities undertaken have no maintenance effect.[7] Local governments can often get away with such behavior because they control the information about local conditions.

It is also true that, at least in some developing countries, many facilities provided by local governments are produced by private contractors.

Such arrangements require well-defined contracts to ensure that all parties are satisfied with the results. Preparing these contracts entails considerable transaction costs, as do monitoring and auditing contract implementation. Unfortunately, maintenance activities (especially in routine maintenance) do not lend themselves easily to specific tender offers. Why is this? It should be easy to specify in a contract that a particular pothole is to be filled with a certain quality of bituminous material according to certain specifications. Writing a contract for every pothole, however, is expensive. Furthermore, a contract to ensure that all bridge railings needing new paint are actually painted during the dry months is extremely hard to enforce, due to the costs the monitor must bear to learn whether and how well the railings were repainted. Hence, information asymmetries necessitate more complex contracts to guarantee that routine maintenance is carried out. The cost of writing these contracts may actually discourage such contracting efforts. Often, the end result is inadequate routine maintenance.

Information asymmetries are the root cause of another major problem in organizing mutually productive activities—shirking. Many goods involve *interdependent production processes,* whereby the marginal contribution of any one input factor cannot be simply determined (Alchian and Demsetz 1972). In an interdependent production process, individual cooperating inputs do not yield identifiable, separate products that can be summed to measure the total output. Thus, the individual efforts of each contributor are not directly observable.

Each member of a production team knows how much effort he or she contributes but may not know how much others contribute without making the effort to monitor their activities. And each is tempted to reduce his or her effort somewhat—to shirk—when efforts are interdependently related. Part of the effects of this shirking is borne by others. To solve this problem, Alchian and Demsetz argued that production teams prefer to abandon market exchanges and rely instead upon the organization and monitoring skills of an entrepreneur-monitor who retains the residual income or profits after all the input factors have been paid. The residual claimant is thus highly motivated to monitor production behavior and reduce shirking. The costs of metering or ascertaining the marginal products of the team's members are what calls forth new organizations and procedures (Alchian and Demsetz 1972:780). In essence, Alchian and Demsetz saw a firm, with its monitoring capabilities, as a counteracting institution superior to the market in limiting shirking.[8]

Alchian and Demsetz claimed that a private firm is the most efficient institution at counteracting the problem of shirking. The firm's owner (through a single manager) retains residual income, is the central party to all contracts with suppliers of labor or other inputs, and can sell part or all of the ownership rights. But their claim has not gone without challenge (see Marglin 1974; Leibenstein 1983; Williamson 1975). Leibenstein, in particular, identified the importance of shared norms about the quality and pace of work. He also contended that workers themselves may be the most effective monitors of other workers' efforts if they care about the quality of the outputs they are producing.

Profit-making firms are not the only counteracting institutions used to reduce shirking in production activities. Many well-developed, common-property institutions have also devised rules and monitoring strategies that reduce incentives to shirk. The *zanjeras* of the Philippines (described in more detail in Box 4.2) provide a good example of indigenously designed institutions that use a remarkable array of rules to limit shirking during the construction and maintenance of diversion structures and irrigation canals. This is obviously a substantial task: In one zanjera in 1980, an average of 37 days of arduous labor were contributed by each of the 431 members (Siy 1982).

The use of work teams for all major construction and maintenance tasks on the irrigation system helps members of a zanjera to overcome the temptation to shirk. These teams all work at the same time, competing in a friendly way among themselves to finish their portion of the work first. The work teams are kept relatively small so that each member can monitor the inputs of others, and the competition among work teams stimulates each to check the work of the others. Such monitoring is crucial because shoddy work could result in the collapse of the diversion dam. Careful records of attendance at work sessions are kept in account books that are open for inspection by anyone—a provision that deters shirking because information about everyone's contribution is available to all. Positive rewards are given immediately to those who contribute—food and drink are provided at the end of each workday. And fines are assessed at the end of the year—in a public meeting—on members who have not contributed their share of labor and materials. The mixture of positive and negative sanctions, combined with the opportunities for all members to monitor what others are doing, has enabled a communal, nonprofit organization to limit shirking quite effectively.

Although Alchian and Demsetz originally pointed to the problem of interdependent production processes as a key source of information asymmetries, the possibility of an asymmetrical distribution of information also arises whenever one person or group (a principal) employs someone else (an agent) to undertake activities on the principal's behalf. The principal faces the problem of rewarding or punishing the agent in order to motivate him or her to pursue activities that are most congruent with the principal's own interests. How to design an appropriate set of rewards and punishments in an environment where random events (such as the weather or changes in the preferences or actions of other actors) affect the outcomes of interest to the principal has been the subject of an extensive body of literature (see Ross 1973; Mitnick 1974, 1980; Harris and Raviv 1978). This literature underscores the difficulty of designing precise contracts that specify exact incentive systems to ensure that agents are fully motivated to carry out activities in their principals' interests. After all, agents who are strongly motivated to cheat on their principals are rarely constrained by a contract alone.

One form of principal-agent contract is tax farming, wherein private entrepreneurs compete for the right to collect the revenues statutorily due to a governing authority. The winning bidder pays the amount bid directly to the authority for the right to collect the outstanding taxes. Such systems were used in ancient Rome (see Levi 1988:71–94) and are still used to collect certain fees and taxes in South Asia and North Africa (see McCullough and Steubner 1985; Azabon and Nugent 1989). With tax farming, the principal (the government) is assured of obtaining revenues, and the agent (the winning bidder) is strongly motivated to collect all taxes due. The risk of such arrangements is that agents may use their positions to extract revenues in excess of those legally due; hence, monitoring is still necessary if the arrangements are to result in a just system.[9]

KINSHIP NETWORKS AS
COUNTERACTING INSTITUTIONS

In light of the pervasiveness and significance of information asymmetries, one would expect individuals to have devised a wide array of institutions that counteract their impact. The extended family and the broader ethnic group constitute what is probably the most widely used category of such institutions. Due to the basic biological functions the family performs, it can be thought of as an example of an institution that has, to some extent, been generated spontaneously. But the different forms that the extended family has taken in each historical period in similar natural environments indicate that this institution is also, to a degree, the product of conscious design. Institutional analysts explain that familism—the reliance upon kin networks for organizing activities that extend far beyond raising children and supporting the elderly—reflects either (1) ignorance of alternative institutions that counteract the problems caused by the information asymmetries mentioned earlier or (2) an inability to create such institutions (Ben-Porath 1980;

Datta and Nugent 1989; Landa 1981; Pollak 1985; Popkin 1979; Sabetti 1984; Yang 1987). These analysts use the tools of transaction-cost economics to explain many of the familiar features of patron-client relationships that characterize the patrimonial or mercantilist regimes operating in much of Southern Europe, Asia, Africa, Latin America, Eastern Europe, and what was the Soviet Union (see also de Soto 1989; Jackson and Rosberg 1982; Pipes 1974; Powell 1970; Young and Turner 1985).

That the family is an effective institutional arrangement for carrying our numerous important transactions accounts for the continuing importance of kinship relationships in all cultures and all types of economies. Even in highly industrialized countries, people buying used cars, choosing business partners, or making personal loans often prefer to rely on kin or other people they know well. But the absence of effective institutional arrangements that permit individuals to contract confidently with others outside their family or ethnic group severely limits the efficiency and dynamism of an economy. Improvements in the entrepreneurial opportunities of all members of a political economy depend critically upon creating institutional arrangements that facilitate transactions among nonkin.

The advantages of using the family as a governance mechanism for contractual relationships lie in this institution's capacity to limit opportunistic behavior and reduce transaction costs and information asymmetries (Ben-Porath 1980; Pollak 1985; Jagannathan 1987). Box 3.3 illustrates an example of this in the Sudan. There, the childhood socialization process that takes place within all family groups provides opportunities to shape individuals who can work well together. This process produces powerful ties of affection and instills family loyalty. Feelings of guilt generated by acts of disloyalty limit opportunistic behavior among kin. And ties of affection among group members also mean that families have sanctions to use against members guilty of misconduct that are both independent of and more powerful than those available to public officials.

Opportunism and moral hazard are also reduced by the fact that members of a kin group frequently have a significant stake in the success or failure of their joint efforts. Landa (1981, 1988) has shown how trust between Chinese businessmen decreases as a function of the distance of their kinship relationship. Shared language, moral standards, and expectations mean that efforts to reach agreement—even about a new activity—will have low transaction costs. Members of a family who have known each other for long periods of time are well acquainted with the character traits of fellow members that cannot be readily evaluated by outsiders. When choosing a factory worker, a contractor to maintain drainage ditches beside a road, or a person to control

BOX 3.3   Using Primordial Ties to Reduce Transaction Costs

In a transaction-cost analysis of informal markets, Vijay Jagannathan emphasized how often the persons involved in exchanges in these markets are also linked by close kinship or ethnic ties. The existence of long-standing social relationships among a group means that the actors concerned can expand the number of joint activities in which they participate without paying much in the way of additional information and monitoring costs. In the example that follows, Jagannathan showed how, in a colonial African setting, ethnic ties were used to guarantee production but minimize transaction costs.

> The Gezira Scheme in the Sudan involved opening up vast tracts of the desert to cotton cultivation through irrigation by the Nile River. Because of the reluctance of Sudanese peasant families to offer their services in the labor markets, the initial demand for labor greatly exceeded labor supply at the inception of the project in 1925. The British colonial administrators overcame this problem by inducting groups of the Fulani tribe from Nigeria. These tribal groups were housed in relative isolation in exclusively Fulani settlements in the project area, and were encouraged to maintain their traditional social groupings. The groups obviously had elaborate networks of conventions through which all members could be controlled and utilized for various stages of cotton cultivation. . . . Local Sudanese farmers were able to utilize the dependable Fulani labor for many decades to produce a very profitable cash crop. The system was, however, very exploitative, with these laborers not receiving any wage increases for four decades. (Jagannathan 1987:33–34)

Informal market relationships may be productive, but they are not as productive as they could be. Jagannathan noted that

> while transactions costs within groups are lower, between groups they continue to be high. Unlike the Coasian framework, in a less-developed country the economic system as a whole is not a smoothly functioning competitive model. High transaction costs between groups imply that economic exchange between groups or segments may have varying degrees of inefficiency. Benefits of economic growth could therefore have very uneven spreads across different segments of the population. (Jagannathan 1987:34–35)

the gates of an irrigation channel, an individual knows in advance whether he or she is getting a lemon or a peach if that employee, contractor, or gatekeeper is a close kinsman. The employer's monitoring costs in these cases are reduced by the fact that both the employer and the employee are likely to have a similar stake in the proper performance of the assigned task, however that may be defined.

An exclusive reliance on kinship networks can, however, significantly constrain the efficiency of the individual firm and the economy as a whole (Pollak 1985). Although ties of affection among family members help to bind the group together, conflicts among members may spill over into decisionmaking, with adverse consequences. Some inheritance rules, such as primogeniture, may provide strongly divergent incentives for siblings, depending upon their sex and birth order. Although family members may have better information about the character of kin than an outsider will, they may also, as a result of ties of affection, be less willing than an outsider to discipline family members guilty of shirking.

In many cases, the extended family offers the necessary complementarity and specialization of labor (Rosenzweig and Wolpin 1985), but in others, the labor or credit supply it provides may be too small to benefit from economies of scale in production. Succeeding generations may fail to have the aptitudes and experiences needed by the family to support the enterprises upon which it depends. An entrepreneur who is dependent upon kin as suppliers, distributors, creditors, and laborers is especially likely to suffer when rapid technological changes occur and when he or she attempts to establish a type of business never before tried by anyone in the wider family group.

And finally, as providers of insurance, kin groups may be able to cope well with the problems of moral hazard and adverse selection, but they form a relatively small group across which to pool risk (Datta and Nugent 1989; Nugent 1985). In addition, because many members may face similar risks, a single localized disaster could devastate all people contributing to an insurance pool.

NEPOTISM AND CORRUPTION

Exclusive reliance upon kin to staff a government bureau or to construct and maintain roads has these same advantages and disadvantages. Kin are particularly easy employees or contractors with whom to communicate, their strengths and weaknesses are well known, and most have a stake in the operation of a public enterprise similar to that of their employer. On the other hand, it may be more difficult for a superior officer to fire a family member, and he or she may not be the most qualified candidate for a job. The disadvantages of nepotism detract from the long-term productivity of a public or private enterprise. Thus, both the employer and the political economy as a whole would be better off if the employer were able to rely on institutions that minimize exposure to hazards in drawing upon a wider population of employees and contractors.

In most less-developed countries, individuals who achieve or acquire positions of considerable influence may well have done so with the help of kin; as a consequence, they may feel morally obliged to award jobs and contracts to other family members.[10] There is no doubt that this makes it more difficult to improve the governance of these countries (Leonard 1984). But though this sense of obligation is a *common* feature of these diverse cultures, the moral force of this obligation is not, however, a *natural* feature. The force with which kinship obligations are felt derives in large part from situations in which (1) other employers are expected to select employees and contractors only from among their own kin and (2) the cost of holding public officials to account for their actions is quite high (see Loveman 1973). If the cost of nepotism and poor performance on the official's part were increased and made more certain, the moral force of the kinship obligation would be counteracted, as it has been in many industrialized countries. The fundamental unfairness of nepotistic systems is keenly felt in all cultures where capable persons cannot succeed without cultivating connections.

James Scott (1976) stressed that corrupt behavior is not limited to nepotism. In many cases, public service positions and other favors within and beyond the discretion of public officials to distribute are often exchanged for extrasalarial benefits with anyone willing to pay the price, regardless of family or ethnic status (see Wade 1985; Theobald 1990). Feelings of obligation to kin are absent from these breaches of the law. Corruption covers a wide range of activities—from efforts to extort money for expediting telephone connections to the purchase of civil service positions to attempts to persuade legislators to adopt laws that will protect a monopoly position. Coralie Bryant provided a cogent overview of the tragically sustainable patterns of corruption that pervade some governance structures.

> The ways by which government leaders manage to make personal use of public office displays a perverse creativity. It is not just the bribery extorted from the poor for services—licenses, custom clearances, permission to carry on with peddling, etc.—it is the wholesale tax evasion by otherwise reputable middle class citizens and the hijacking

of a percentage of government contracts by senior officials—that further impoverishes poor countries. This institutionalized corruption (not absent it must be said from, e.g., big city governments around the world) scares off potential investment, erodes trust, hence legitimacy of government, and slows down financial and commercial activity. (Bryant 1991:11)

Institutional analyses of corruption (Buchanan, Tollison, and Tullock 1980; Jagannathan 1987; Rashid 1981; Tollison 1982) emphasize the temptations that situations exhibiting one or more of the following characteristics present to individuals who are prone to behaving opportunistically:

- decisionmaking authority is concentrated in a few national government positions;
- public goods are often provided free or at subsidized rates, and demand greatly exceeds supply;
- public officials often determine access to these goods and otherwise play an extensive role in the economy as regulators or production managers;
- institutions that provide contractual certainty (such as independent courts) are absent; and
- public service salaries are low.

Institutional reforms widely adopted in less-developed countries to reduce corruption, alleviate the effects of low incomes, and enhance equity have created many such situations. Provisions are sometimes made to transfer authority from numerous local traditional authorities to a few civil servants in order to improve the accountability of public officials. The officials installed by such policies, however, are no more accountable to ordinary citizens than their predecessors, and in addition, they have insufficient access to and little interest in acquiring time and place information. In fact, some of these officials may even extract rents from individuals seeking control of monopolies or access to scarce subsidized or free goods. Efforts to provide equal, low-cost access to telephone service, for example, have created a huge backlog of unserved customers who are eager to offer extrasalarial rewards to accommodating telephone installers (Rashid 1981). In other cases, in the name of protecting consumers, very high commercial building code standards have been adopted, raising product prices, increasing the entry costs to prospective new entrepreneurs, and inviting payoffs to safety inspectors. Moreover, legal traditions shielding civil servants from liability, as well as the absence of independent judicial authorities, make it extremely costly for ordinary citizens to bring charges against officials or enforce contracts against those who enjoy the protection of politically powerful allies. And finally, efforts to contain the rise in civil servant salaries as a means of overcoming large budgetary deficits have further increased the temptations to which public officials are exposed.

One method of reducing the officials' incentives to engage in corrupt activities is found in the Nepal suspended bridges case discussed in Box 3.4. Rather than transferring monetary resources to localities, ministry officials transferred the raw materials needed for the bridges. Because it is much more difficult to extract building materials—especially things like steel cable that have few alternative uses—than it is to extract money, local officials were constrained from skimming the transferred resources.

CONCLUSION

In this chapter, we have argued that contracts or governance arrangements are necessary to enable a large number of individuals with different preferences, resources, and stakes in the outcome to design, construct, operate, manage, and use rural infrastructure facilities. It is costly, however, to negotiate, conclude, and implement such contractual arrangements. Ex ante and ex post transaction costs are always involved in communicating preferences, in negotiating alternative means of solving problems, and in allocating the side-payments that may be necessary to gain agreement. These costs will exist whether or not participants engage in opportunistic behavior. The level of transaction costs associated with infrastructure coordination activities will depend on a variety of factors, including the attributes of the individuals involved, the specific kind of infrastructure in question, and the type of institutional arrangements used to organize decisionmaking by multiple individuals.

In addition, errors are likely to arise in all multiactor decisions about the design, construction, operation, maintenance, and/or use of rural infrastructure facilities. These errors can be attributed to both the fallibility of humans and the difficulty of obtaining an optimal blend of technical expertise and knowledge of the local people, their needs, and the physical systems involved. The costs of these errors are affected by the same variables that affect coordination costs: attributes of the individuals involved, attributes of the infrastructure facility, and attributes of the institutional arrangements.

We have also examined the strategic costs of opportunistic strategies that may be adopted by individual parties to an agreement. These costs exist because information and power are not always symmetrically

BOX 3.4 Banglung Suspended Bridges Project

In 1958, His Majesty's Government of Nepal (HMG) initiated a program to build suspension bridges in order to spur rural development. Due to substantial technical and financial constraints associated with the construction of this type of bridge, however, the program proceeded very slowly. Searching for ways to speed up the improvement of transportation services in his area, a local political representative from Banglung, a mountainous district in western Nepal, eventually realized that a simpler construction technology for suspended (rather than suspension) bridges was widely available at the local level in mountainous parts of the country. Indeed, suspended bridges had been constructed over short spans for centuries. Because this was a widely understood technology, the limited technical staff at the district level would not be needed to oversee construction.

The suspended bridges projects that were eventually adopted beginning in 1972 were directed by one district-level committee and a host of subcommittees operating at the village level. All operated outside the framework of the regular local government institutions (*panchayats*) of Nepal, although panchayat members known for their ability to mobilize villagers served on the committees. The projects required that local communities provide all the inputs for the bridges (except for specialized construction materials that were not available locally). These consisted primarily of used steel cable and the iron for the fittings needed to anchor the cables. Materials themselves, rather than monetary grants, were made available to committees formed in each locality where a bridge was to be built, thereby reducing the amount of financial oversight required by the project. This technique also reduced the villagers' fears that local government officials were profiting illegally from the undertaking.

Villager confidence was critical to the success of the projects because residents supplied all the labor and local materials. Communities served by the bridges also assumed responsibility for bridge maintenance, which, for at least the first ten years of the life of the bridges, would be minimal. Labor was the principal local resource contributed to the projects: Considerable effort was required to carry the heavy coils of cable from the nearest road to the construction site, rock had to be moved, and excavation work was needed to anchor the cables properly. A local tradition of mutual help made it easier to organize this level of effort. Writing about the bridge projects, Pradhan (1980:32) noted that "contributions of voluntary labor have also been a part of the culturally recognized system of *Parma* (a household labor exchange system on a reciprocal basis). Parma takes place mostly during the planting and harvesting seasons and during the construction of individual

(continues)

BOX 3.4   (continued)

homes in a village. So, the sharing of labor is a part of the culture in this region." Such a system helps to ensure a reasonably equitable sharing of the burden of constructing infrastructure facilities. Furthermore, households that were not able or willing to participate directly in the effort were asked to contribute food or money to those who did participate. Additional cash contributions were also mobilized locally, primarily to pay local skilled workers—masons, carpenters, and blacksmiths—for their efforts.

The methods used for local resource mobilization were successful because they took the incentives of all participants into account. Pradhan (1980:36) reported that a total of sixty-two bridge projects were ultimately completed in the two phases of the bridge building program, with direct costs to HMG of only about US$50,000. The value of villagers' contributions was substantially higher. These public bridges provided net benefits to the communities involved, and apparently, nearly everyone participated in the efforts on a reasonably equitable basis. The project was not carried out in the spirit of "the government" providing the facility; instead, community responsibility was emphasized, including responsibility for all the engineering expertise required. Given local economic circumstances, the bulk of resources mobilized came in the form of nonmonetary inputs rather than in cash, which would have been much more difficult to safeguard from misappropriation. Finally, because the decisions concerning the location of the bridges were made locally, because the villagers themselves had participated in their construction, and because the consequences of not replacing inexpensive rope and planks was potentially catastrophic, it is not surprising that the bridges continued to be maintained even though no formal provision for maintenance was made.

---

distributed to all participants. The asymmetry provides opportunities for some individuals to use information or power opportunistically in order to reap personal benefits at the expense of others. We have examined four types of opportunistic behavior in this chapter that can substantially increase the cost of infrastructure development and maintenance: adverse selection, moral hazard, shirking, and corruption. We will discuss a fifth type of strategic cost—free riding—in Chapter 4. And again, the factors that affect strategic costs are identical to those that affect other transaction costs—attributes of the individuals, of the infrastructure facilities, and of the institutional arrangements. The next several chapters will further expand this analysis.

NOTES

1. This is not to imply that all private owners of capital behave identically in making their maintenance decisions. Different persons face different relative prices, possess different types and amounts of information, perceive the benefits of maintenance differently, use different discount rates, and are willing to assume differing levels of risk.

2. These analyses are based on the seminal work of Knight 1921; Coase 1937; Commons 1959; Simon 1946, 1972; Williamson 1975, 1985; and North 1985, 1986.

3. See Adelman and Thorbecke (1989) for a review of this literature as applied to the role of institutions in economic development. See also Nabli and Nugent (1989).

4. Cheung (1983:3) defined transaction costs as the costs of operating institutions. The origins of modern transaction-cost analysis is frequently traced to the work of Ronald Coase (1937), who recognized the pervasiveness of transaction costs in all forms of coordination and argued that the choice of one form of contracting (the organization of a firm) would be selected over another form of contracting (exchange in a market) when the transaction costs of the first type of contract were lower than those involved in the second.

5. This is neither a recent nor a highly localized problem, as is reflected in the following assessment by Crosson (1975:522): "The management of large irrigation projects is in the hands of public officials who are far too removed from the on-farm situation to know the conditions of efficient use, who lack incentives to achieve it even if they knew how, and who typically are bound by inflexible operating rules of water allocation impeding their response to economic incentives even if they had them."

6. An interesting series of articles examined the types of contracts used in the transportation sector of developing countries. These contracts reflect the different information asymmetries that are present and the various institutional arrangements that have been established to reduce the costs of these asymmetries (see, for example, Heston et al. 1985; Otsuka, Kikuchi, and Hayami 1986).

7. See Schroeder (1987) for a discussion of this phenomenon in Indonesia, and Bahl (1984), who noted the lack of oversight on the part of the government of Bangladesh regarding its maintenance mandate in the rural works program.

8. As Steven Cheung (1983:8) graphically illustrated, members of a team may be willing to hire a monitor themselves in order to reduce shirking, even when this involves the imposition of severe sanctions. Teams of Chinese workers who towed heavy wooden boats along a shore used to hire a monitor to whip those who shirked.

9. Ferris and Winkler (1991) applied the principal-agent model to the more general issue of decentralized governmental relationships. They noted that national levels of government often wish to achieve objectives that are to be implemented by regional or local governments acting as agents.

10. As Peter Ekeh (1975) pointed out, the *only* moral ties that such officials may feel are to their primordial groups. The same individuals who will engage in corrupt practices in their governmental position would not think of breaking a promise, accepting a bribe, or in any manner defrauding the primordial groups to which they belong.

4

Provision and Production of Rural Infrastructure

The information problems discussed in Chapter 3 characterize many situations in which individuals face incentives that lead them to jointly produce unintended and undesirable outcomes. Without counteracting institutions to ameliorate the problems of shirking, adverse selection, moral hazard, corruption, and inadequate blends of time and place information with scientific knowledge, individual achievement is limited. These problems are far more frequent than a casual reading of most introductory political science, public administration, or economics textbooks suggests.

The problems reviewed in Chapter 3 arise in the creation of public as well as private goods. Private goods are used primarily by a single individual or firm, which can exclude others from consuming the goods; and potential users of such goods have considerable choice as to whether to consume. Rural infrastructure facilities, on the other hand, are used by many individuals or firms. They are costly to fence off in order to preclude potential beneficiaries from enjoying benefits without paying. In other words, because of their specific attributes, rural infrastructure facilities are often provided by public institutions, rather than private enterprises. To complete our discussion on the challenge of designing institutions within which sustainable infrastructure can be developed, we now consider the set of attributes shared to a greater or lesser extent by all jointly used facilities. These attributes further increase the difficulty of designing counteracting institutions to offset the perverse incentives that result in the construction of unsustainable rural infrastructure.

As the title of this chapter suggests, it is useful to distinguish between *provision* and *production* activities when considering the attributes of jointly used goods or services. This distinction is elaborated upon in the following section. We will then discuss the various attributes

73

of rural infrastructure that first complicate provision decisions and then complicate production decisions. Because different infrastructure facilities have different combinations of characteristics complicating their provision and production, we will conclude the chapter with a set of hypotheses about the relative difficulties of developing different kinds of infrastructure.

DISTINCTION BETWEEN PROVISION AND PRODUCTION

In private economic exchanges, little attention is paid to the difference between provision and production activities, probably because that difference is so obvious. Individuals and households decide which private goods they want to provide for themselves and how they are going to provide them. As was suggested in the earlier discussion of the sorts of decisions faced by the builder of a garage, individuals can decide whether to produce the goods or services in their own household or to purchase them from someone else. The distinction between provision and production is, however, of considerable importance in the public realm.[1] Sometimes, the unit of government that provides a facility or service is also the producer of the facility and of the flow of services it yields. This is the situation, for example, when a school district both owns and operates a school: Provision and production are each undertaken by the same public agency. A unit providing for rural infrastructure facilities need not, however, also produce them. Frequently, an agency will rely on a private company or even another public authority to construct and/or operate a facility. For example, the unit of government that provides for a road may hire a private contractor to construct it.

Thus, throughout this volume, the term *provision* will refer to decisions made through collective-choice mechanisms about:

- the kinds of goods and services to be provided by a designated group of people,
- the quantity and quality of the goods and services to be provided,
- the degree to which private activities related to these goods and services are to be regulated,
- how to arrange for the production of these goods and services,
- how to finance the provision of these goods and services, and
- how to monitor the performance of those who produce these goods and services (ACIR 1987).

The organization of provision, therefore, relates primarily to consuming, financing, and arranging for and monitoring the production of goods and services. It is important to recognize that these activities must be carried out whenever the good or service is provided by a collectivity, be it a unit of government or a group of private citizen-users. In the provision of rural infrastructure, the collectivity must concern itself with determining the demand for the service, arranging for and monitoring the work of those who construct and maintain a facility, and financing all of these activities.

Production refers to "the more technical process of transforming inputs into outputs—making a product, or, in many cases, rendering a service" (ACIR 1987:7). Once a unit of government or other collective decisionmaking body has decided to "provide" a particular type of infrastructure, it must then decide whether it will produce the infrastructure facility itself or have it produced by others. If the latter alternative is chosen, several possibilities are available. Governmental or nongovernmental units might contract with private or even with public agencies to construct the facility and/or operate it. Governmental units may also have the power to mandate other enterprises to produce the service. Or governments may encourage its production by offering financial incentives to other units of government.

The organizational arrangements for the construction of a facility may differ substantially from those related to its maintenance. For example, a single agency may design and finance the construction of large-scale infrastructure projects, and it may or may not involve the ultimate users in the process. Once an infrastructure facility has been built, there may be few, if any, ways for someone to articulate a demand for infrastructure maintenance or a willingness to finance it. This is particularly likely where deterioration due to a lack of maintenance is a slow process and competing needs are much more obvious. The allocation of resources to maintenance may be more likely where the organization in charge of the facility is exclusively responsible for that activity—for example, a special district or an irrigation system users' group. The implication of this line of reasoning is that maintenance efforts are more likely to be financed and performed where organizations provide one or a few closely related goods and services, rather than a diverse set of goods.[2]

Financing the construction, operation, and maintenance of a facility is another critical part of provision. But, as we will explain, mobilizing the resources to finance these activities is greatly complicated by the nature of the goods and services being provided collectively. Nongovernmental groups must rely on the willingness of users to contribute money or other resources for financing the services. Governmental units can utilize direct payments by facility users; in addition, they often have the power of taxation to coerce payments from users and nonusers alike. The authority to tax, however, does not always automatically produce actual resources—potential payers may refuse to comply with the tax laws or find ways to dodge licensing fees. Collective decisions regarding appropriate financial instruments are further complicated by the fact that different instruments have different effects on a local or national economy that may or may not be desirable.

In many instances, considerable resources are made available to local units of government through grants and loans from other governmental entities, including bilateral and multilateral donor organizations. The flow of these resources may, however, be extremely uncertain, thereby jeopardizing the longer-term sustainability of a facility. Furthermore, because grants do not generate a direct burden on facility users, they can discourage a collectivity from mobilizing its own resources.

Various attributes of rural infrastructure can greatly complicate both provision and production decisions and create a variety of difficulties in designing appropriate counteracting institutions. It is useful to separate those attributes that primarily influence the provision or consumption of infrastructure facilities from those that principally affect their production. The next two sections consider each in turn.

ATTRIBUTES OF RURAL INFRASTRUCTURE PRIMARILY AFFECTING PROVISION

We will first consider a set of four attributes that distinguish goods and services that normally are provided by public rather than private institutional arrangements. Publicly provided goods and services generally yield benefits that can be enjoyed jointly and simultaneously by many people. Consumption cannot be withheld easily from any individual; indeed, individuals may have little choice about their consumption regardless of whether the service is deemed to yield benefits. Making the provision process even more complex is the fact that there are often difficulties in estimating the potential benefits of infrastructure facilities, as well as in measuring the extent of usage. Finally, public provision of goods and services can also elicit counterproductive strategic or rent-seeking behavior by bureaucrats and others attempting to influence collective decisions in order to secure unearned benefits. Thus, in this section, we will consider the problems resulting from the characteristics of nonexcludability and joint use of goods and services, together with the difficulties of measuring the quality of physical structures, assessing the level of benefits they generate, and forestalling rent seeking.

Nonexcludability and the Free-Rider Problem

The nonexcludability of the benefits generated by a good is cited by scholars as the hallmark of a good that must be provided publicly, rather than privately. A good whose benefits can be withheld at low cost by the owner or provider displays excludable benefits (Cornes and Sandler 1986:6). When the benefits of a good are available to a group, whether or not members of the group contribute to the provision of the good, that good is characterized by nonexcludability. When it is very costly to exclude individuals from enjoying benefits from an infrastructure facility, private, profit-seeking entrepreneurs, who must recoup their investments through quid pro quo exchanges, have few incentives to provide such services on their own initiative.[3] And because it is difficult to exclude people from enjoying the benefits of rural infrastructure, profit-seeking entrepreneurs are likely to under-invest in such facilities.

The attribute of nonexcludability can thus lead to the problem of free riding and to underinvestment in capital and its maintenance. Because the public sector possesses the authority to finance a good using taxes and fees and to regulate usage of the good, this attribute, therefore, often requires that sector to actively participate in the provision of the good. Public sector involvement, however, raises difficult questions concerning (1) the design of collective-choice mechanisms that accurately reflects the desires of those who will benefit from the good and (2) the means to be used to finance the construction and maintenance of the good.

Free Riders. Where exclusion is costly, those wishing to provide a good or service face a potential free-rider or collective-action problem (Olson 1965). Individuals who gain from the maintenance of a local road, for example, may not wish to contribute labor or taxes to maintenance activities, hoping that others will bear the burden. This is not to say that all individuals will free ride whenever they can. But there definitely is an incentive to be a free rider in all situations where potential beneficiaries cannot be excluded for failing to contribute to the provision of a good or service.[4]

As mentioned previously, the benefits of maintenance are frequently quite subtle and time delayed. When they can be shared by all users, whether or not they have contributed to maintenance, we can begin to see how truly difficult this problem is: Why should I use very scarce resources today to slow the rate of deterioration of a facility that will benefit not only me but also everyone else using it? It takes an extraordinarily well-crafted set of institutions to offset the many incentives to invest resources in almost any other way than in the maintenance of an infrastructure facility that benefits a large group of individuals.

A variety of institutional arrangements help beneficiaries of collective action to prevent free riding. Provision by an agency of a local, regional, or national government is one strategy to overcome free-rider problems, but it is not the only available approach. Private groups that can control their own membership are also able to overcome some of the problems of collective action.[5] Strictly private institutions can prevent free riding if they have coordination mechanisms assuring their members that (1) the benefits they receive will be greater than the costs they pay, (2) their contributions are necessary to achieve the collective benefit, and (3) most beneficiaries will contribute their share of needed inputs (Popkin 1981; Frohlich and Oppenheimer 1971, 1974; Frohlich, Oppenheimer, and Young 1971). Nevertheless, as discussed in Box 4.1, designing voluntary arrangements to overcome free-rider incentives is quite difficult, particularly without the ability to make and enforce laws. Voluntary arrangements are also especially hard to use for the construction and maintenance of large-scale, capital-intensive projects, where free riding is likely to be easier than in small-scale, labor-intensive ventures.

Determining Preferences. Public sector provision of an infrastructure facility that yields nonexcludable benefits raises additional problems in determining preferences and organizing finances. When exclusion is feasible, preferences are revealed as a result of many quid pro quo transactions. Producers learn about preferences through the consumers' willingness to pay for various goods offered for sale. Where exclusion is not feasible, designing mechanisms that honestly reflect beneficiaries' preferences and their willingness to pay is complex, regardless of whether the providing unit is organized in the public or the private sphere. In very small groups, those affected are usually able to discuss their preferences and constraints on a face-to-face basis and to reach a rough consensus. In larger groups, decisions about infrastructure are apt to be made through mechanisms such as voting or the delegation of authority to public officials.

Expressing preferences through voting involves several key difficulties not found in quid pro quo transactions:

BOX 4.1   The Importance of Being a Government
(Rather Than a Voluntary Organization)

Although voluntary organizations can and do accomplish much in
the way of collective action, they have limits. In a recent study of
community management of renewable natural resources, James Thomson
(1991) explained why solving a local fuelwood crisis in the Sahel requires
that a local "public" be authorized to exercise some autonomous authority
to make and enforce laws.

The thing that most obviously distinguishes a government from
a non-governmental organization is the government's capacity to
make binding, non-voluntary decisions. In CILSS [Comité Inter-
état de Lutte Contre la Sécheresse au Sahel] countries, such power
has been reserved almost exclusively to the national government
and its local agents. . . . Thus, since the colonial era few sahelian
communities have enjoyed legal authority to engage in self-government.
. . .
The legal incapacity of local publics to constitute themselves
as jurisdictions authorized to exercise certain collective powers
means *no one can afford to deal with these problems.* Nobody in
overriding administrative jurisdictions—the *cercle*, the *arrondissement*,
or the *poste administratif*—has the finances, personnel or time.
Cantons, which in many sahelian states used to be viable units
of government (and were often based on pre-colonial local governments)
have been stripped of authority to engage in governmental activities
except when functioning as agents of the civil administrator of
the next largest jurisdiction. The same is true of village communities,
and their leaders, village headmen and elders. These same constraints
have been applied to pastoral ethnic groups as well, with their
different governmental structures.
Without capacity to make rules, "public entrepreneurship"—
identifying problems that create publics and then trying to devise
solutions to them—become prohibitively expensive. In such
circumstances, all decisions are voluntary and have to be taken
on the basis of a unanimity rule. That means any single person
can veto a collective decision. Trying to organize local governments
on the same basis as private voluntary associations is impractical.
Someone usually has a good reason to reject the decision, either
because they prefer the status quo or because they wish to extract
some benefit from the community in return for their consent.
Many people are subject to social pressure, but some generally
have reason and resources to resist it.

(continues)

BOX 4.1   (continued)

For example, someone proposes to deal with a fuelwood crisis in an area by keeping all livestock out of a hundred adjacent fields. By simply protecting regeneration of officially unprotected trees farmers can, in seven or eight years, encourage a canopy of trees on their fields. . . . Assume that most of the concerned farmers agree with the proposal. They believe the solution is an appropriate one to deal with fuelwood and building pole supply and soil conservation problems. But several farmers, all of whom own many goats and a few cattle, refuse. They want to continue allowing their animals to roam freely over village lands in the dry season, to save themselves the cost of paying a herder. These few persons can frustrate the desire of the large majority of farmers.

Nothing prevents the majority of farmers from controlling their own animals, but so long as the local community has no legal authority to make binding land use rules, the few with many animals can still allow them to roam and destroy most of the seedlings protected by the first group. Farmers who would have willingly controlled their own animals to help promote natural regeneration will let their stock continue to roam free. To do otherwise would be to make themselves suckers, whose attempts to improve the environment, in the absence of an ability to make binding land use rules, would only benefit the free riders. (Thomson 1991:13–15)

1. Voting mechanisms do not automatically translate diverse citizen preferences into a well-defined preference order for a variety of goods for a community as a whole (Arrow 1951). In fact, the order in which alternatives are presented and other aspects of the voting procedure strongly affect outcomes (Shepsle 1979).
2. Even if voting mechanisms adequately translate individual preferences for single goods, voting decisions are rarely confined to provision decisions concerning one and only one good. Citizens must usually vote for officials who make many decisions regarding the provision of different goods and services. Consequently, an official may represent a citizen closely in regard to one type of infrastructure but not in another (Bish 1971).
3. All votes are given equal weight, no matter how intense the preferences of some voters. Voters with strong preferences and

    indifferent voters could all be better off in settings where vote trading is possible (Buchanan and Tullock 1962).

4. Voters may lack a sense of responsibility for their choices and therefore invest little in searching for information about issues. A voter who perceives that his or her vote is of little consequence to the outcome has little incentive to invest time in analyzing issues and may well make poor choices (Buchanan 1960).

5. Those who will benefit more than others from the provision of a particular type of good are more motivated to advocate its provision through interest groups and other political activities.

6. If the costs of provision are spread evenly over a population, opposing the provision of a good that benefits one group disproportionately more than others may be more costly in time and energy than bearing the added costs of taxation.

7. Groups that are already effectively organized may be able to mobilize political support, leading to an overinvestment in rural infrastructure and generating a disproportionate benefit for themselves.

8. On the other hand, groups that are not effectively organized, such as poor farmers living in isolated rural areas of a developing country, may not be able to mobilize enough electoral support in national or provincewide elections to obtain investments in rural infrastructure facilities that would generate substantial economic benefits as compared to costs.

Use of nonvoting mechanisms to transmit information about citizen preferences is also problematic. Relevant time and place information is embedded in citizen preferences and may be very difficult for even highly motivated officials to access without preference-aggregating institutions. But, as suggested in the previous chapter, delegating authority to make decisions about infrastructure to officials who are organized hierarchically in public agencies generates distortions as information is transmitted up and down organizational channels (see Williamson 1975; Downs 1967; Campbell 1974).

Problems of exclusion may derive from several sources, including the property law relevant to particular types of infrastructure facilities. Local farmers, for instance, may have the physical capability to exclude potential beneficiaries from an irrigation system at a relatively low cost, but they may be legally precluded from doing so. Institutional arrangements can thus reinforce incentives to free ride, thereby creating situations in which free riding is rampant, or they may help to counteract the force of these incentives so that the problem of free riding is reduced.

Issues of Finance. The inability to exclude also has profound effects on financing infrastructure. Indeed, because public sector intervention is often required for many kinds of infrastructure, it is not surprising that much of public finance economics is predicated on the existence of public goods. If nonpayers truly cannot be excluded from using the infrastructure services, public finances cannot be raised through charges placed on users. Instead, some form of taxation, which may or may not reflect actual or potential usage, must be employed. Some forms of public taxation can do a reasonably good job of reflecting usage and, in turn, may help to ration infrastructure use (although this is certainly not always the case). For example, taxes on gasoline, lubricant, and tires, which are subsequently used to finance roads, may reasonably approximate the costs of providing road services. And property taxes imposed on the value of real property may approximate the relative benefits derived from protecting the property from fire damage (including damage caused by fires originating on neighboring property).

Where the benefits of publicly provided goods and services cannot easily be withheld from nonpayers, potential taxpayers will have strong incentives to evade the tax. This means that for a tax instrument to work well, it must be administered properly. Tax administration, however, is costly. Furthermore, if a taxpayer feels that he or she is bearing a tax burden that other, free-riding service beneficiaries are avoiding, they will have even stronger incentives to avoid the tax rather than become a "sucker."[6] Tax avoidance is also endemic in many developing countries where taxes are still associated with the tribute given to conquerors, rather than with the price paid by citizens of a free country to obtain needed public goods and services (Guyer 1991).

Another attribute of some goods with nonexcludable benefits is that, once they are provided, consumers may have no choice whatsoever as to whether they will consume. An example is the public spraying of insects. If an individual does not want this public service to be provided, there are even stronger incentives not to comply with a general tax levy. Thus, compliance with a broad financing instrument may, in turn, depend upon the legitimacy of the public-choice mechanism used to make provision decisions.

We are not arguing that all rural infrastructure facilities create nonexcludable services. In fact, they vary greatly as to how costly it is to exclude potential beneficiaries from accessing them. The costs of excluding potential beneficiaries from a well, for example, are usually quite low, and it is not at all unusual to find wells owned by individuals who require that nonowners pay for the water they draw.

But it is not always easy to introduce water fees in the operational phase of a project if users were not involved in the design or construction phases. Bigelow and Chiles (1980) described a USAID-funded project in Tunisia in which project funds were used to purchase water pumps and to pay guardians to operate and maintain them. The project did not, however, supply the fuel needed to run the pumps. Interestingly, the users in some areas organized themselves into a provision unit, decided on a fee schedule, collected fees, and kept good financial records. At other sites, attempts by the guardians to establish fees were resisted by users, and the guardians were removed. The study illustrates the feasibility of user fees for such small-scale infrastructure projects, and also the capability of even poorly educated and resource-poor individuals to organize themselves effectively. But the experience also demonstrates the problems that can arise when projects are designed primarily by officials of a centralized national government or donor agency who ignore questions of how the facility is to be operated and maintained.

In contrast to wells, it is very costly to fence a major highway connecting many villages to marketing centers or to construct and operate tollbooths at limited-access points along the highway. If the road is not used heavily, the costs of collecting tolls could easily exceed the revenue generated. Furthermore, excluding potential beneficiaries from some types of infrastructure, once provided, may not only be infeasible but may also result in inefficiencies.

Some analysts use the difficulty of excluding beneficiaries as the single attribute to distinguish goods and services most appropriately provided through market mechanisms from those that must be provided by a government. This leads to policy proposals that suggest the use of market mechanisms for all rural infrastructures where low-cost exclusion is feasible, including community wells, elementary schools, and primary health care facilities. However, there may be good reasons for public sector involvement in the provision and, potentially, in the production of such services. We therefore view the feasibility and cost of excluding potential beneficiaries from rural facilities as but one of several important attributes that need to be considered when designing institutions to provide these facilities. The capacity to exclude is necessary, though, if direct user charges are to be relied upon to finance all or part of the provision of the facility or its operation and maintenance. When the costs of exclusion are low, diverse forms of user fees can be considered as one means of paying for part or all of the provision of such services. When the costs of exclusion are extremely high, user fees drop out of serious consideration in the design of appropriate financial arrangements.

In summary, problems of exclusion exacerbate the difficulty of designing institutions that motivate individuals to make economic investments in maintenance activities in several ways. The following points are relevant here:

1. When those who benefit from maintenance cannot be excluded from receiving the benefits of these activities, they are motivated to ride free on the contributions of others.
2. Without counteracting institutions, the incentives to ride free lead to an underinvestment in the provision and maintenance of rural infrastructures.
3. To overcome the free-rider problem, decisions about infrastructure provision must be made collectively either by a governmental unit authorized to force beneficiaries to contribute money or other resources to provide for infrastructure maintenance or by a private organization that can exclude nonmembers from enjoying benefits.
4. Voting mechanisms that are frequently used to make collective decisions are quite imperfect methods for translating individual preferences into collective choices.
5. Reliance on simple voting mechanisms, unless they are crafted with considerable care, can lead to substantial over- or underinvestment in rural infrastructure and its maintenance.
6. The inability to exclude nonpayers at a low cost precludes utilization of private prices or publicly imposed user charges and, instead, requires some form of general taxation to mobilize the resources necessary to build and maintain infrastructure.

Rural infrastructure facilities vary considerably, however, with regard to the severity of the problems of exclusion involved. Whenever institutional arrangements can be designed to allow for effective exclusion of nonbeneficiaries, it is possible to rely both on more effective modes of revealing preferences and on diverse methods of resource mobilization, including user charges.

Problems of Joint Use

Another attribute that all rural infrastructure share is the considerable extent to which the flow of services they produce can be used simultaneously by multiple individuals or firms. Because infrastructure facilities are jointly used, the characteristics of the users and the effect one individual's use of the facility has on other users are important factors affecting the incentives of the joint users.

Distinguishing the infrastructure facility (the capital stock) from the flow of services produced by the facility helps to clarify the nature of the problem of developing rural infrastructure that can support joint use. Infrastructure facilities include many different types of capital assets, such as roads and bridges, community wells, schools, irrigation canals, and sewers. These can all be thought of as capital stocks that are capable, under appropriate conditions, of producing flows of services over their expected life.

Individuals consume (use) the flow of services produced by infra- structure facilities, rather than directly consuming the facilities themselves. Thus, farmers in a rural community consume transport services, not a local road. Irrigators consume water, rather than an irrigation system. And children consume the teaching services of a school system. Hence, the expected life of rural infrastructure facilities is always longer than the period of time in which consumers make use of the services they provide. Some users may return to use the flow of a particular facility many times; others may use it only once. The relevant time perspective of users may, therefore, vary markedly from that of the designers and financiers of the facility itself. These differing perspectives make it difficult to match benefits and costs to provide proper incentives in collective decisionmaking.

Characteristics of the Users. The number of individuals using a single facility may range from the twenty to fifty families that jointly use a community well or piped water system in a small village to the thousands of individuals who use the main artery of a rural road system. The size of the group receiving joint benefits is a variable that has been given considerable attention in the theoretical literature (see Olson 1965; Chamberlin 1974; McGuire 1974; Hardin 1982). In a very small group, the problem of reaching agreement about what patterns of use reduce the wear and tear on a facility and of how to provide adequate maintenance may be resolved in an informal, purely voluntary, face-to-face manner. But even in a very small group, incentives to free or easy ride on the contributions of others are still quite strong (as anyone who has shared living quarters with others will understand).

Without some form of organization in which individuals accept a set of mutual responsibilities and monitor each other to be sure that these responsibilities are carried out, everyone will tend to wait for someone else to undertake the onerous tasks involved in maintain- ing a facility. Organizing individuals to carry out mutual responsibilities is much easier in a small group than it is in a large group. In a small group, individuals have better information about each other's preferences; they are also more apt to know who will benefit the most from various ways of providing for a facility, and they have a more realistic understanding of the costs of constructing, operating, and maintaining it. Thus, the decisionmaking costs borne by a smaller group are less than those facing a larger group. A smaller group may, therefore, be able to solve the problem of how to assign rights and responsibilities to one another using informal or very simple institutional arrangements. A large group, on the other hand, will have to rely on formal mechanisms and sanctions to accomplish the same tasks.

The degree of concentration or dispersion of joint users also affects the ease of designing and adopting methods to sustain infrastructure. If most of the users live in the same village and see one another regularly as they use a facility, they can more easily recognize authorized users and communicate about use and maintenance as they go about their daily work. If those who jointly use the same facility are highly dispersed, mechanisms for determining how the facility should be used to reduce the rate of deterioration and how maintenance activities should be undertaken and paid for must be specially designed. Thus, solving the problems of maintaining roads used by many widely dispersed users requires far more effort than organizing to maintain a road used exclusively by a few farmers living near a road.

The relative homogeneity of the joint users of an infrastructure facility is a third characteristic affecting the ease with which users can organize to provide for the development and maintenance of the infrastructure. Individuals with relatively homogeneous assets and reasonably similar preferences will be affected in a similar way by rules that allocate responsibilities. Thus, where all farmers have plots at both the head *and* tail ends of an irrigation system, as is the case in the zanjeras described in Box 4.2, there is a greater homogeneity of interests than where each farmer has land only at the headwaters or at the tail end.

A single set of rules followed by heterogeneous users produces different stresses and tensions. If all the users of a rural road, for example, rely on bicycles or light vehicles, open-access rules for all weather conditions may produce reasonable levels of wear and tear on the road. Similarly, if nearly all road users own heavy vehicles that, if used during the rainy season, cause deep ruts in the road and increase transport costs to all, the users may jointly decide it is in their best interest to close the road for that season. Conflict over the rules of road use can arise, however, if some users rely

BOX 4.2   Self-Governing Philippine Irrigation Community

The term *zanjera* is a word of Spanish origin meaning "cooperative irrigation society"; it is also used to refer to the irrigation system managed by such a society. The organization of these societies and systems probably reflect both Spanish and precolonial indigenous cultural influences. Zanjera members are all landless farmers who have entered into a contract with a landlord that permits them to cultivate land as long as they construct and maintain an irrigation system for themselves and the landowner.

Zanjera Danum (a pseudonym) is one of 686 communal societies operating irrigation systems in the Philippine province of Ilocos Norte; this particular system is located on the extreme eastern edge of the coastal lowlands of the province (Coward 1979). It irrigates 1,500 hectares of land, which is divided into 32 named field areas (*sitios*). A fixed number of membership shares (*atars*) was assigned to each sitio when the zanjera was created. In Zanjera Danum, there are 564 atars. Each share has one or more claimants, with some claimants owning more than one share. The claimant holds the right to till the land associated with the atar and has responsibilities and privileges that the irrigation association assigns to each atar. The right to a portion of the system's water is the main privilege; providing labor and construction materials is the principal responsibility.

Each sitio is divided into two or more sections, one at the head of the lateral canal and one at the tail. The land associated with each atar consists of noncontiguous strips located in each of these sections; the holder of one atar thus farms two or more strips of land laying perpendicular to the canal feeding his or her fields. A few strips of land are set aside for the use of the sitio's zanjera leaders as compensation for the effort they expend on behalf of the zanjera membership. These strips are, however, located at the tail of each sitio, which means that, unless the irrigation water flow is adequate, the leaders will not be compensated for their efforts!

The operation and maintenance of the zanjera is governed by institutional arrangements that represent the three levels of the physical system: the canals serving the sitio, the branch, and the zanjera as a whole. One of the tasks of the leaders at all three levels of the association is to organize and monitor work details of differing sizes. The membership of the entire system is mobilized to repair the diversion structure and to clean the main canal. Each sitio is required to organize its members into five *sarungkar* groups, which are assigned a three-and-one-half-day duty period, in sequence. Thus, on a routine basis, a holder of one atar contributes three and one-half days of work every

(continues)

BOX 4.2   (continued)

two weeks, doing maintenance tasks or helping to rotate and distribute water in the system. Each of the five sarungkar groups of Zanjera Danum is composed of individuals from every sitio in the system; each sitio contributes two members to each sarungkar group for every ten atars in the sitio. Along with the rule that distributes the fields of an atar holder at both the head and tail ends of the canal, this way of forming work groups ensures that the interests of all the sitios are protected in the operation of the system.

Elaborate records of work contributions of each atar holder guarantees that rules concerning labor contributions are enforced. Atar holders who do not show up for work are fined. Conflicts do arise, and appeals up through the three levels of the zanjera are possible.

Unlike most administered systems, the zanjeras make efficient use of water through well-maintained structures of local design. The complex, multilevel organization of the zanjeras makes it possible to accurately represent the interests of each member in the different portions of the irrigation facility itself. It also facilitates the mobilization of appropriate amounts of labor for reconstruction, maintenance, or operational tasks that differ dramatically in scale. In some parts of the Ilocos region, several zanjeras have joined in a federation that permits them to exploit a single, large-scale diversion structure (see Siy 1982).

---

on heavy trucks and others on bicycles and light vehicles. This is particularly true if users of light vehicles do not have the power (political or physical) to prevent users of heavy vehicles from using the road inappropriately.

Homogeneity of interests also reduces the problems involved in using voting mechanisms to translate individual preferences into expressions of collective choice. The difficulties of reaching a stable consensus that can occur where heterogeneous preferences are present are reduced when a more homogeneous group is involved in joint use (see Plott 1967; McKelvey 1976).

Subtractability of the Flow. Jointly used infrastructure facilities can generate a flow of services that is entirely subtractable upon consumption by one user; in other instances, consumption by one does not subtract from the flow of services available to others.[7] In a survey of the literature on public goods, Cornes and Sandler (1986:6) defined rivalry in consumption, or perfect divisibility, as a characteristic of situations in which one person's consumption of a unit of the flow of benefits produced by a good fully eliminates any benefits that others can obtain from that same unit. The distinction between the joint use of an infrastructure facility and the partly or fully subtractive use of units of the flow of services from that facility is frequently not made in the literature and has resulted in substantial confusion.

The services produced by infrastructure facilities are not often consumed entirely by one individual, but the subtractability of the flow of services from facilities may vary substantially (see Blomquist and E. Ostrom 1985 and E. Ostrom 1985 for discussions of the difference between the facility and the flow). The withdrawal of an acre-foot of water from an irrigation canal by one farmer means that there is one acre-foot of water less for anyone else to use.[8] Most agricultural uses of water are fully subtractive, whereas many other uses of water— such as for power generation or navigation—are not. Most of the water that passes through a turbine to generate power, for instance, can be used again downstream. When the use of a flow of services by one individual subtracts from what is available to others and when the flow is scarce relative to demand, users will be tempted to try to obtain as much as they can of the flow for fear that it will not be available later.

Effective rules are required if scarce, fully subtractive service flows are to be allocated in a productive way. Charging prices for subtractive services obviously constitutes one such allocation mechanism. Sometimes, however, it is not feasible to price services. In these instances, some individuals will be able to grab considerably more of the subtractive services than others, thereby leading to noneconomic uses of the flow and high levels of conflict among users.

Allocation rules also affect the incentives of users to maintain a system. Farmers located at the tail end of an irrigation system that lacks effective allocation rules have little motivation to contribute to the maintenance of that system because they only occasionally receive their share of water.[9] Similarly, farmers located at the head end of such a system are not motivated to provide maintenance services voluntarily because they will receive disproportionate shares of the water whether or not the system is well maintained.

Consequently, for infrastructure facilities whose flows are highly subtractive, institutional arrangements related to the allocation of the flow of services are intimately tied to the problem of maintenance. It is highly unlikely that one can solve maintenance problems without careful attention to the efficiency, fairness, and enforceability of the rules specifying who can appropriate how much of the service flow, at what times and places, and under what conditions. Furthermore, unless responsibilities for maintenance are linked in a reasonable fashion to benefits obtained, the beneficiaries themselves will resist efforts to insist that they take responsibility for maintenance.

When multiple uses are made of infrastructure facilities, consumption by one user may seriously interfere with consumption by others. Use of a rural farm-to-market road by heavy trucks, for example, may make the road impassable for others. Similarly, allowing farm animals to use a community water source may rule it out as a domestic water supply. A system that produces a flow of positive benefits under one set of use conditions may produce a flow of negative costs under other conditions (Buchanan 1970).

Problems of Measurement

Although measuring some attributes of virtually all goods is difficult, measuring the demand for, the attributes of, and the benefits produced by an infrastructure facility presents numerous challenges to those responsible for provision. Measurement problems occur in all phases of infrastructure development—design, construction, operation, use, and maintenance. Furthermore, if the resources mobilized to pay for these activities are to be related at all to the benefits generated, measurement is crucial to devising adequate public financing schemes.

Ascertaining the level of demand for a facility is fraught with difficulties, particularly in the rural areas of developing countries where it is unusual to find authorized public institutions in which local preferences can be translated into independent taxing and spending decisions. One common approach to this measurement problem has been to rely on external assessments of the willingness of beneficiaries to pay, compared to the expected construction and/or maintenance costs of a particular facility. As is discussed at some length in Box 4.3, however, securing a valid measure of a community's willingness to pay is itself a difficult task. Analysts have learned by experience to discount reported willingness to pay in order to derive a more accurate estimate. In the case of water supply and sanitation projects, for example, a higher level of willingness to pay as demonstrated by a willingness to support higher levels of maintenance costs appears to be characteristic of communities whose residents enjoy greater incomes and thus are usually better educated. Over the past few years, CARE/Indonesia has also learned that villagers who face difficulties in accessing water value a piped water system more and therefore actually pay more for construction and maintenance than villagers who have an adequate but contaminated water supply (see McGowan, Rahardjo, and Ritchie 1991).[10]

BOX 4.3   Ascertaining Willingness to Pay for Water

If infrastructure facilities are to yield efficient outcomes and costs are to be recovered, reasonably accurate estimates of demand are crucial. When project planners greatly overestimate demand, cost recovery is highly unlikely because revenues will be less than expected; if demand is underestimated, the facility is unlikely to be built at an efficient scale. Demand is, of course, dependent on both the willingness and the ability of consumers to pay for the services generated by a facility.

One approach to estimating demand uses econometric estimation of actual behavior. As Whitting, Briscoe, and Mu (1987:23) argue, the approach is often limited due to its substantial data requirements. Information on household water use for different purposes, time spent collecting water, and socioeconomic characteristics of the households are all necessary. Also, the data should be obtained from villages already served by a variety of sources so that households face some real choices. These constraints are often difficult to overcome in developing countries.

The "contingent valuation method" is an alternative method that involves asking individuals what they would be willing to pay. The approach is not costly, it focuses on the village in which the project may be implemented, and it enhances participation in the planning process. It may, however, yield biased responses. Overstatements of willingness to pay can occur if respondents feel such answers will result in the project being built. Or they may understate willingness if they anticipate their responses will determine how much they actually *have* to pay. Question phrasing is, therefore, crucial to the quality of the results.

In spite of potential biases, the contingent valuation method has been used to estimate the willingness to pay for water in rural villages. One experiment was conducted in 1986 in two villages in Haiti— Laurent and St. Jean du Sud. The researchers attempted to determine how much villagers would be willing to pay each month for either a public standpost (a public fountain) near the home or a private connection within the house (with the respondent paying for the connec-tion). Because the researchers were also interested in the possible biases resulting from different types of questions, some respondents were simply asked to state how much they would be willing to pay, while others participated in a "bidding game" where respondents were requested to say whether they would be willing to pay several different monthly charges.

From the analysis, several findings emerged (Whittington, Briscoe, and Mu 1987:42–43):

1. There was no evidence of any systematic bias on the part of the respondents.

(continues)

BOX 4.3   (continued)

2. The bidding game format was more effective than direct, open-ended questions.
3. The willingness to pay (WTP) bids (at least in Laurent) corresponded to consumer demand theory. "For example, households farther away from their existing source were willing to pay more for a new public tap than a household close to the traditional source. Similarly, higher-income households were willing to pay more than low-income households."
4. "The mean of the WTP bids in the village of Laurent for public taps was $1.15 US per month, approximately 1.5 percent of per capita income and significantly lower than the 3 percent to 5 percent of income rule of thumb [often used by the World Bank]. The mean of the WTP bids for private connections (assuming the public taps were already in place [and were being paid for by the villagers]) was not significantly higher: $1.40 US per month."
5. A comparison of the data collected from the interviews with actual water use information showed that the survey data were "reasonably accurate."

The researchers concluded that "WTP bids offered by individuals are meaningful and not simply numbers 'pulled out of the air.' . . . Such information could be particularly helpful in (1) identifying communities which could meet specified cost-recovery targets, (2) determining prices and connection fees to charge for the improved water services, and (3) determining the appropriate level of service and the water system capacity required."

The authors acknowledge that villagers might state that they are willing to pay prior to a project and still not actually pay once a system is in place. If payments are actually to occur, those administering the water system must be willing to impose penalties on noncompliers, a task that, in the case of water, is considerably easier when each household has its own private tap that can be turned off by the authorities in the event the household refuses to pay.

In the design phase, it is often extremely difficult to obtain a reliable estimate of the benefits likely to result from the investment in a particular facility. Making such an estimate requires the following information:

- an estimate of the life of the facility, given assumptions about the patterns of use and the level of maintenance expected,
- an estimate of the units of required inputs and service output whose quality may vary over time,
- an estimate of the value of the flow of services to beneficiaries, and
- the adoption of an appropriate discount rate for converting future flows of benefits into present values.

The first three items are subject to substantial errors, and rules of thumb are often used for all four types of information. For example, fifty years is frequently used as the estimated life of irrigation systems, notwithstanding the extreme variation in the useful life of previously constructed systems. Fifty years may be a reasonable time horizon, given debt financing and interest rates, but there is nothing of special merit in the fifty-year period as such. Furthermore, different actors may use different time horizons and different discount rates in their implicit or explicit calculations. Also, for many infrastructure facilities (such as roads) the ultimate useful life will depend crucially upon the maintenance regime that is employed. Hence, the expectation that a road will yield twenty years of service prior to requiring reconstruction is likely to be entirely too optimistic if the assumed maintenance does not occur.

The quantity and value of use depend on many factors also unknown at the time the project is designed and evaluated. Rarely indeed does the number of hectares of land irrigated by recently constructed irrigation systems in the developing world approach the number specified in the original project plan (see, for example, Harriss 1984). Given all the rules of thumb and gross estimates that are involved in project evaluation, the actual benefits derivable from investment in an infrastructure facility are not often measured with much certitude or reliability.[11] Developing reasonably accurate estimates of expected costs and benefits is probably easier for smaller-scale projects than for larger ones. This is particularly true if the anticipated consequences of long-term projects are quite uncertain. For example, although there are analytical techniques capable of estimating the benefits of road improvements, they can be extremely complex to implement and can require considerable data. Beenhakker (1987:200–201) reviewed eight different estimation procedures and listed eighteen different types of data required for one or more of the techniques. Obviously, the larger the project, the harder it is to derive reasonably accurate estimates for such variables as production costs of agricultural products with and without the road project. The ambiguities of such measurements mean that overly optimistic assessments of project benefits may quite easily result, particularly if those basing decisions on the outcomes of such benefit-cost calculations (for example, agents of development assistance institutions) are required to spend large amounts of money.

A recent analysis of more than 1,000 World Bank projects completed between 1974 and 1987 concluded that "World Bank appraisal estimates are biased, that is, too optimistic" (Pohl and Mihaljek 1992:274). The authors compared the estimated rates of return from projects when they were being appraised (during the project planning) with estimated rates of return after the project construction phase had been completed (generally four to six years later). Their analysis showed great uncertainty associated with these estimates. Although cost overruns and delays explained a small portion of the uncertainty, they found that external market forces and domestic policy changes were particularly important factors.

Difficulties in measurement are also encountered in the construction phase. Whether a physical facility will survive over a long period of time depends critically on the quality of the construction process and the materials used. In many cases, a simple examination of the completed facility will not reveal, even to a trained observer, whether important steps were omitted in construction. Any facility using cement, for example, will deteriorate rapidly unless the cement has been reinforced, cured, and sealed properly. Unless construction contractors plan to remain in business and therefore know they might be identified with substandard construction, they have strong incentives to shirk. Posting bonds may be one means of reducing this incentive, but the problem of determining cause and culpability for faulty construction work remains. Incentives to shirk, steal materials, distort records, bribe inspectors, and generally avoid complying with costly construction specifications frequently exist.

Again, smaller-scale construction projects may be less vulnerable to such behavior. In smaller projects, it is easier for participants to discover who is responsible for inadequate construction. Most larger-scale construction projects utilize inspectors to examine key steps in the process before the next step covers up earlier work. But if inspectors are poorly paid and operate in a setting where public corruption is the normal way of doing business, inspection requirements may accomplish little more than give inspectors opportunities to line their pockets.

The frequency and quality of maintenance activities also may not be easily observable. To be most effective, many types of routine maintenance must be completed before the need for maintenance is obvious. Equipment requires regular oiling and the replacement of worn parts; potholes in roads require filling to prevent the road subgrade from becoming saturated with water, causing the entire roadway to give way; irrigation canals need to be desilted and weeded each year or the operational efficiency of these facilities will begin to decline. The effects of neglecting maintenance are often difficult for users of a system to detect until maintenance has been deferred too long.

Good maintenance requires well-tailored rules that provide incentives encouraging those responsible for maintenance to conduct these activities in a timely and appropriate fashion. Examples of maintenance activities successfully carried out over long periods of time by organized user communities are described in Boxes 4.2 and 9.2. These commonly involve small teams of users who are assigned well-demarcated tasks that can easily be monitored by team members and by others (Coward 1980; Siy 1982).

Unfortunately, measuring techniques themselves may be inappropriate and create undesirable incentives. For example, manual labor is generally used in Bangladesh to excavate soil and pile it up to form the earthen embankments that support the road surface. Though it is easy to measure the amount of earth moved and to compensate workers on that basis, successful road building requires considerable compaction of the earth (particularly in a delta area, where the soil is dominated by clay and contains large amounts of vegetable matter). By calculating compensation on the basis of the volume of earth moved and ignoring the degree to which it has been compacted, public authorities create no incentives for workers to compact the soil they move. The result is earthen roads that may lose up to 40 percent of their volume by the end of only a single monsoon season (Connerley et al. 1989b).

The ease of measuring patterns of use also varies from one type of rural infrastructure to another, and these patterns affect the type of resource mobilization instruments that can be employed. Without adequate measures of patterns of use, it is extremely difficult to determine the benefits derived from a system and thus to develop efficient and equitable forms of direct or indirect payment. Users have every incentive to underestimate the value they will receive from an infrastructure facility if they are required to pay for the services generated by it. Conversely, providers have strong incentives to overestimate the value to users. One of the most challenging institutional design tasks is devising low-cost means of monitoring patterns of use and assigning benefits and costs. For irrigation systems, this may mean that payments (either monetary or in-kind) are proportioned according to the number of acres actually irrigated. Again, however, ensuring that the data concerning these patterns of use are accurate is simpler for smaller facilities than for those that cover a large area.

Problems of Rent Seeking

All three of the attributes discussed here, particularly nonexcludability, provide a rationale for public sector involvement in the provision of an infrastructure facility. Assigning responsibility for a facility to a government agency helps considerably to reduce the opportunities for consumers to free ride. Similarly, where the services generated by the facility are not easily measured or are nonsubtractable, general financing mechanisms like taxes are required. Public authorities then have the power to penalize those who enjoy benefits but do not pay their taxes—that is, those who attempt to free ride.

Free riding on the part of ordinary consumers, however, is not the only possible strategic behavior associated with the public provision of infrastructure facilities. If governmental decisions concerning the nature and location of an infrastructure facility and its use can yield unearned advantages to particular individuals, those individuals may engage in what has been termed "rent-seeking" behavior. As Krueger (1974:291) noted, rent seeking can take many forms, including bribery, corruption, smuggling, and black markets.

In the case of public infrastructure, certain groups of potential users, such as large landowners, may stand to gain so much from infrastructure projects that they actively seek out public funds for projects generating disproportionate benefits for themselves.[12] A few individuals may benefit tremendously from a project even though its total costs exceed total benefits. Similarly, government officials may stand to benefit from investment in a facility of greater scale and complexity (and, therefore, greater cost) than would be warranted by a sober prediction of the returns expected from the investment (see especially Repetto 1986).

Rent seeking makes the productivity of any particular investment secondary to the private gains of the rent seeker. For example, irrigation officials may actively seek out donor funding for the development of an irrigation system. They do this not with the expectation of improving their own access to water (although this may also happen) but to improve their own position within a government agency. For example, large loans or grants for a new high-tech irrigation system to be built by an irrigation ministry may serve ministry officials better than a smaller loan for selective improvements in an existing system (for an example, see Box 7.1). This may be true in spite of the fact that the latter investment would come closer to generating returns that outstrip the costs of the investment. For many officials the main concern is that a large influx of funds supports the employment of more subordinates, thereby increasing his or her power and prestige (see Niskanen 1971). Projects also offer opportunities for officials to draw extrasalarial benefits from vendors of the equipment and construction materials that the agency will purchase to complete the facility. Because project funds come as bilateral country-to-country or multilateral agency-to-country transfers, frequently neither officials nor farmers personally bear any risk for repaying loan funds invested in ways that produce few benefits. In such a context, severe biases, with few checks, work to favor large, expensive infrastructure projects operated through public agencies.

Rent seeking is not specifically an attribute of rural infrastructure; it is a problem commonly associated with publicly provided facilities. But this does not mean that such structures should not be publicly provided simply because many such facilities yield benefits that are nonexcludable and/or nonsubtractable. What is required are institutional arrangements that severely limit the opportunities for rent-seeking behavior. Such institutions are considered in greater depth in subsequent chapters.

ATTRIBUTES OF RURAL INFRASTRUCTURE PRIMARILY AFFECTING PRODUCTION

The attributes just discussed primarily influence the provision or consumption side of infrastructure development. Nonexclusion, nonsubtractability, and difficulties of measurement are all frequently cited as reasons for public provision of much rural infrastructure. Deciding how infrastructure facilities are to be constructed, operated, and maintained is also a responsibility of the provider. And again, several production attributes affect how such activities can best be organized and, in turn, influence the sustainability of the investments. The particular attributes featured here include scale economies, asset specificity, and the rate at which the infrastructure deteriorates. We will close this section with a brief discussion of how the provision and production of public services can be considered analogous to a private sector industry.

Economies of Scale

Infrastructure facilities can vary markedly in the extent to which economies of scale exist in their design and construction and in regard to their operation, use, and maintenance. Economies of scale are present where the per unit costs of output decline as the level of output rises. These economies have three important implications for capital infrastructure design and operation.

Natural Monopolies. First, where per unit costs decrease as levels of output increase, the operation of normal market mechanisms will lead to monopolistic production and the allocative inefficiencies that monopolies create. This is the classic case of natural monopolies discussed at length in the public finance literature (Stiglitz 1986). In such cases, public sector intervention is considered necessary to overcome market failure. This argument underlies public provision of services such as urban water supply or telephone and electric utilities, which, though not characterized by problems of nonexcludability or nonsubtractability, still require public sector intervention in order to increase allocative efficiency.[13]

Organization of Production. The second implication of decreasing costs concerns the most efficient organization of activities associated with capital infrastructure development and maintenance. Again, it is important to consider the design, construction, and operation (including maintenance) of facilities separately because the potential for economies of scale are often not identical for all of these activities. The planning and design of infrastructure facilities may very well entail some economies of scale. Similar designs for bridges, for instance, may be utilized throughout a country or at least throughout regions experiencing similar climatic conditions. There is little reason for each bridge to be designed from scratch, particularly if the design process requires the use of skilled engineers, who usually are quite scarce in developing countries.[14]

Infrastructure construction may also yield economies of scale. This is particularly likely if the construction process requires substantial amounts of capital, for example, in building hard-surface roads. Construction economies of scale may be much less common in instances where labor-intensive techniques are as efficient as capital-intensive approaches. In some successful development projects, the initial design is undertaken by a large-scale agency but the actual construction of specific subsections of the project is carried out by small-scale, locally organized groups. The Malawi self-help water supply program discussed in Box 4.4 is one such project.

Perhaps even more important is the fact that the most appropriate scale for organizing design and construction may not be equally appropriate for operating and/or maintaining an infrastructure facility. For example, the maintenance of field canals is frequently best done by relatively small groups of irrigators who are intimately familiar with the canals and thus know where silt accumulates, which channels are weakened

BOX 4.4   Malawi Village Water Supply Systems

The village water systems completed in Malawi from 1968 to 1988 are now famous for the simplicity of the waterworks and for the amount of community labor mobilized to construct and maintain the systems (Hill and Mtawali 1989; Chauhan et al. 1983; Glennie 1983; Liebenow 1981). The villages served by these systems consist of clusters of homesteads that surround one of the many low, uninhabited mountains scattered throughout the country. Water for these gravity-fed systems is diverted from unpolluted rivers originating at high elevations. Each system consists of an uptake pipe, storage tanks, and a network of pipes and valves that feed tap stands. The Mulanji West water supply project, for example, contains 143 miles of pipeline that feeds 460 taps serving 75,000 users in 120 villages (Glennie 1983).

The system design for all the projects, as well as the specialized construction materials (polyvinyl chloride [PVC] and asbestos cement pipe), were supplied by the Ministry of Works and Supplies (MOWS), which was supported financially by a variety of public and private donors. Because the technology was entirely new to the villagers, ministry personnel supervised construction and maintenance work. Village residents supplied the remainder of the inputs, principally the labor needed to dig and refill trenches, excavate tank sites, carry pipe from deposit sites, and plant grass over the pipeline.

The support of village leaders, who still exercise great influence in Malawi, was crucial to the success of the projects. These people formed a project committee, which assisted engineers in fitting a design to a particular local area and oversaw the organization of labor. Separate committees were formed for each section, branch, and tap in each project. Project assistants worked with the committees at these levels to assist in organizing the workers and advising them on technical matters.

Arrangements for distributing the burden of work were critical to the successful mobilization of labor. Villagers were organized into work teams supervised by project, branch, and village committees representing differing communities of interest in the water system. All villagers contributed to the construction of the intake and the trenches needed for the large pipes that carried the water from the intake down the mountain to the point where it was diverted into branches. Each branch of the system was constructed by residents of the villages it served. The system that distributed water to standpipes within a village was constructed by village residents. A project committee and tap committees handle maintenance and repair. The project committee supervises branch repair teams, tap committees, and intake caretakers; raises small sums

(continues)

BOX 4.4 (continued)

for repairs and to pay the caretaker; and reports any repair work that cannot be handled by repair teams to the ministry's Rural Water Section. Members of project committees and repair teams contribute about one day per month to complete their tasks; members of tap committees donate about one-half day per month.

These institutional arrangements for construction and maintenance have been important to the success of the project. They have combined good time and place information about the construction site with modern engineering expertise in a productive manner. They also have represented the different communities of interest associated with a network-type infrastructure facility.

The effort is not, however, without problems. The government now faces the task of raising revenues to meet an increasingly higher proportion of maintenance costs as donors withdraw funding. It has not, however, succeeded in putting in place appropriate arrangements to finance these long-term maintenance activities (Gearheart 1990; Warner et al. 1986). Newer schemes pose an even greater challenge than the earliest ones. These recently developed systems have been built in periurban areas, whose populations find it more difficult to mobilize labor for construction and maintenance because they lack the social cohesion of villages. Also, the new systems have been much more complex. Because easily accessed water sources have all been tapped, the new systems must draw water from distant sources that are polluted. This means that more extensive piping systems and water treatment facilities are necessary. In their enthusiasm for a design that worked well in one type of social and physical setting, ministry engineers may well have replicated the design in settings for which it is not well suited.

by heavy flows of water, and where tree roots and weeds are likely to be a problem. The actual construction of the same field canals may most economically be accomplished by a fairly large engineering firm that can amortize specialized construction equipment over many such projects. (The knowledge of the farmers themselves about the lay of their own land and the pattern of rainfall and runoff in their area may, however, be very important in the design of these canals.)

Furthermore, in any large and complex infrastructure project, different parts of the system may require different maintenance strategies and different scales of operation. In regard to irrigation projects, Abeywickrema

(1986:23) pointed out that maintaining the headworks requires a highly trained technical staff to perform regular upkeep and to handle emergency repairs rapidly when breakdowns occur. The operation and maintenance of large distributor canals may require the presence of full-time paid personnel. Few farmers observe more than a limited section of a canal, and they are not motivated to handle either operation or mainten- ance activities on the main canals. Thus, farmers and official guards complement one another on the large canals. On the other hand, both the operation and maintenance of field canals may best be undertaken by the farmers themselves, both because they have the time and place information necessary to keep these parts of the systems working as efficiently as possible and because the improved performance of these canals may be sufficiently noticeable to the individual farmer that he or she will be motivated, given appropriate institutional arrange- ments, to keep them in good condition.

The preceding examples of farmers participating in the maintenance of irrigation systems illustrate another attribute related to at least some public services. This is the concept of "coproduction." Some services, such as education, cannot be produced unless the consumer actively participates in production (see, for example, Davis and E. Ostrom 1991). Although some infrastructure facilities can be produced by a government agency or a contracting firm without the active participation of those who will consume the flow of benefits from them, beneficiaries themselves may have to participate in related production activities. Farmers served by a new farm-to-market road are active coproducers of lower transportation costs when they transport their own produce to market. Consequently, rural infrastructure facilities that are designed, sited, and funded with the active participation of at least some of the future users are more likely to be effectively used.

Different scales of production can also be used advantageously in cases where various types of road maintenance do not require similar amounts of capital investments by those carrying out the maintenance. This is a feature of a maintenance-by-contract scheme implemented on national highways in Pakistan (Kampsax International, A/S 1986). There, a two-tier contracting procedure was utilized. One tier was used for simple, routine maintenance tasks; the other was used for more complex, periodic ones. Because routine maintenance includes simple activities like vegetation control, drain cleaning, and basic repairs to shoulders, culverts, and bridges, contractors did not need to own expensive, specialized equipment to fulfill their contracts. Hence, small contractors were eligible to bid on these jobs. To offer performance incentives, contracts were also restricted to bidders residing within the area through which the highway passes. Area residents could be expected to exert pressure on local contractors to carry out their responsibilities properly. The more complex types of maintenance—repaving, regraveling, and major repairs to bridges—were reserved for larger contractors who could demonstrate greater technical competency and who enjoyed access to more capital. This demonstrates that even maintenance efforts can take advantage of economies of scale if such economies are significant.

Nested Institutional Arrangements. Economies of scale have important implications for the organization of all of the public sector. Specifically, they may affect the efficiency of public service provision through the reliance upon several different tiers or layers of governmental organizations. Simply because production is characterized by substantial economies (or diseconomies) of scale does not mean that the provision unit has to be at the same scale as the production unit. It is possible for small-scale provision units (for example, local units of government) to arrange for production with large-scale production units (for example, large private contractors or even the national government). Alternatively, it is also possible for large-scale provision units (for example, national units of government) to arrange for production with small-scale production units (for example, local contractors or the residents of a particular village).

It is sometimes argued that when economies of scale characterize production, a large (for example, national) government should also provide for that service. In fact, service assignments may be most efficiently organized if some aspects of the service are controlled at the national level, while others are the responsibility of local units. We refer to such institutional structures as "nested" arrangements because smaller jurisdictions are encompassed within but not the subordinates of the larger ones.

Asset Specificity

Many of the assets used in creating and maintaining rural infrastructure facilities are general-purpose assets that can be redeployed in other activities without cost. Examples include dump trucks used to build roads that can also be used in many other kinds of construction projects. A contractor purchasing a dump truck for a road project is not investing in an asset that must sit idle in the future if he or she does not obtain another road-building contract.

On the other hand, some capital equipment used in producing roads, such as large road rollers, cannot easily be redeployed in other construction activities. Contractors investing in this type of equipment are exposed to considerable losses if they fail to win future road construction contracts. Williamson (1985) argued that parties to a transaction that involves the use of highly specific assets will desire safeguards in their contractual relationships before they are willing to make major investments. Monies allocated to such assets would be lost if the contractors cannot continue to make productive use of them. Therefore, one argument in favor of both public production and public provision for some facilities suggests that the assets used in production are so specialized that private contractors cannot afford to acquire them.

Even if the specificity of the equipment precludes private ownership, arrangements can be made to allow private production of construction or maintenance. For example, although assets like large road rollers may be owned by the government, they may be used by private contractors under lease arrangements in which the lease payments include all operating costs plus amortization. To avoid improper use of the equipment, the leases can also specify that the government will provide an operator to ensure that the private contractor does not misuse the equipment or fail to maintain it properly.

Another important institutional arrangement that promotes efficient production even if the public sector retains ownership of highly specialized assets is one that allows all public as well as private organizations to bid on construction and maintenance projects. For example, a public authority, such as a district, that owns a road roller should be able to bid to provide road-rolling services to another jurisdiction. This helps to ensure that the equipment is utilized most fully and enhances competition that can drive down the costs of carrying out the construction or maintenance activity.

It may also be possible to increase the likelihood that assets purchased for one purpose can be put to alternative use. For example, instead of relying on specialized bulldozers, ordinary tractors with grader blades can be used, albeit less efficiently, for road construction. The efficiency loss associated with the road-building activity can be offset by an overall greater utilization of the tractors in alternative pursuits.[15]

Rate of Deterioration

Infrastructure facilities differ greatly in terms of how sensitive their continued survival is to the patterns of use and maintenance they experience. In some instances, lack of maintenance can bring on rapid deterioration; in other cases, the rate of deterioration is so slow, at least initially, that it is imperceptible to the user. Consider, for example, the maintenance of capital equipment. If a bearing on a road roller is not greased, it will soon burn out and may render the entire piece of capital equipment inoperable. On the other hand, failure to change the oil in a truck will slowly decrease the lubricating efficiency of the oil, but only after some period of time will the engine finally fail to operate.

The rate at which rural infrastructure deteriorates may also depend on the original design and construction of a facility. A road built with a thick bed of crushed rock and several layers of surfacing materials may survive use by light vehicles and trucks for a much longer period of time, even without maintenance, than a gravel road constructed in the same location and subjected to a similar pattern of use. The initial construction costs of the gravel road, on the other hand, may be a fraction of the investment needed to build the sturdier road.

The differences in rates of deterioration and the perceptibility of a decline in the effectiveness of a facility are also likely to affect the willingness of users to undertake maintenance activities. For example, users of an irrigation system soon realize that, unless certain activities (such as clearing weeds and silt out of field channels) are carried out annually, the system will fail. It is much more likely that these activities will be undertaken as opposed to actions like patching cracks in a cement dam that will enhance the effectiveness of the system only over the longer run.

Public-Private Industry Structure

Although development projects are often organized around the production of one type of facility—roads, village water systems, health clinics, or schools, for example—little consideration has been given to the nature of these facilities other than the fact that they are usually public. The provision of such facilities, which are characterized by considerable difficulty in excluding consumers, generally requires some form of collective organization.

An alternative way of looking at the provision of public goods and services stresses the variety of goods provided by government. In their efforts to evaluate how different patterns of interorganizational arrangements affect performance, economists have long used the concept of an industry to refer to a "group of sellers of close-substitute outputs who supply a common group of buyers" (Bain 1959:6). It is assumed that the structure of an industry will vary considerably for different types of private goods and services and that given attributes of goods, combined with the structure of an industry, will affect how well industry participants perform.

The term *industry* is also useful for conceptualizing public sector organization in which many separate enterprises develop interdependent patterns of behavior. Some organizations in a public service industry perform provision activities; others are production agencies. We can think of the public sector as comprising many public service industries—roads, education, police, and water industries, among others. The governmental component in some industries, such as national defense or police, is proportionately larger than in others. The boundary of a public service industry includes those enterprises participating in the production or provision of a related set of goods or services that share similar technologies and production methods and are jointly consumed by a defined set of individuals.

When visualizing patterns of relationships that apply to the organization of governments, scholars frequently use a pyramid. The apex of the pyramid is occupied by some center of authority that exercises sovereign prerogative and has the last say in making governmental decisions. In visualizing the interorganizational structure of public service industries, however, a matrix is a more appropriate representation.[16] Collective-consumption units can be arrayed as the columns in a matrix, and producers form the rows. The specific arrangement between providers and producers in a particular service, such as a contract between a highway department and a private road construction firm, can be entered in the cells of the matrix. Once the organizational elements are arrayed in this manner, it is possible to develop a quantitative measure of the structure that can be used in predicting the incentives that industry participants will face and the likely behavior of those participants. For a rigorous comparison of the performance of public service industries that are organized differently, measures must be developed to quantify attributes like the number of different providers and producers involved or the proportion of total provision or production carried out by any one firm or governmental unit in the different structures.

CONCLUSION

Rural infrastructure development is a complex phenomena, due to the many attributes of infrastructure that make it difficult for individuals to design, construct, operate, and maintain these facilities effectively and efficiently. Some problems stem simply from the fact that infrastructure facilities by nature have potentially long, useful lives during which the circumstances of users may change. Thus, decisions concerning their initial design and subsequent maintenance are extremely difficult to perfect.

Even greater problems arise, however, because the sustainability of the bulk of the rural infrastructure in the developing world is influenced greatly by public sector decisionmaking. We agree that there are often good reasons for public sector involvement in the *provision* of rural infrastructure facilities. This chapter has shown, however, that the arguments favoring public sector *production* are less convincing.

Provision-related attributes of the services of at least some rural infrastructures include nonexclusion, nonsubtractability, and problems of measurement. When one or more of these attributes is present, there are valid reasons to expect that some form of collective-provision arrangements will have to be made if the good is to be provided.[17] But as was also noted earlier, when public sector provision is warranted, strong incentives may be created for individuals to seek rents or unearned private benefits from provision decisions.

The nature of the production process also affects the desirability of collective, rather than purely private, decisionmaking. If there are substantial economies of scale obtainable from a production process, as in the generation of electricity, public sector involvement in the process is necessary to avoid welfare losses associated with monopoly production. Similarly, if asset uses are highly specific, collective ownership may be required. Finally, we recognize that the slow deterioration of assets, particularly where collectively provided, creates strong incentives to defer maintenance.[18]

It is important to recognize that all rural infrastructure facilities do not share the same set of provision and production attributes. Thus, we cannot make any general statements about the long-run sustainability of all infrastructure facilities. Furthermore, as will be emphasized in subsequent chapters, the institutional arrangements used to provide and produce infrastructure services affect their sustainability.

Consider, for example, cases of rural road networks and small irrigation facilities. A single small farmer in a developing country is unlikely to be willing or able to produce such facilities on his or her own. Instead, the farmer would find it beneficial to join with others in providing for the construction and maintenance of these capital facilities. But, again, there is no good reason to think that all aspects of the production of the facility and its upkeep will *have* to be provided in an identical manner. The design of each may entail economies of scale or require specific assets (such as highly trained civil engineers) that are often in short supply in low-income countries. On the other hand, if the proposed facility is sufficiently simple or if it replicates existing facilities, it may be designed entirely by the local people who will use it. Similarly, high-quality construction may be attained entirely through the use of local inputs, without external assistance of any sort; other facilities, however, may require highly specialized construction inputs, such as heavy machinery, that are not readily available locally.

The characteristics detailed in this chapter probably have the most profound effect on the willingness and ability of a collectivity to mobilize the necessary resources and allocate them to maintenance. As we will stress in the final chapter, the characteristics of the infrastructure facilities and the services they yield create different types of challenges for those attempting to design diverse institutional arrangements to provide rural infrastructure.

Consider a network of local rural roads. Roads generally deteriorate at very slow rates, and even as they deteriorate, the additional costs of transportation to most users are likely to be relatively small, so that no single user finds it in his or her best interest to undertake maintenance. Even a small group of road users may be unwilling to handle the required maintenance if they feel that the bulk of the benefits of their efforts would accrue to users outside the group (as is the case with arterial roads).[19] Adding to the difficulty of ensuring the maintenance of rural roads is the fact that it is often very difficult to measure and monitor road usage. Even resource mobilization techniques, such as taxing gasoline, cannot reach owners of animal-drawn carts that often do great damage to earthen road surfaces.

Unlike the users of rural roads, which have strong public good attributes, users of small irrigation facilities may have a distinct interest in ensuring that water continues to flow through the system. Although the deterioration of irrigation canals resulting from silt accumulation is not particularly rapid, tail-enders (those living at the tail end of the system) probably recognize quite quickly that the flow of irrigation water has slowed. Because their entire livelihood may be at stake, farmers tend to be quite willing to contribute resources to ensure an adequate flow of water. And if the irrigation system serves a relatively small number of reasonably homogeneous users, a collective approach to system maintenance is likely to be perceived by all to be in their self-interest. All recognize that irrigation water is a fully subtractable resource.

Where an irrigation system or other infrastructure facility is large and serves many people, it is probably much easier for individuals to free ride and hope that others will maintain the system. This is especially likely when facilities are provided for by "the government" and participants expect that public resources will be utilized to maintain them. Only very careful crafting of institutional relationships in such instances can overcome incentives to ignore maintenance. We will return to the differences between the problems posed by large-scale facilities with many participants and those of smaller-scale facilities with fewer participants in Chapter 10.

NOTES

1. For an early discussion of these concepts, see Musgrave (1959) and V. Ostrom, Tiebout, and Warren (1961). For applications of these concepts, see E. Ostrom, Parks, and Whitaker (1978); ACIR (1987, 1988); and V. Ostrom, Bish, and E. Ostrom (1988).

2. In the United States, where some communities use single-purpose funds to finance services that, in other locations, are financed from a general fund, there is some evidence that proprietary fund administrators are more sensitive to long-term costs (including maintenance) than are general fund managers, who pay more attention to the immediate budget constraints facing the jurisdiction. Sharp (1986) attributed a portion of this difference to the fact that proprietary fund accounting requires reporting of asset depreciation.

3. This is the classic market failure argument made by Musgrave (1959) and others following in his footsteps.

4. The incentive to shirk is closely related to the incentive to free ride. Shirking is a strategy used by producers of goods; free riding is a strategy used by consumers of goods. Where the same individuals engage in both provision and production of the same infrastructure, as well as its maintenance, the distinction is difficult to make.

5. The theory of clubs has evolved in analyses of situations where strictly private arrangements suffice to overcome free-rider problems (see Buchanan 1965; Sandler and Tschirhart 1980; Cornes and Sandler 1986).

6. These issues were considered by Levi (1988:52–53), who emphasized the "quasi-voluntary" nature of tax compliance. It is voluntary because taxpayers choose to pay. It is quasi-voluntary because noncompliants are subject to coercion, if they are caught. Voluntary compliance is, in turn, influenced by the confidence taxpayers have that (1) decisionmakers will actually provide the services being paid for and (2) other constituents will also comply.

7. This attribute has been given many names in the technical literature, including divisibility and jointness of consumption. At low levels of use, a facility producing subtractive use-units may not be characterized by rivalry, however, because many use units are available to potential consumers. As the demand for subtractable use units rises, rivalry increases.

8. An acre-foot is the volume of water required to cover one acre of land with one foot of water.

9. See Harriss (1977) for a grim description of the lack of effective allocation rules and maintenance of irrigation projects in Sri Lanka. Perera (1986) and Uphoff (1985a, 1985b, 1985c) described a major effort to change the institutional

structure and the basic relationships among farmers on the Gal Oya project in Sri Lanka, which dramatically reversed what had been a hydrological nightmare.

10. In recent years, CARE/Indonesia has steadily increased the demands made on villagers to contribute to the construction and maintenance costs of water projects it supports. In 1988, CARE launched a five-year pilot project that requires participating communities to pay 100 percent of construction and maintenance costs, including skilled and unskilled labor, local and imported materials, and equipment. CARE contributes only technical assistance and logistical support. As of June 1991, fifty communities had agreed to participate in the program, twenty-three water committees were operating, sixteen systems had been completed, and another eighteen were in process. Evaluators considered these projects to be among the most successful community water system development efforts currently in operation (see McGowan, Rahardjo, and Ritchie 1991).

11. Irrigation experts are frequently uneasy about the effect of using discount rates of 10 or 15 percent in estimating flows of benefits and costs. This is sometimes responsible for "the haste to get benefits, the dropping of components to lower early costs, the ignoring of large late-arising benefits and costs . . . and worst of all, the fraudulent manipulation of forecasts to ensure that the project arithmetic produces the minimum cut-off rate of return" (Carruthers 1988:25).

12. One form of rent seeking engaged in by large-scale developers involves encouraging a national government to set up a large development agency to provide roads and other facilities for massive development of previously undeveloped areas. Given the tax breaks associated with many of these projects, they are unsustainable economically and environmentally. Emilio Moran's recent account of the effects of creating a large-scale development agency (SUDAM) and a regional development bank (BASA) in the Amazon gave a dramatic picture of the perverse incentives created.

> By going through SUDAM and BASA, it was possible to have 50 percent of personal and corporate income tax liability invested in an approved development project. Developers not only escaped paying taxes to the federal government, but in addition they received three dollars from their tax liabilities for every dollar invested. They were able to keep all four dollars, and the capital gain was tax-free. . . . Most of the deforestation in the southeastern portion of the Amazon Basin is traceable to this specific policy.
>
> Not only was this tax holiday and subsidy attractive in its own right, but the great majority of the projects ratified by SUDAM were extensive cattle ranches. The conversion of forest to pasture took place at a rate of approximately 8 to 10,000 square kilometers per year in the 1970s. Conversion increased to 25,000 square kilometers in the late 1980s. . . .
>
> A recent simulation of a typical 20,000 hectare ranch receiving a 75 percent subsidy demonstrates that livestock activities are profitable

only when they receive the full array of tax holidays. Without them, the ranches are not profitable and can achieve positive internal rates of return only through overgrazing. (Moran 1992:8–9)

13. Problems still arise, however, because the marginal cost pricing rules that are required to achieve allocative efficiency lead to a failure to cover the total operating costs of utilities.

14. Uniformity of design can, however, also be inefficient. For example, in a country where quite different building materials are available in different regions, it may make little sense to create a single design calling for concrete schools if local conditions make cement expensive relative to other building materials, such as wood.

15. For a discussion of various technologies in the road sector, see Swaminathan and Lal (1979).

16. See E. Ostrom, Parks, and Whitaker (1974, 1978) for examples of how matrices are used to measure the structure of polycentric interorganizational structures.

17. We recognize that there can be exceptions to this. For example, if a road with relatively little traffic yields very important benefits to a single user, the user may be willing to provide that road and not attempt to exclude others from using it. In this instance, the private benefits from the "public" good exceed the costs and bring additional uncompensated benefits to nonpayers.

18. The disincentive to maintain privately owned infrastructure is considerably less than that for collectively provided infrastructure because owners recognize that their investments will depreciate much more rapidly without adequate maintenance and that they will bear the entire cost. Therefore, it is not surprising to find that in many developing countries with poorly maintained public infrastructure, private owners of vehicles, houses, or animals take very good care of these assets.

19. Small groups of road users, specifically bus owners, were willing to invest in repairs on roads in Bangladesh when members of the group recognized that they personally would benefit significantly from improved roads (see Connerley et al. 1989b).

5

Evaluating Institutional Performance

We have learned in the last two chapters that perverse incentives are endemic in the development of rural infrastructure facilities. Without effective, counteracting institutions, major problems in the provision and production of rural infrastructure are likely to occur. Chapter 3 emphasized the types of transaction costs that arise when many individuals with different preferences, resources, and stakes are involved in the numerous decisions associated with developing and maintaining infrastructure. Chapter 4 explained how the attributes of the provision and production of jointly consumed infrastructure facilities further complicate decision processes. All these problems combined could easily lead to the creation of infrastructure that cannot, for a variety of reasons, be maintained.

In Chapters 6 through 9, we will analyze alternative institutional arrangements designed to reduce one or more of the transaction costs and the perverse effects of attributes of goods reviewed in the previous chapters. To evaluate the performance of these alternative institutional arrangements, however, it is necessary to specify a set of *valuative criteria*. This is the task of the current chapter.

We begin by explaining the overall performance criteria that we will use to evaluate the outcomes of institutional performance—efficiency, equity (including both fiscal equivalence and redistribution), accountability, and adaptability. Trade-offs obviously exist among these criteria, and different institutional arrangements are capable of yielding outcomes with higher or lower scores on each criteria. We argue that these criteria significantly affect the sustainability of infrastructure investments.

The cost of sustaining infrastructure depends crucially on the institutional arrangements used. For example, if an institutional arrangement provides no incentive to monitor contractor performance, profit-maximizing, opportunistic contractors are likely to shirk in their performance by producing substandard infrastructure. Such infrastructure will, in turn, deteriorate at a more rapid rate than was envisioned by designers.

Given the key role of transaction costs in determining the sorts of incentives associated with alternative institutional arrangements, it is necessary to examine these costs in considerable depth when analyzing the institutional arrangements. We believe that it is critical to study a set of intermediate performance criteria that, together, constitute the transformation (production) and transaction costs associated with the provision and production of facilities with public good characteristics. A discussion of intermediate performance criteria is found in the second section of this chapter.

In the final section of this chapter, we will summarize our argument and explain how the full set of criteria are used in subsequent chapters. Throughout this chapter and the remainder of this volume, it is important to keep in mind that a change from one type of institutional arrangement to another usually reduces some transaction costs and increases others. Whether the net effect of a change in institutional arrangements is positive, neutral, or negative depends on how the costs and benefits of several effects balance out.

OVERALL PERFORMANCE CRITERIA

It may be tempting to think that maintaining rural infrastructure is the one and only objective to be sought when considering the impact of alternative institutional arrangements for providing and producing these facilities. This would, however, be fallacious. Some facilities are simply inappropriate for the situations for which they were built and should not be maintained. If substantial environmental harms are generated, for example, the benefits produced by the facility may not exceed the total construction and environmental costs, and the project would be unsustainable even before the costs of operation and maintenance are calculated. Instead, it is necessary to consider a variety of objectives for institutional arrangements that can lead to sustainable *development*. The five that we focus upon are (1) economic efficiency, (2) equity through fiscal equivalence, (3) redistributional equity, (4) accountability, and (5) adaptability.

Economic Efficiency

Economic efficiency is determined by the magnitude of the change in the flow of net benefits associated with an allocation or reallocation of resources. When an economy operates efficiently, no reallocation of resources will improve the welfare of some person or group without making someone else worse off. This concept is, of course, intimately related to rural infrastructure sustainability. A project is sustainable only if the benefits of operating and maintaining facilities exceed the full set of direct and indirect costs. Indeed, it would be better to allow a structure to deteriorate if the resources necessary for operating and maintaining it exceed the benefits to be gained from such activities.

The concept of efficiency plays a central role in studies estimating the benefits and costs or rates of return to investments, which are often used to determine the economic feasibility or desirability of infrastructure projects. Economic efficiency also provides the rationale for a careful consideration of the issues addressed in the previous two chapters. A principal reason for government intervention in an otherwise competitive market is the existence of public goods; as suggested in Chapter 4, a private market is generally not capable of efficiently allocating goods with public goods attributes (nonexcludability and nonsubtractability). Similarly, opportunistic behavior like shirking can lead to an inefficient allocation of resources. When considering alternative institutional arrangements, it is, therefore, crucial to consider how revisions in the rules affecting participants will alter behavior and, hence, the allocation of resources.

Finally, alternative methods of financing infrastructure development can have differential impacts on the allocation of resources. Several tax and fee instruments have nonneutral effects on behavior. And because the particular tax or fee adopted can affect subsequent allocations of resources, it may improve or worsen the general level of welfare in a society and consequently affect economic efficiency. For example, greater economic efficiency can result if taxes are used to discourage activities that produce undesirable externalities or side effects, as might be deemed the case with taxes on alcohol. On the other hand, if product prices already accurately reflect the costs to society of the consumption of these products, tax-induced changes in prices—which, in turn, alter consumers' or producers' decisions—can result in a net loss in social welfare. In fact, issues like this are central to studies in the field of public finance.[1]

Equity

Economic efficiency is not always the sole criteria for judging institutions responsible for creating sustainable capital infrastructure.

Equitable treatment for all people is often of equal importance. Equity or fairness can, however, be judged in different ways. There are two principal means to assess equity: (1) on the basis of the equality between individuals' contributions to an effort and the benefits they derive and (2) on the basis of differential abilities to pay. We will consider each in turn and utilize both concepts in our overall evaluation of institutional arrangements.

Fiscal Equivalence. The concept of equity that underlies an exchange economy holds that those who benefit from a service should bear the burden of financing that service. And those who derive greater benefits are expected to pay more. This concept essentially expresses a concern for fiscal equivalence between the benefits derived from a public service and the costs of providing that service.[2]

Perceptions of fiscal equivalence or a lack thereof can affect the willingness of individuals to contribute toward the development and maintenance of rural infrastructure. If infrastructure users feel they are being asked to contribute monetary or nonmonetary resources significantly different from those provided by other users in similar circumstances, they will be less willing to comply. Thus, when taxpayers observe or perceive that some of their neighbors are not paying a local tax, they, too, may decide not to pay, thereby resulting in ever-lower tax compliance. On the other hand, in-kind contributions of labor to "finance" the construction or maintenance of rural infrastructure are directly observable by all. It is, therefore, easier for participants to monitor fiscal equivalence if this resource mobilization technique is used, rather than if monetary charges are imposed on users. This is especially true if the participants are unable to read and understand financial accounts.

Redistribution. Policies that redistribute resources to poorer individuals are of considerable importance in developing countries where distributions of wealth are highly skewed. Thus, although efficiency would dictate that scarce resources be used where they produce the greatest net benefit, equity goals may temper this objective, resulting in the development of facilities that benefit particularly needy groups. Likewise, redistributional objectives may conflict with the goal of achieving fiscal equivalence. Only wealthier individuals may have the wherewithal to contribute resources that fully reflect the benefits they derive from using infrastructure.

Redistributional goals are often stated as the rationale for infrastructure investment in low-income countries, and for that reason, such activities are frequently subsidized. Caution must be exercised, however, in presuming that the poor are the primary beneficiaries of subsidized services. In fact, it has been asserted that "it is often the middle class and the rich, not the poor, who benefit most from free services" (Akin, Birdsall, and de Ferranti 1987:27). Furthermore, the objective of income redistribution is often used by those engaging in rent-seeking behavior to legitimize public sector activities that, in reality, disproportionately benefit those with lesser needs.

These two views of equity can lead to quite different conclusions regarding the equity of institutional arrangements, particularly those used to finance goods and services. For example, if a water pump provides benefits to all users, the benefit or fiscal equivalence principle would hold that everyone using the pump should be required to pay the marginal costs associated with their use of the facility. But under the ability-to-pay principle, such fees may be deemed inappropriate because they would reduce low-income individuals' access to the pump. This view would suggest that the service be subsidized through other means (which will have equity implications of their own).

Accountability

We also stress that officials must be accountable to citizens concerning the development and use of a public facility. In the absence of accountability, the provision decisions discussed in Chapter 4 are likely to be made without much regard for the desires of the final users. Furthermore, without accountability, actors can engage successfully in the various strategic behaviors considered in Chapter 3. Ultimately, the failure to hold officials accountable can result in the construction of inappropriate rural infrastructure.

Accountability regarding the use of scarce resources is often of paramount concern, particularly in the case of donor-financed facilities. Without adequate accountability, the targeted groups are unlikely to receive the benefits of donor-assisted projects, and resources can more easily be wasted.

Much policy analysis takes as a given that the institutional arrangements being considered promote accountability. Consequently, these analyses focus primarily on the performance objectives of efficiency and equity. Developing countries, however, often lack competitive elections, a free press, and an independent judiciary, and ensuring the accountability of public officials in particular can be much more difficult in such nations.

In fact, the accountability objective need not conflict greatly with efficiency and equity goals. Indeed, achieving efficiency requires that information about the preferences of citizens be available to decisionmakers, as does achieving accountability. Institutional arrangements that effec- tively aggregate this information assist in realizing efficiency at the same time that they serve to increase accountability and to promote the achievement of redistributional objectives.

Adaptability

Finally, unless institutional arrangements are able to respond to ever-changing environments, the sustainability of infrastructure invest- ments is likely to suffer. Rural areas of developing countries are often faced with natural disasters and highly localized special circum- stances. If an institutional arrangement is too inflexible to cope with these unique conditions, it is unlikely to prosper. For example, if an irrigation system is centrally controlled and allocates only a specific amount of resources for annual and periodic maintenance, it may not be able to meet the special needs associated with a major flood that destroys a section of the canal system. Institutions subject to greater local control might have anticipated such an emergency and would have had a reserve fund and rules that made it possible to respond appropriately to such a crisis.

The adaptability of resource mobilization instruments is similarly desirable. An instrument should be sufficiently adaptable to mobilize resources in the face of changing economic conditions. Particularly important in this regard, a monetary tax or fee should be capable of generating revenues in the face of increased demands for infrastructure services or in response to increased operating costs due to inflation. Taxes or fees that must be altered through explicit policy decisions are much less adaptable than are revenue instruments that automatically yield additional revenues as price levels rise, as the local economy grows, or as the number of public service users increases.

Trade-offs Among Criteria

Trade-offs are often necessary when using the various performance criteria as a basis for selecting from alternative institutional arrangements. Particularly common in that regard are choices between the goals of efficiency and of redistributional equity.[3] Although we do not dispute the crucial importance of redistribution in many contexts, the primary focus in this volume is on an efficient allocation of resources. In fact, this objective does not necessarily conflict with distributional goals. Infrastructure investments may be targeted toward particular segments of society, such as the poorest of the poor, and these facilities should still be operated so that the target groups can derive the largest benefits possible from the investment. Although any ultimate decision regarding trade-offs between equity and efficiency must be made by the citizens and officials of each country, maximizing returns from targeted investments is still preferable to a total lack of concern for the efficiency of investments of scarce resources.

Another trade-off issue arises most explicitly in considering alternative methods of funding infrastructure maintenance. Economically efficient pricing of the use of an existing facility should reflect only the incremental maintenance costs and any external or social costs associated with its use. This is the well-known efficiency pricing rule that requires that prices equal the marginal costs of usage. It is especially problematic in the case of goods with nonsubtractability attributes. In such instances, the marginal cost of another user utilizing the good is zero; hence, the efficient price is also zero.

Consider the case of a rural road. Because congestion costs are likely to be zero in the case of rural roads, economically efficient user charges should equal only the marginal maintenance costs associated with each additional user (assuming that it is feasible to administer such charges). Imposition of charges exceeding the marginal cost of maintenance restricts use of the road below the level that would be economically efficient, to the point where benefits would be suboptimal.[4]

Total maintenance costs, however, may be considerably greater than the costs of maintenance due solely to traffic because much road maintenance in low-income countries is required simply to slow deterioration caused by aging and weather. This means that charging efficient prices (prices equal to the marginal, use-related maintenance costs) will yield revenues that fall short of the total amount needed to maintain the road. Hence, efficient prices result in inadequate revenues; adequate use-based prices result in inefficiently low road utilization. If efficient prices are imposed, some alternative incremental revenue source must be found to generate the additional funds needed.[5]

In spite of the potential for efficiency losses to an economy, we argue that there are good reasons for user prices to sometimes be set at levels greater than use-related marginal maintenance costs. First, from a practical standpoint, user fees may link payments to beneficiaries and achieve fiscal equivalence. Second, from a purely theoretical perspective, one must recognize that insisting on marginal cost pricing in one portion of an economy does not necessarily mean that the overall allocative efficiency of the economy will be improved. This concept, known as the theory of the second best (Lipsey and Lancaster 1956), limits the generality of theoretical conclusions concerning economic efficiency in an economy characterized by numerous market failures, such as many administered prices, extensive sectoral subsidies, and substantial noncompetitive factors. The theory suggests that piecemeal (single-sector) analytic work cannot confidently rely upon the first-best allocative rules or the observed prices in the rest of the economy to evaluate efficiency consequences in the sector or area under study (Friedman 1984:415).

Given these important trade-offs, we suggest the following pragmatic advice. If the benefits of maintaining an infrastructure facility exceed the costs, one should first determine whether a resource mobilization instrument or combination of instruments can generate adequate resources to meet the costs after accounting for administrative expenses. If that criterion is satisfied by several instruments, those instruments that closely link the resources generated with benefits received should be considered most appropriate because they are equitable on the grounds of benefits received. If redistribution concerns are important, efforts must be made to ensure that subsidized services are actually made available to those least able to pay full costs and in a manner that will avoid permanent dependency.

INTERMEDIATE PERFORMANCE CRITERIA

Systematic comparison of the performance of institutional arrangements for providing and producing goods and services with diverse characteristics is a recently developed and still evolving field of inquiry.[6] In the zero transaction-cost environment of neoclassical economics, one can easily demonstrate that open, competitive markets push producers to seek combinations of land, labor, and capital that produce private goods at their lowest possible cost per unit. Similarly, consumers obtain and pay for the best mixture of goods and services obtainable, given the resources available to them. Thus, compared to other institutional arrangements for providing and producing private goods, an open, competitive market keeps production costs at as low a level as is feasible and distributes goods to those who have the highest marginal value for them. The dual goals of economic efficiency and fiscal equivalence are attained. However, although markets generate substantial incentives to create wealth, they do not redistribute current resources from wealthier to poorer individuals without some sort of subsidy. That is, the market is not an effective institutional device to achieve redistributional goals.

Comparing the performance of institutional arrangements is a more complex undertaking when the various transaction costs discussed in

Chapter 3 are recognized. In addition to production costs, the coordination, information, and strategic costs involved in transacting must be added to the analysis. When transaction-cost analysis is combined with production-cost analysis, some institutional arrangements that had previously been misunderstood or considered inefficient have been evaluated more positively (see Williamson 1985). Furthermore, transaction-cost economists do not conclude that markets are always the best institutional arrangements, even for private goods.[7]

The situation is made even more complex when the additional characteristics of goods and services normally provided by public sector institutions are included. Thus, for a systematic comparison of the costs and benefits of diverse institutional arrangements used to provide and produce rural infrastructure, substantially more variables must be taken into account. Both production costs and transaction costs can be used as intermediate criteria to evaluate performance. The results of such analysis can then be used to judge institutional arrangements on the basis of the five overall criteria discussed earlier.

Evaluating how institutional arrangements compare across overall criteria is quite a challenge. Because these criteria require a summary of all costs and all benefits, only very detailed studies can even begin to derive approximate measures of efficiency, equity, and accountability. Thus, an analytical examination of the likely trade-offs between intermediate costs is valuable in attempting to understand comparative institutional performance.

In the remainder of this section, we will summarize the diverse types of costs that we will use as intermediate criteria in comparing institutional arrangements in subsequent chapters. Unfortunately, the terminology gets a bit cumbersome because, in keeping with the arguments of Chapter 4, it is necessary to examine both the production and the provision of rural infrastructure. Rather than use the more common term *production costs* for the costs of creating outputs from a set of inputs, we use the term *transformation costs* for this activity because, in fact, production involves "transforming" inputs into outputs (also see North 1990). We also consider transaction costs on both the provision and the production side of infrastructure decisions.

Costs of Provision

Providing goods and services involves both transformation and transaction costs. These costs are frequently ignored in private sector institutional arrangements because they are largely borne by those who consume the goods and services. Those who bear these costs control their investment in provision activities, to a large extent.[8] Provision costs in the public sector are usually more substantial than they at first appear because they are often recorded in many different locations and are extremely difficult to identify and measure. In regard to provision, we will distinguish between transformation and transaction costs and define them as follows:

- *transformation costs*—the costs involved in (1) transforming citizen preferences about outcomes and their willingness to pay into articulated demands for packages of publicly provided goods and services, (2) arranging for financing and producing these packages, (3) monitoring the performance of producers, (4) regulating the use patterns of consumers, and (5) enforcing compliance with taxation and other resource mobilization measures, and
- *transaction costs*—increases in transformation costs associated with coordination, information, and strategic behavior.

Transformation costs are those associated with the provision of jointly provided goods and services. As such, they are directly affected by the characteristics of the goods and services involved, by the scale of the provision unit, and by the technologies used in aggregating interests, arranging financing and production, monitoring producers, regulating users, and enforcing compliance. Transaction costs on the provision side are incurred as the result of attempts to counteract incentives associated with strategic behavior.

We distinguish among three different types of transaction costs involved in provision:

- *Coordination costs* are the sum of the costs of the time, capital, and personnel invested in negotiating, monitoring, and enforcing agreements about provision among actors.
- *Information costs* are the sum of the costs of searching for and organizing information and the costs of errors resulting from a lack of or an ineffective blend of knowledge about time and place variables and general scientific principles.
- *Strategic costs* are the increased transformation costs produced when individuals use asymmetric distributions of information, power, or other resources to obtain benefits at the cost of others. The most frequent kinds of strategic costs related to provision activities are free riding, rent seeking, and corruption.

As with transformation costs, transaction costs of provision are directly affected by the characteristics of the goods and services involved, by the scale of provision units, by technologies used for interest aggregation, monitoring, regulating, and policing, and by the particular rules used to govern transactions.

It is most important to recognize that trade-offs exist between most of these costs and even within broad categories of costs. For example, reducing the costs of errors resulting from a lack of information about time and place variables (such as the immediate destruction of a water diversion project because irrigation design engineers had insignificant knowledge about local conditions) requires an investment of resources to obtain better information about local conditions. Thus, as shown in Figure 5.1, the total cost of time and place information has two components: the cost of errors due to a lack of information and the cost of acquiring and using information.

In an environment where one could make a careful estimate of both the cost of error and the cost of search, it would be possible to make an optimal investment in acquiring information up to the point at which the marginal cost of new information just equaled the marginal benefits of reduced error (Lee [1989:5] makes a similar argument). But, participants in infrastructure development rarely have such complete information about costs. Therefore, we cannot assume that optimal investments are made. Instead, we must assume that the level and shape of the total cost of time and place information vary across physical domains and institutional arrangements. Thus, farmers with many years of experience in irrigating lands from a river acquire intimate knowledge about the velocity of that river at different times of the year and about the soil types present in their fields. This time and place information is acquired as a by-product of other activities, without much investment of resources in information search activities. When these farmers then engage in design, construction, and maintenance activities, total costs of time and place information are low because both the costs of error due to lack of place-specific information and the costs of information acquisition are relatively low.

It is far more costly for employees of national ministries to acquire time and place information than it is for locally elected officials. This is because this type of information cannot be obtained as a by-product of day-to-day activities unless these officials are assigned to a particular location for a long period of time (something that rarely happens) and are highly motivated to seek it out. Consequently, we can assume that the costs of error due to a lack of time and place information are higher in a national bureaucracy. On the other hand, we would expect that the costs of acquiring relevant scientific information would be lower than in a farmer-managed irrigation system. A centralized ministry is likely to have well-trained engineers on

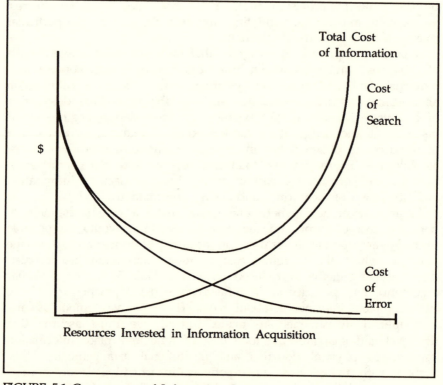

FIGURE 5.1 Components of Information Costs

staff who have access to current technological information not available to local farmers.

Recognizing that there are trade-offs between intermediate costs is an essential component of comparative institutional analysis; it is never possible to reduce all costs to zero. Thus, if one institutional arrangement has lower costs with regard to one intermediate criteria, it is apt to have higher costs somewhere else. The key question is whether the differences associated with alternative arrangements simply offset one another or whether a net gain in efficiency is achieved in moving from one arrangement to another.

Costs of Production

On the production side of infrastructure development (including design, construction, operation, and maintenance), we also distinguish between general transformation costs and transaction costs. Specifically for production, we define:

- *transformation costs* as the costs of transforming inputs (land, labor, and capital) into outputs (the design and construction of an infrastructure facility or its operation and maintenance) and
- *transaction costs* as increases in transformation costs associated with coordination, information, and strategic costs.

Transformation costs are the direct costs associated with using inputs to create outputs. The level of these costs will be directly affected by the characteristics of the goods or services involved, the scale of production, and the type of technology adopted, including its susceptibility to breakdown. Transaction costs, on the other hand, derive from steps taken to achieve coordination, find and analyze information, and counteract various types of opportunistic behavior. As in the case of provision, we identify three types of transaction costs:

- *Coordination costs* are the sum of the costs of the time, capital, and personnel invested in negotiating, monitoring, and enforcing agreements among actors.
- *Information costs* are the sum of the costs of searching for and organizing information and the costs of errors resulting from a lack of or an ineffective blend of knowledge about time and place variables and general scientific principles.
- *Strategic costs* are the increased transformation costs produced when individuals use asymmetric distributions of information, power, or other resources to obtain benefits at the cost of others. The most frequent kinds of strategic costs related to production activities are shirking, corruption (or fraud), adverse selection, and moral hazard.

Again, transaction costs are affected by the characteristics of the goods and services involved and the scale of production and technology used. Furthermore, the particular rules used to govern transactions (that is, the institutional arrangements used) will greatly influence the extent of these transaction costs. Although analytically separate, transaction costs are normally recorded simply as part of the transformation or production costs of an enterprise. The time and personnel allocated to transacting within a production firm or bureau and across production enterprises to organize production can vary substantially from producer to producer, even among those producing the same mix of outputs and using similar technologies.

TABLE 5.1 Criteria to Be Used in Judging the Comparative Performance of Alternative Institutional Arrangements

---

Intermediate performance criteria, provision costs

Transformation costs
Transaction costs
   Coordination costs
   Information costs
      Time and place
      Scientific
   Strategic costs
      Free riding
      Rent seeking
      Corruption

Intermediate performance criteria, production costs

Transformation costs
Transaction costs
   Coordination costs
   Information costs
      Time and place
      Scientific
   Strategic costs
      Shirking
      Corruption
      Adverse selection/moral hazard

Overall performance criteria

Efficiency
Fiscal equivalence
Redistribution
Accountability
Adaptability

CONCLUSION

This chapter has presented five overall performance criteria against which alternative institutional arrangements can be evaluated. These criteria include economic efficiency, two indicators of equity (fiscal equivalence and income redistribution), accountability, and adaptability. Such objectives, particularly efficiency and equity, are common to nearly all assessments of public policy. But rather than focus exclusively on these five criteria, we argue that the complexities of alternative institutional arrangements make it useful to consider an additional set of intermediate performance criteria. These criteria focus particularly on the costs necessary to reduce the various types of strategic behavior engaged in by opportunistic individuals.

In the following chapters, we will utilize this entire set of intermediate and overall performance criteria in evaluating a variety of institutional arrangements. Specifically, we will consider each of the intermediate performance criteria noted in the upper portion of Table 5.1, as well as the five overall performance criteria shown in the lower portion of the table. We will show explicitly how alternative institutional arrangements yield advantages with respect to *some* of the criteria, while producing disadvantages with respect to others.

NOTES

1. For further discussions of the welfare costs of taxation, see public finance textbooks, such as Stiglitz (1986).

2. The fiscal equivalence principal, per se, has most commonly been applied to the question of assigning public service responsibilities to different governments, especially within a federal governmental framework. See, for example, Olson (1969), where the term appears to have first been used. A similar concept of fiscal correspondence was used by V. Ostrom, Tiebout, and Warren (1961) and by Oates (1972).

3. For additional discussion of the trade-off between efficiency and equity, see Okun (1975) or most public finance textbooks, for example, Stiglitz (1986).

4. Walters (1968:18) provided a simple numerical example that illustrates the losses involved if prices greater than the marginal costs of use-related maintenance are imposed.

5. Newberry (1989) illustrated how, by imposing road-use charges that reflect the external social costs of congestion (primarily in urban areas) in England, sufficient resources could be mobilized to yield enough revenues to maintain the entire system while using economically efficient prices.

6. The work of institutional economists, such as Coase and Commons, can be considered foundational for comparative analysis between markets and firms; the work of V. Ostrom and Tiebout is foundational for comparative analysis in the public sector.

7. A brief review of the questions pursued in the *Journal of Law, Economics, and Organization* reveals the complexity of variables and analyses involved.

8. Consumers may organize into buyers' cooperatives or information acquisition groups to reduce individual costs related to provision. Some free riding may occur, whereby nonmembers of these organizations acquire benefits without paying. As consumers demand that government agencies take a more active role in consumer protection, the costs of providing private goods begin to resemble more closely those associated with providing public goods.

6

Analyzing Institutional Arrangements

Although a diverse array of institutional arrangements currently operate in both developed and developing countries, academic disciplines use an extremely sparse vocabulary to describe them. Apart from the usual market-versus-state or centralization-versus-decentralization dichotomies, there are few well-accepted terms to describe the variety of institutions that operate—sometimes quite successfully—to sustain rural infrastructure. Moreover, considering only the extreme dichotomies severely handicaps analyses of social problems, as well as efforts to design and redesign institutions.

In this chapter, we begin the analysis of some of the diverse institutional arrangements used in the contemporary developing world to provide and produce rural infrastructure facilities. We ask how three specific arrangements—a simple market, a differentiated market, and a user group—counteract or exacerbate the intermediate costs discussed in the previous chapter.

In analyzing the structure of an institutional arrangement, the analyst investigates what participants are involved, what their stakes and resources are, and how they are linked to one another and to outcomes in the world. Specifically, the analyst identifies the types of actions that actors can take, the type of information available to them, how actions lead to outcomes, and how rewards and punishments are allocated in light of the outcomes achieved and the actions taken. Then the analyst predicts the actions and aggregated outcomes that are most likely, given the structure of the incentives. When the predicted actions and outcomes are verified in an empirical setting, the analyst has provided an initial explanation for what is being observed. The welfare outcomes can then be evaluated using the criteria defined in the previous chapter.[1]

INSTITUTIONAL ARRANGEMENTS FOR
PRIVATE INFRASTRUCTURE DEVELOPMENT

In this section, we consider two alternative arrangements that would allow a group of citizen-consumers to benefit from the development and maintenance of private infrastructure facilities. These arrangements— a simple market and a differentiated market—differ in the way infrastructure users interact with a group of potential designers, builders, and operators-maintainers of these facilities.[2] (See Malone 1987 for a discussion of the general modeling technique we use in this chapter.)

A Simple Market

If the *sole* institutional arrangement available to a group of citizens for developing infrastructure facilities is a simple market, we can envision the processes of providing and producing, as shown in Figure 6.1. Each individual citizen-consumer is responsible for provision, and each must seek out the producers (designers, builders, and operators-maintainers) necessary for each and every infrastructure project he or she wants undertaken. Infrastructure financing is accomplished through a series of quid pro quo exchanges between citizen-consumers and the various artisans involved. Similarly, the demand for various types of infrastructure design, construction, and operation-maintenance activity is articulated directly by citizen-consumers to the producer involved.

Such a simple market could easily be used for organizing the provision and production of private capital investments used by a single household, such as owner-occupied housing. In this scenario, each family unit is completely responsible for its own provision, deciding whether it wants to undertake a task itself or hire someone else to do it. Each is also free to negotiate with potential designers, search for builders, and formalize a contract with one particular builder. Finally, a family unit either selects the gardeners, plumbers, electricians, and housecleaners who will be hired to maintain the house over the long term or decides to produce these activities within the household.

The rules underlying such a market are relatively simple. All artisans and citizen-consumers are permitted to be buyers or sellers at their own initiative. No one is allowed to take the property of others without a mutual agreement on acceptable terms of exchange. Essential to the operation of a simple market is the availability both of monitors to enforce property rights and of arenas in which

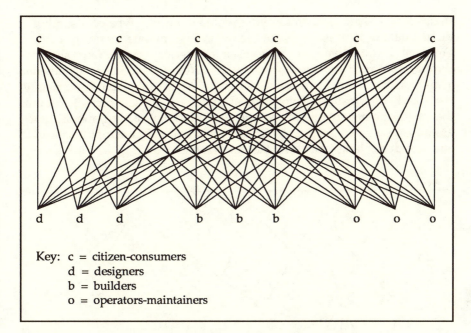

FIGURE 6.1 A Simple Market for Infrastructure Development

conflicts about property rights can be resolved. Further, parties to contractual agreements must be able to hold each other accountable for their actions.

A Differentiated Market for Infrastructure Development

If the only institutional arrangement available was a simple market, information asymmetries would reduce the number of beneficial trades actually transacted in the process of providing and producing even a private investment like housing. Families vary substantially in their earning capacity and their credit worthiness. And without financial institutions that can aggregate funds, share risk, hold property under various types of mortgage arrangements, and screen out unreliable family units, many long-term transactions related to housing would not occur. Similarly, designers and builders vary substantially in their skills, knowledge, integrity, and capacity to bear risk. Establishing firms to combine the skills of several different workers, monitor internal performance, share risk, and build a reputation is one type of institutional differentiation that is likely to occur in the private housing market. Financial institutions may also insist on certain monitoring activities during construction before they will agree to credit arrangements. Thus, many of the problems deriving from contractual uncertainty, risk, and information asymmetries discussed in Chapter 3 prompt the development of more complex institutional arrangements, such as those illustrated in Figure 6.2, when individuals attempt to provide and produce long-term, capital investments.

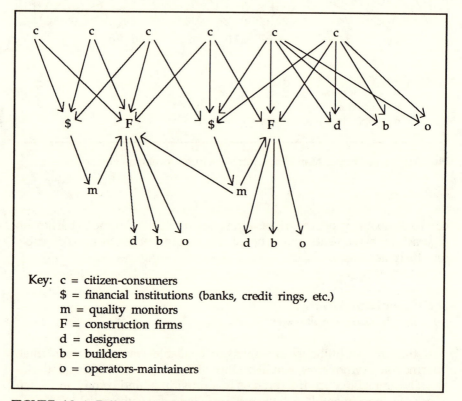

Key: c = citizen-consumers
      $ = financial institutions (banks, credit rings, etc.)
      m = quality monitors
      F = construction firms
      d = designers
      b = builders
      o = operators-maintainers

FIGURE 6.2 A Differentiated Market for Infrastructure Development

In a differentiated market, each consumer no longer has to negotiate personally with numerous artisans. Instead, consumers may choose from a smaller number of construction firms that employ artisans on longer-term contracts, monitor their performance, and attempt to build reputations for high performance. Some consumers may be able to choose from a full array of potential producers and financial institutions; others may face a more limited set. (We assume there is sufficient competition among producers and financial institutions so that no one has a monopoly position.) In addition to firms, some independent artisans will continue to offer services as well. Consumers who wish to make a large investment may obtain funds from financial institutions after they have established credit worthiness and offer sufficient property to secure a loan. And financial institutions are likely to inspect the construction to ensure that quality standards are met. The underlying rules of a differentiated market enable individuals to hostage property in exchange for credit and to enter into long-term employment contracts involving mutual responsibilities and duties.[3]

Comparative Evaluation

As we have argued previously, the performance of institutional arrangements depends on the type of goods and services that individuals attempt to provide and produce. For private capital investments like housing, rough estimates can be made of the intermediate costs of provision and production discussed in the second section of the last chapter.

On the provision side, for example, transformation costs are low for both simple and differentiated markets because each family unit decides for itself how much and what type of housing is desired. Coordination costs will be lower in a differentiated market because the number of producers with whom a family would need to communicate has been reduced. Obtaining information about specific preferences involves few costs in either case. Without intermediate organizations on the provision side (such as consumers' unions), individuals may not have access to scientific information (for example, about the health dangers of using particular building materials) in either case. Free riding, rent seeking, and corruption are not problems in either a simple or a differentiated market because a family unit is arranging for its own housing.

On the production side, the transformation costs generated by a differentiated market are likely to be lower than those produced by a simple market because construction firms can capture economies of scale unavailable to individual artisans. Coordination costs are also likely to be lower in the differentiated market because the number of potential linkages involved in completing a project is lower. Individuals involved in either a simple or a differentiated market would have access to accurate time and place information, conveyed through the medium of prices. One could surmise, however, that artisans operating in a simple market would be less likely to have access to the latest scientific information than firms operating in a differentiated market because firms can more easily afford to invest in the acquisition of technical information. Moreover, costs due to adverse selection, moral hazard, fraud, and shirking are apt to be higher in the simple market than in the differentiated market, where counteracting institutions have been devised specifically to reduce these problems.

The total level of benefits in the simple market is likely to be lower than in the differentiated market because many potentially beneficial transactions would not be completed without the help of the counteracting institutions of the differentiated market. Thus, the differentiated market is likely to be more efficient (providing greater benefits *and* lower costs). In both types of markets, those who pay the costs are the primary beneficiaries of the investment, and no redistribution is likely to occur. The addition of banks, firms, and monitors in a differentiated market is apt to increase the overall accountability of all participants in provision and production transactions. Finally, both arrangements are highly adaptable.

In Table 6.1, we have presented scores for both types of market arrangements on the intermediate and the overall performance criteria. Based on the previous analysis, the entry in each row in the upper portion of the table indicates whether the associated costs or performance levels would be low (L), medium (M), or high (H). An L should be interpreted as positive or desirable because it represents a judgment that an intermediate cost will be comparatively low. By comparing the entries in the two columns, it is therefore possible to predict or hypothesize the relative advantages of the two institutional arrangements according to each of these intermediate criteria.

In the lower portion of the table, we summarize the performance scores on the overall evaluation criteria anticipated from the two institutional arrangements. There, we have used numerical notation to represent performance evaluations on the five overall criteria. A differentiated market should yield greater economic efficiency due to the specialization and various institutional arrangements that arise to offset opportunistic behavior; thus, a 1 is entered in the cell for the economic efficiency of the differentiated market, whereas a 2 is entered for the efficiency of the simple market. Each of the arrangements yields high fiscal equivalence but little or no redistributional equity.[4] Similarly, both arrangements are highly adaptable. The differentiated market provides greater accountability because safeguards against opportunistic behavior are built into the institutional arrangements.

TABLE 6.1 Comparative Performance of Institutional Arrangements Related to the Provision and Production of a Private Infrastructure

	Simple Market	Differentiated Market
Intermediate performance criteria, provision costs		
Transformation costs	L	L
Transaction costs		
Coordination costs	H	M
Information costs		
Time and place	L	L
Scientific	H	H
Strategic costs		
Free riding	L	L
Rent seeking	L	L
Corruption	L	L
Intermediate performance criteria, production costs		
Transformation costs	M	L
Transaction costs		
Coordination costs	H	M
Information costs		
Time and place	L	L
Scientific	H	M
Strategic costs		
Shirking	M	L
Corruption	M	L
Adverse selection/moral hazard	M	L
Overall performance criteria		
Efficiency	2	1
Fiscal equivalence	1	1
Redistribution	3	3
Accountability	2	1
Adaptability	1	1

Note: L = low, M = medium, H = high (L is most desirable).
    1 = high, 2 = medium, 3 = low (1 is most desirable).

INSTITUTIONAL ARRANGEMENTS FOR
PUBLIC INFRASTRUCTURE DEVELOPMENT

Now let us consider how these institutional arrangements would perform in the provision and production of an infrastructure facility subject to joint consumption. In this chapter, we focus on the case of a small-scale irrigation system that benefits a small set of citizen-consumers. (Large-scale systems are the topic of the following chapter.) We contrast the simple market and the differentiated market with user groups.

User Groups

User groups constitute a third type of institutional arrangement found in some settings to provide for and produce small-scale irrigation systems. A simplified representation of this type of institutional arrangement is presented in Figure 6.3.

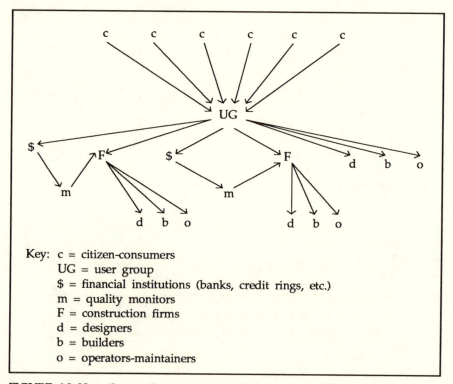

Key: c = citizen-consumers
     UG = user group
     $ = financial institutions (banks, credit rings, etc.)
     m = quality monitors
     F = construction firms
     d = designers
     b = builders
     o = operators-maintainers

FIGURE 6.3 User Group Organization for Infrastructure Development

The production side of the differentiated market structure remains the same. The major change between Figures 6.2 and 6.3 is the organization of the citizen-consumers themselves (the provision side). The following is a sketch of the rules that structure such an organization. A group of farmers (the citizen-consumers in this situation) decide to construct an irrigation system that will serve only those citizen-consumers who initially buy shares in the enterprise (or those who later purchase shares offered by the user group). Those who own shares are then assigned a weighted vote equal to the number of shares they own. The officials of the user group are chosen from among the members of the user group, using some form of voting rule.

When water is obtained, it is distributed according to the amount of shares owned. Each shareholder must contribute a proportionate share of resources to the user group each year (in the form of commodities and/or funds). These resources are used to pay people to operate the control works and to guard the canal so that water is distributed according to an agreed-upon formula. Each shareholder is also responsible for contributing a defined share of the labor each year when the user group collectively cleans out the canals and undertakes routine or emergency repair work on the canals.[5]

The rules governing the operation of user groups often permit the group to respond in appropriate ways to tragedy in an individual household that affects the household's ability to meet its responsibilities for the upkeep of a system. In cases where the head of a relatively poor household dies while his sons are still young, for example, the user group constitution will likely ensure that the dead man's responsibilities are met. Most often, heads of other households assume a greater load of responsibility for a period of time so that the widow's household can continue to receive its share of water. In some cases, the responsibilities of the household are simply waived until the eldest son is old enough to take his father's place in the work group. In others, the widow or her young son joins the work group in the place of the dead man but is assigned lighter tasks consistent with his or her strength. A widow in a wealthier household would, however, be expected to hire a laborer to replace her husband in the appropriate work team (for examples, see Benjamin 1989; Development Research Group 1986:110–142).

Comparative Performance

Assuming that the construction and operation of a small irrigation system are within the technical competence of local designers, builders, and operators, any of the three sets of institutional arrangements described earlier could potentially be used to provide and produce such a system. In general, the differentiated market performs better than the simple market, and the user group structure built on top of the differentiated market has the potential to perform better still. All of the intermediate costs on the production side remain the same for a differentiated market and for a user group organization atop a differentiated market, as shown in Table 6.2.

The major difference between a user group and individual family units interacting with a differentiated market is the potentially lower costs of free riding. As long as the user group is able to exclude noncontributors from enjoying irrigation water and to monitor and enforce the required contribution of monetary, commodity, and labor inputs so that conformance to the rules is relatively high, the user group arrangement will solve the free-rider problem; the two types of market arrangements will not.[6]

Free riding, particularly in the provision of maintenance activities, is relatively infrequent when a user group is effectively organized. The absence of members who fail to join the others on the day set aside to clean out the channels, for instance, is easily noticed. These individuals' reputations as reliable members of the group, of considerable importance in small communities, are adversely affected. Thus, although overt sanctions are employed in user groups to reduce free-riding behavior, the reduction results, in large part, from the increased information that all members have about each other's activities and the importance of a good personal reputation in such settings.

On the provision side, transformation costs inevitably increase somewhat for a user group, as contrasted to a simple or differential market. Farmers must now discuss their preferences and come to a common agreement about design and operating characteristics and maintenance strategies. If the farmers involved have similar interests (for example, if they own roughly the same size farms, grow similar crops, and share religious values and if tail-enders are not strongly disadvantaged), coordination costs will remain relatively low. These costs will always be higher when consumers are organized, rather than when they can act independently; how much higher will depend on the homogeneity of the individuals involved and the rules they use for aggregating preferences. Of course, efforts to coordinate also yield benefits by developing solutions to provision problems.

Both rent seeking and corruption should be low when a user group organizes for collective provision. The resources needed to provide the infrastructure come from the group that benefits, rather than a public treasury to which nonbeneficiaries also contribute. Thus, investment

TABLE 6.2 Comparative Performance of Institutional Arrangements Related to the Provision and Production of Small-scale Irrigation Systems

	Simple Market	Differentiated Market	User Group
Intermediate performance criteria, provision costs			
Transformation costs	L	L	L+
Transaction costs			
Coordination costs	H	M	M+
Information costs			
Time and place	L	L	L
Scientific	H	H	H
Strategic costs			
Free riding	H	H	L
Rent seeking	L	L	L
Corruption	L	L	L
Intermediate performance criteria, production costs			
Transformation costs	M	L	L
Transaction costs			
Coordination costs	H	M	M
Information costs			
Time and place	L	L	L
Scientific	H	M	M
Strategic costs			
Shirking	M	L	L
Corruption	M	L	L
Adverse selection/moral hazard	M	L	L
Overall performance criteria			
Efficiency	3	3	2 or 1
Fiscal equivalence	3	3	1
Redistribution	?	?	2
Accountability	2	1	1
Adaptability	1	1	1

Note: L = low, M = medium, H = high (L is most desirable).
1 = high, 2 = medium, 3 = low (1 is most desirable).

decisions are made with the knowledge that those making the investment will be able to use *only* their own resources, not those of others. Given this close association between the source of input resources and the benefits, it is unlikely that a group would overinvest in new facilities. Indeed, in such settings, underinvestment due to uncertainty about benefits and costs is more likely than overinvestment. Underinvestment may also occur if the resources directly available to the user group are insufficient to undertake the investment and if credit on reasonable terms is not available.

As soon as collective provision arrangements are created, it becomes more likely that some individuals will invest in activities to obtain a disproportionate share of benefits, thus spending resources in unproductive activities. But rent-seeking behavior is severely limited where the membership of the user group is relatively homogeneous—although if leaders have a disproportionate say in how benefits are allocated, rent seeking can characterize even these close-to-home institutions.[7] Corruption is also minimized because many user groups do not mobilize large amounts of cash, which is the easiest resource to exploit in corrupt transactions. And farmers have more control over how group resources are utilized if they personally perform required maintenance labor than if they give an official cash to hire laborers to do it. Certainly, crops can be used to pay irrigation officials to deliver more than the authorized amount of water to a farmer's gate, but such a delivery and the subsequent crop payoff are far more likely to be observed when the farmers themselves are part of the operation and maintenance crews.

In regard to the five overall performance criteria, the major differences between the user group arrangements, on the one hand, and either type of market arrangement, on the other, derive largely from the user group's ability to severely reduce free riding. Given the free-riding problems involved in either of the market arrangements, many potential benefits will not be achieved until some form of collective provision is established, with effective sanctions against those who do not contribute. Provision by a user group able to marshal effective sanctions thus makes greater efficiency possible. Provision rules common to many user groups, which assign responsibilities in proportion to benefits received, mean that the groups have more fiscal equivalence and relatively less redistribution in comparison to the two market arrangements. In the case of user groups, redistribution is likely to be better tailored to the needs of the poor than is the redistribution that occurs as a result of free riding. User groups that maintain open records of labor and other member contributions and of monetary expenditures also increase accountability on the provision side and rely on the more accountable production-side arrangements of the differentiated market. Because consumers are closely linked to provision and production decisions in the three types of institutional arrangements, all of these forms are potentially highly adaptive.[8]

CONCLUSION

This chapter has demonstrated how alternative institutional arrangements can be analyzed using the evaluation criteria set out in Chapter 5. In purely private infrastructure development, it was shown that a differentiated market could lead to greater economic efficiency as compared to a simple market. In the development and maintenance of a public good, the analysis suggested that, in both simple and differentiated markets, the costs of free riding are high, a problem that could potentially be overcome by relying on user groups.

The incapacity of individuals relying strictly on market institutions to overcome free-riding problems has led many analysts to recommend that all infrastructure facilities be funded by a national government. Such policy prescriptions are frequently made without distinguishing between facilities that serve a relatively small, well-defined set of individuals (such as small-scale irrigation systems) and facilities that serve a large and less well-defined set of individuals (like large-scale irrigation systems or a highway network). Many small-scale infrastructure projects are designed, constructed, operated, and maintained quite effectively by those most directly affected, relying on some form of user group organization similar to the simplified version analyzed above (see E. Ostrom 1992 and Tang 1992 for examples). It is obvious, however, that this method of organizing provision is not sufficient when the infrastructure serves a large and difficult-to-define set of beneficiaries. In the next chapter, we will consider how effectively centralized national governments provide for such large-scale facilities.

NOTES

1. The method of institutional analysis that we are using is described in Kiser and E. Ostrom (1982) and E. Ostrom (1986). It is applied in E. Ostrom (1990); Schaaf (1989); Tang (1992); Wynne (1989); and Yang (1987).

2. Throughout this discussion, we combine operation and maintenance to reduce complexity.

3. In any particular setting, many specific rules about credit, mortgages, creation of firms, monitoring, and so on may be present. In this section,

we offer highly simplified situations and rule structures to illustrate a mode of analysis, rather than the more detailed analysis one would undertake in an in-depth study of a specific problem.

4. The data in the tables presented in this chapter primarily reflect informed conjecture, rather than tight analytical conclusions. Analytical models like those of Malone (1987) and S. Cohen et al. (1981) have informed our judgment and could be used in developing the arguments more rigorously.

5. This description of a user group rule configuration is a simplified version of the rules used in many such groups in Nepal and the Philippines (see Martin and Yoder 1983; Siy 1982; Bagadion and Korten 1985; Coward 1985).

6. The user group must, however, be able to sanction its own members by threatening to withhold water, charge fines, and/or impose social sanctions on nonconformers.

7. Traditional leaders who exert undue influence in village affairs in the rural areas of some developing countries are, thus, rent seekers.

8. Many indigenous institutions, like the zanjeras described in Box 4.2, have extensive internal mechanisms to assure accountability. When user groups are created by external authorities and rely primarily on monetary rather than in-kind resources, accountability can be much more difficult to achieve.

Centralized Institutional Arrangements

In Chapter 6, we demonstrated how alternative institutional arrangements can be systematically evaluated to determine how well they are able to provide and produce, first, a purely private good and, second, a small-scale irrigation system. In this chapter, we consider the problem of designing, constructing, operating, maintaining, and using *large-scale* infrastructure facilities. To do so, we must examine a fourth type of simplified institutional arrangement—that of a centralized, national government bureau.

In fact, a substantial portion of all rural infrastructure investment in Third World countries is organized with heavy reliance upon highly centralized national governments. For that reason, most of this chapter is devoted to a consideration of how well a highly centralized institutional arrangement will perform the provision and production tasks necessary to construct, operate, and maintain large-scale infrastructure. As might be expected, our analysis suggests that centralized arrangements score higher on some performance criteria and lower on other criteria. Because the criteria on which large-scale agencies tend to perform less effectively are frequently ignored by policy analysts, we argue that most institutional analyses recommending that centralized institutional arrangements play the dominant role in infrastructure development are truncated or incomplete.

Finally, we recognize that in many low-income countries, a large portion of government capital development budgets is funded by grants and loans from a long list of "donor" organizations. Multilateral organizations such as the World Bank and regional development banks such as the Asian Development Bank or the African Development Bank, as well as bilateral donors like the USAID, annually provide support for extensive development of infrastructure in low- and middle-income countries. These organizations, which are generally authorized to negotiate only with the national government of recipient countries, create additional institutional linkages that can have profound effects on the success of infrastructure development efforts. The role of such organizations is the final topic of the chapter.

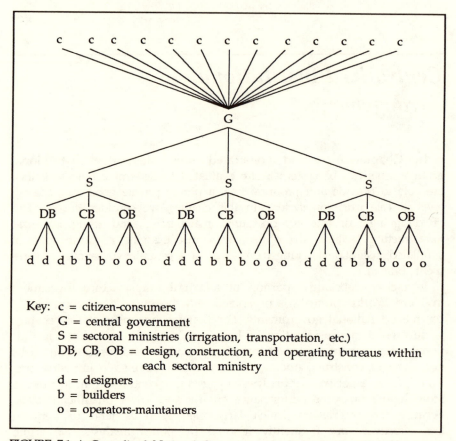

Key: c = citizen-consumers
      G = central government
      S = sectoral ministries (irrigation, transportation, etc.)
      DB, CB, OB = design, construction, and operating bureaus within
                   each sectoral ministry
      d = designers
      b = builders
      o = operators-maintainers

FIGURE 7.1 A Centralized National Government for Infrastructure Development

CENTRALIZED INFRASTRUCTURE DEVELOPMENT

The institutional structure of a centralized national government hierarchy is shown in Figure 7.1. The organization of both sides of the provision-production nexus in this case is radically different from that of the three types of institutional arrangements we considered in the previous chapter. On the provision side, instead of a few citizen-consumers who act independently (as in the two market-based situations) or collectively (as in the user group situation), a large number of citizen-consumers residing throughout an entire nation face a constrained set of choices. At periodic intervals, these citizen-consumers select full-time officials to act as their representatives in making infrastructure provision decisions, as well as many other provision decisions. Between elections, groups of citizen-consumers can try to influence those officials to use their authority in obtaining desired benefits for their supporters. On the production side, another group of officials work in specialized production bureaus within ministries or departments that are usually organized along sectoral lines.

Both sets of officials are full-time employees, and their future careers depend on pleasing superiors who help them retain and/or advance their positions. The incentives facing these officials in a centralized regime can compound perverse consequences regarding decisions about the infrastructure facilities to be designed and constructed and the investments to be made in operation and maintenance activities.

The actual costs of providing and producing rural infrastructure facilities under a large-scale central agency will vary substantially from one project to another. To focus our discussion, we will examine the incentives involved in the construction and the operation and maintenance of a large-scale irrigation system.[1] But large-scale investment projects in infrastructure such as roads are likely to yield similar outcomes. The anticipated performance results for both production and provision of construction and O&M are summarized in Table 7.1. We will first examine the production side.

Anticipated Performance on the Production Side

Whether a national bureau contracts with private enterprises to build large-scale irrigation systems or constructs them with its own personnel, we assume that it is able to capture economies of scale. Thus, we presume the transformation costs related to construction will be low.[2] Although it is more difficult to justify an assumption of low transformation costs for operation and maintenance tasks, we make this assumption in order to focus attention on differences in coordination, information, and strategic costs (see Table 7.1).

We expect coordination costs on the production side to be higher for a centralized national government than for the institutional arrangements considered earlier because lower-level bureaucrats in a centralized agency must obtain permission from higher-level colleagues before proceeding with many tasks. Furthermore, efforts to enhance the accountability of governmental agencies frequently entail substantial

144

TABLE 7.1 Performance of a Centralized National Government Bureau Related to the Construction and O&M of a Large-scale Irrigation System

	Construction	Operation and Maintenance
Intermediate performance criteria, provision costs		
Transformation costs	M	M
Transaction costs		
Coordination costs	M	M
Information costs		
Time and place	H	H
Scientific	H	H
Strategic costs		
Free riding	L to M	L to H
Rent seeking	H	L
Corruption	H	L
Intermediate performance criteria, production costs		
Transformation costs	L	L
Transaction costs		
Coordination costs	M to H	M to H
Information costs		
Time and place	H	H
Scientific	L	L
Strategic costs		
Shirking	M	H
Corruption	H	H
Adverse selection/moral hazard	L	L
Overall performance criteria		
Efficiency	1-3	2-3
Fiscal equivalence	3	3
Redistribution	?	?
Accountability	2-3	2-3
Adaptability	2-3	2-3

Note: L = low, M = medium, H = high (L is most desirable).
1 = high, 2 = medium, 3 = low (1 is most desirable).

increases in coordination costs. All stages of an infrastructure project will be reviewed by various officials. Establishing a proper paper trail requires that significant resources be devoted to coordination efforts. Thus, coordination costs will vary from medium to high, depending on the particular administrative procedures used.

Costs involved in securing relevant time and place information would be high in most national bureaus with respect to both construction and maintenance. The problems that design engineers encounter in obtaining accurate information about water flow from the maps and other data available to them have already been discussed; securing accurate and timely information related to maintenance is even more difficult for a centralized bureau. Minor failures in an irrigation system can occur anywhere, at any time, and a local flash flood can cause a small washout within an hour. Yet maintenance personnel located one or two hours away from this site may not even know it rained. By the time the information about a small problem reaches repair crews, a minor repair job may have become a major reconstruction project.

The costs of securing relevant scientific knowledge, on the other hand, should be relatively low in a national bureau. With responsibility over several large-scale infrastructure projects, a single agency can justify hiring several well-trained civil engineers, capable of designing most features of these complex irrigation systems. Similarly, more highly educated engineers are likely to know what sorts of maintenance requirements are associated with such systems.

We expect the amount of shirking in a national bureau to be higher than in simple or differentiated markets or user group arrangements. When coordination costs are high, individuals have strong incentives to keep their jobs as easy as possible. Thus, civil servants with the best of intentions often find themselves in situations where the demands on their time and energy require them to reduce, as much as possible, the effort they spend in supervising projects. If monitoring procedures for all projects are fixed, regardless of their size, total project monitoring time can be reduced by approving a smaller number of larger projects. A shift to larger projects may occur, therefore, regardless of whether this project mix results in higher or lower direct costs for producing infrastructure facilities.

An example from the Philippines illustrates how high coordination costs and the incentive to reduce personal effort can work against selecting low-cost projects. The governor of Laguna Province offered the National Irrigation Administration 50,000 pesos to be used for improving the operation of the region's irrigation systems. Funding hinged on the plans being approved by the University of the Philippines College of Agriculture. NIA engineers proposed spending all the funds on a single project to line the main canal of one system with concrete. A review conducted before the project began revealed that the water leaking from this canal was used anyway by the farmers in the project area and that, consequently, the proposed expenditure would not improve the system's operation. The review instead proposed several smaller projects (such as constructing small-scale drainage checks and building additional farm ditches) that *would* increase productivity at the same cost. These suggested small-scale improvements were, however, rejected by the NIA, so that the funds ultimately reverted to the provincial treasury. This episode led analysts to conclude, "It was clear that the burden on the limited staff in planning and overseeing many small implementation activities, plus the intensive involvement with individual landowners and tenants over rights-of-way, etc., were such that it was in the bureaucracy's, if not the farmers' interest to refuse the money" (Barker et al. 1984:46–47). Whether the bias toward supervising large projects is considered the result of shirking, high coordination costs, or a combination of both, overall efficiency is reduced when small but productive projects are rejected in favor of large projects, especially when the larger projects produce no net benefits.

We also expect shirking to be higher in operations and maintenance divisions than in design and construction divisions. All employees are likely to find some tasks more fulfilling than others: Most engineers, for instance, gain greater satisfaction from their involvement in the design and construction of a system than from overseeing the maintenance of completed systems. Furthermore, bureaucratic rewards are more likely to go to those engaged in highly visible and successful design and construction projects, rather than to those with the harder-to-evaluate jobs of organizing effective maintenance regimes. Thus, internal and external incentives tend to counteract shirking to a somewhat greater extent in regard to construction. On the other hand, few internal or external incentives counteract shirking in O&M. Because it is difficult to monitor how maintenance engineers or their staffs spend their time, few bureaucratic punishments can be administered to those who work on personal tasks rather than maintenance.

Public officials responsible for both construction and O&M encounter opportunities for corruption; those in construction stand to gain the larger amount of illegal subpayments.[3] Jagannathan described how this is accomplished in South Asia.

> Suppose tenders are called for a highway construction project worth $1 million. Tender papers and award of contract to the lowest bidder will be perfectly in order. Informal agreement (before or after the

contract finalization) will, however, be reached by which the contractor is allowed to use substandard material and pad up labor costs so that his costs amount to only $750,000. The balance of $250,000 is then shared between the concerned individuals. (Jagannathan 1987:111)

Opportunities for illegal side-payments are not limited to the letting of contracts. Employees who hold positions as operators and maintainers of large-scale irrigation projects, for example, might receive side-payments on a regular basis. The difference in the quantity and quality of crops that can be grown with a regular supply of water versus those grown with an irregular supply means that many farmers are perfectly willing to pay a "personal fee" to a lower-level irrigation official to ensure the predictable delivery of water to their field gates. Robert Wade (1984, 1985) has documented the prices that irrigation officials illegally charge farmers for various types of public services, as well as those that higher-level officials charge lower-level officials for lucrative postings.

The incentives that public officials face must be understood in the context of the generally low salaries they receive, their limited career advancement opportunities, their poor working conditions, and the opportunities (both legal and illegal) available to them in different types of work assignments. Most central government employees prefer to live in the capital of their country. There, they can obtain a better education for their children and enhance the next generation's opportunity for a brighter future. Health services for themselves and their families are usually better. And their own career prospects can be improved by working where they can be observed by superiors, rather than in the countryside where their activities may go unnoticed. These factors all generate a strong employee preference for work in the design and construction of large systems, which lead to many employment positions in the national bureau.

Jobs in the operation and maintenance of infrastructure projects typically are located in the countryside. Many administrative officials posted to smaller rural communities attempt to maintain two households— one for their family living elsewhere and a minimal living arrangement for themselves on-site. Once assigned to the countryside, many devote considerable time and energy to arranging for reassignment in the capital city.

The working conditions of officials assigned to an O&M division in the countryside are also considerably more difficult than those of their peers working in the capital. In many developing countries, governments are committed to using the national treasury to ensure continued employment for a substantial proportion of the educated population; this, combined with the extreme budgetary constraints of these countries, has meant that the budgets of many administrative bureaus are almost totally committed to salaries. As a result, few funds are available to purchase the supplies officials need to carry out their duties. Thus, O&M officials are frequently assigned to large districts without a gasoline budget or even a bicycle. It is hardly surprising that public officials responsible for infrastructure O&M are not able to supervise these processes properly when they lack the money to simply visit the roads, water supply systems, or irrigation works within their jurisdictions.

Given the low salaries and the high costs of keeping two households, the official's incentive to search out opportunities to earn extra funds in the countryside (while urgently maneuvering to get reassigned) is understandable. Clearly, there are relatively few opportunities for career advancement or extrasalarial benefits in maintaining an existing facility. The opportunities for additional income arise when goods and services can be withheld from potential beneficiaries unless side-payments are made. Officials may also supplement their incomes via side-payments associated with the award and supervision of contracts to construct or maintain infrastructure. Thus, national government irrigation officials responsible for the O&M of an irrigation system may devote more energy to allocating water to individual farmers who are willing to contribute funds or commodities in return, rather than to maintaining structures that benefit many users in a diffused manner.

This is not to say that all administrative officials in centralized regimes are necessarily corrupt or shirkers. One finds many devoted public officials everywhere—men and women who resist the temptations afforded by the systems in which they work. What this analysis does suggest, however, is that centralized regimes produce incentives that enhance the opportunities for corruption and shirking. At the same time, the regimes generate few counteracting pressures that discourage officials from engaging in these practices. Furthermore, once shirking and corrupt practices are well established in large, centralized bureaucratic systems, those who attempt to fight the problem from within are vulnerable to recriminatory actions both by their peers and by their superiors. Consequently, corrupt behavior occurs with considerable frequency in both construction and O&M.

Anticipated Performance on the Provision Side

In the preceding discussion, we focused exclusively on the performance of centralized national government agencies in producing large-scale irrigation systems. Now, let us examine the provision side. Recall that provision includes (1) the transformation of preferences and willingness to pay into specific infrastructure development processes and (2) the monitoring and enforcement of procedures related to operation and use. Assuming a competitive, democratic selection process, each citizen-consumer participates in general elections to choose national officials, who run on platforms representing their promised positions regarding future investments of public funds. Many campaign promises involve projects that are strongly preferred by a particular set of supporters, such as the members of an electoral district or a relevant group (urban voters, ethnic groups, individuals sharing specific economic interests, and so forth).[4]

One cannot presume, however, that the outcome of a national election provides a clear indication of majority preferences about the proposed investments and allocations to be made from a national treasury. Nor can one assume that elected officials can make credible commitments to voters or to external donor agencies. More realistically, the outcome is the selection of a set of actors who will each try to obtain as much as possible for the group he or she must please in order to stay in office. Even if this behavior were not endemic, the problems of aggregating the preferences of a heterogeneous population discussed in Chapter 4 lead to this conclusion: The outcome of a national election neither provides a reliable indication of the most preferred set of public policies to be pursued nor binds officials to keep the promises they have made.[5]

The costs of obtaining time and place and scientific information are high when provision is organized by one very large national unit. Residents of one town or village cannot know much about what is needed elsewhere. Likewise, officials know little about the preferences of any citizens other than those who are highly motivated and organized in an effort to obtain disproportionate benefits or rents. Even gaining reliable information about the expected effectiveness of various proposed policies (scientifically grounded policy knowledge) is extraordinarily costly when all policies have to be adopted for an entire country without benefit of the results of prior experimentation by smaller subnational units of government.

The financing arrangements associated with national government projects also can significantly affect provision costs. The bulk of public revenues collected in most developing countries tend to be amassed by the national government and placed in a general fund from which most expenditures are allocated. There are several reasons for this. One principal reason is that it is very costly to collect many types of taxes in developing countries. Direct personal taxes, such as income and property taxes, and sales-based taxes collected at the retail level are so costly to administer as to be infeasible. Because of these collection costs, developing countries have traditionally relied much more heavily on trade-based taxes, particularly import duties, than have industrialized nations.[6] Typically, there are relatively few points of entry for imported items, so collecting such duties is considerably cheaper than attempting to raise revenues from thousands of taxpayers. In much the same way, excise taxes imposed primarily at the manufacturing level have the advantage of reducing the number of units from which taxes must be collected. During the past two decades, value-added taxes (VATs) have gained considerable popularity, in developed and developing countries alike.[7] Although they are more expensive to administer than excise taxes, they provide a strong incentive for business firms to report tax liabilities: A firm can deduct from its tax liabilities all VATs that were included in the prices of its inputs, which encourages officers of the firm to file a tax return in order to receive a rebate. Each firm pays the VAT only on the value added during the production stage for which it is responsible. And because VATs, manufacturers' excise taxes, and trade taxes are not particularly amenable to collection at a local level, these broader-based taxes are generally imposed only by national governments.

Another reason many developing countries prefer to mobilize the bulk of all public sector taxes, rather than permit local (state, province, or city) governments to do so, is that they can thereby retain greater control over the fiscal affairs of the country. Of particular importance in this regard is control over the macroeconomic policy objectives of stabilization and growth. Given the scarcity of capital in most developing countries, national governments do not wish to compete with local jurisdictions for a limited tax base. This competition is generally reduced by national government policies that greatly restrict the taxing authority of local governments.

When national governments collect the bulk of all public revenues, which are then placed in a general-purpose fund, the fund becomes a common pool for all national government officials. Because the source of funds is not directly related to particular public sector activities, all elected officials are motivated to obtain as much of the general fund as possible for projects that benefit their constituents. Each official also weighs the observable benefits of specific projects more heavily than the costs. (Benefits are visible and can be directed toward specific sets of supporters; costs are relatively hidden and can be spread across all taxpayers.) Some form of logrolling among elected officials will occur—the particular form depends on the specific set of rules used to make national government decisions. If strong institutional constraints on logrolling processes do not exist, it is quite likely that such efforts will lead to substantial overinvestments in some types of public projects and major underinvestments in others.[8] Further, local governments do not have to raise local taxes in order to undertake new projects. Public moneys are viewed more like "someone else's money" than like "our money." Thus, representatives are judged more for the resources they bring to an area than for how well they use the resources mobilized for public purposes. As Jane Guyer (1991) pointed out, representation without taxation can lead to irresponsible behavior.

Let us now turn to the problem of free riding. A presumed advantage of governmental provision over private provision is a government's capacity to prevent free riding. Yet this certainly is not always the case. As Repetto's data show, the actual revenue collected from farmers in many developing countries does not even begin to cover the O&M costs of government-run irrigation systems, let alone contribute to capital costs (see Box 2.2). It is difficult to interpret the repeated findings that farmers do not actually contribute required fees; however, as we noted in Chapter 4, if there are no sanctions against nonpayers or if participants discover that the national government will subsidize the operations, individual farmers are likely to attempt to avoid paying fees. Finally, the farmers must perceive that the benefits they derive from complying are at least as great as the required assessment. What *is* obvious is that governments in many developing countries do *not* solve shirking problems on the production side nor willingness-to-pay problems on the provision side.

Anticipated Overall Performance

Given their poor performance on the intermediate criteria outlined above, it is not surprising that national government agencies in most countries cannot be expected to perform at a high level with regard to any of the four overall performance criteria arrayed in Table 7.1. The description of the Mahaweli project in Sri Lanka, presented in Box 7.1, provides a good illustration of problems in both construction and O&M commonly encountered by centralized arrangements. A system like this would have to be rated as performing at a low level in regard to overall efficiency, fiscal equivalence, redistribution, accountability, and adaptability. Centralized agencies can perform far better when design, construction, and O&M activities are planned and operated in conjunction with the beneficiaries. This has been documented in the Philippines (see D. Korten 1980; F. Korten 1982, 1985) and elsewhere.[9]

BOX 7.1   The Mahaweli Development Program

In adopting the Mahaweli Development Program, the government of Sri Lanka chose a large-scale, multifaceted approach to improving irrigated agriculture over a less ambitious, piecemeal one. Virtually all current analyses consider this to have been the wrong choice (Chambers 1975; Siriwardhana 1981; de Silva 1987; Ascher and Healy 1990). The Mahaweli project was intended to exploit a major river—the Mahaweli Ganga, which flows for 200 miles from the mountains to the Bay of Bengal— for irrigation and energy generation. The plans envisioned a thirty-year construction period beginning in 1970, during which fifteen new reservoirs, eleven power stations, and many canals to divert the Ganga into the seven rivers flowing through the largely undeveloped dry zone would be built. Some 900,000 acres of land were to be irrigated (of which 650,000 acres were then undeveloped); 200,000 people were to be settled in the area. The projected cost of the scheme in 1970 was six billion rupees (Rs. 6 billion, or US$1 billion). By 1977, 130,000 acres of land were opened and settled at a cost of Rs. 30 billion (1982US$1.9 billion). The investment per family settled on 2.5 acres of land was Rs. 75,000 (1978US$4,800) in a country whose per capita income was roughly $250. Agricultural yields were so low that, by 1981, residents of one of the project areas suffered the highest levels of chronic malnutrition in all of Sri Lanka (Hesselberg 1986).

The World Bank and the Sri Lankan government funded the initial construction of two dams and power stations, begun in 1970. Since then, however, the bank has contributed little to the funding of the project. Bilateral aid agreements, on the other hand, have been extremely generous. Ascher and Healy (1990:6–13, 6–14) calculated that over Rs. 7.6 billion (1982US$365 million) were provided in the form of grants or import support by Britain, Canada, Sweden, West Germany, Japan, Kuwait, and the European Economic Community, for which no repayment was required. A major portion of Sri Lanka's own capital has gone into the project as well. In 1982, for example, the Mahaweli scheme absorbed 40 percent of the country's total capital budget (Ascher and Healy 1990:6–8).

Tragically, adoption of the project meant that alternative irrigation projects that might have yielded higher returns for much smaller investments were neglected. In the late 1960s, for instance, 10,000 small irrigation catchment tanks existed that needed only minor reconstruction or renovation to be functional. It is estimated that 251,000 acres of land could have been made productive if 7,406 tanks had been repaired and maintained. Compared with the Mahaweli project, these smaller tank projects would have had much lower unit costs (Rs. 7,000–10,000/ acre, rather than Rs. 25,000–30,000/acre) and a much lower import

BOX 7.1 (continued)

content (15 percent, rather than 40 percent), and they would have provided many more unskilled jobs. Had the government of Sri Lanka pursued these minor tank projects, however, they likely would not have attracted the support of bilateral donors that the Mahaweli project has.

Mahaweli, like many failed irrigation projects, was based on overly optimistic estimates of (1) the amount of water that could be stored and released and (2) the discipline that would be exercised by Irrigation Department officials and by farmers in scheduling and using water. Feasibility studies paid scant attention to how water would get to the farmer or how the system would be maintained. Planners simply assumed that farmers in each section of the system would, on their own, organize themselves to distribute water equitably and maintain the channels and structures (Jayawardene 1986:79).

Just a few years after construction was completed, the system showed clear signs of decay (Corey 1986). Farmers had built numerous unauthorized outlets because the original ones had been placed too low to permit water to flow onto their fields. The maintenance of structures, ditches, and access roads was poor. Leakage around drop structures initially caused by burrowing animals was often not corrected before serious erosion or the collapse of a structure had taken place. It was impossible to get farmers to clear the ditches of brush more than once a season— and then only if they felt that the brush would seriously reduce their water supply. Many settlers subsisted on government food stamps or rations provided by the World Food Program (Hesselberg 1986). With no attention to the human organizational requirements of appropriate design and operation, the system could not be made to work except at grossly inefficient levels. This project dramatically illustrates the type of failures that characterize a large class of donor-funded irrigation projects initiated in the 1960s and early 1970s.

Without detailed analysis, it is almost impossible to determine whether the poor are subsidized to some extent by the wealthy in this case. As was suggested in Chapter 5, however, all too frequently, careful analyses have shown that redistribution moves in the opposite direction. Whether it actually occurs is difficult to establish theoretically; instead, it must be determined empirically.

The tenuous linkage between national government decisionmakers and the ultimate users of infrastructure facilities makes it difficult for users to hold these decisionmakers accountable. Again, accountability can be strengthened if national officials are required to rely more heavily on local inputs in the decisionmaking process; however, the incentives for them to carry out such mandates are commonly quite weak, and the consequences of ignoring them are minimal.

Centrally controlled, large-scale irrigation systems are often incapable of adapting to changing circumstances or to special local needs. They are much more likely to be constructed and operated with a "blueprint" mentality that ultimately threatens the sustainability of the systems.

THE PROBLEM OF TRUNCATED ANALYSES

The previous discussion has stressed some of the costs of relying on a single, large-scale government to provide and produce the design, construction, operation, and maintenance of rural infrastructure. But though these deficiencies are widely understood, national government provision of much rural infrastructure appears to be the rule, rather than the exception. Why might that be?

The belief that jointly consumed infrastructure facilities *must* be provided and produced by national governments rests primarily on the presumption that this arrangement is best able to limit free riding, capture economies of scale in production, and make the best use of technical expertise. A national government can use its taxing authority to counteract underinvestment in infrastructure facilities due to free riding, as well as reduce the costs of producing capital-intensive goods due to economies of scale achieved by large production bureaus. The technical skills needed to design and construct (and, in some cases, to operate) capital-intensive facilities are presumably possessed by the employees of national government agencies and by no others.

These presumptions have considerable surface validity only if a relatively restricted set of institutional alternatives are considered. If the only institutional arrangements that could be used to provide large-scale infrastructure projects were a centralized governmental regime *or* strictly private arrangements—such as one of the market arrangements or a user group, as considered in the previous chapter—the advantages of the central regime in counteracting free riding and lowering production costs would be impressive (see Table 7.2).

These presumptions are, however, based on a truncated analysis. First, the set of intermediate performance criteria is limited primarily to only three of the fifteen we use in our analysis: production costs, free riding, and costs of securing scientific knowledge. Second, the set of alternative institutions being considered is unnecessarily limited. Third, attention has focused on the design and construction of infrastructure,

TABLE 7.2 A Truncated Analysis of Institutional Performance Related to the Design and Construction of Large-scale Infrastructure

	Central Government	Private Arrangement
Production costs	L	H
Scientific knowledge	L	H
Free riding	L	H

Note: L = low, H = high (L is most desirable).

with little regard to operation and maintenance. Although the production costs of design and construction activities may be lower for larger-scale agencies in major projects, the production costs of operating and maintaining these same projects may be higher when they are undertaken by a centralized agency as opposed to smaller agencies or the users themselves.

This truncated analysis is implicit in the presumption that centralized governmental arrangements are necessary for infrastructure provision and production. If the analysis adequately represented the institutional options, the full array of activities associated with infrastructure, the full set of costs, and actual practice with regard to free riding, then the policy prescriptions of the past would be appropriate. Their inadequacy has, however, been repeatedly demonstrated in assessments that have stressed the unexpected costs of exclusive reliance on centralized governmental agencies (Uphoff 1986b; Chambers 1988; Cernea 1985; Esman and Uphoff 1984). These unexpected expenses include coordination costs, as well as costs due to a lack of time and place information, rent seeking, on-the-job shirking, and corruption. Furthermore, the presumption that economies of scale exist, which is frequently correct in regard to the design and construction of large-scale projects, is frequently incorrect in regard to the O&M of these same projects. And, most importantly, the assumption that national government provision and production is "best" implies that the options for institutional arrangements are limited to a choice between "the market" and "the state." This is decidedly *not* the case: As we will discuss in Chapter 9, a wide variety of institutional options are available.

For some rural infrastructure projects, a careful analysis of all performance criteria and the various possible institutional arrangements would lead to the conclusion that both provision and production by large, centralized, bureaucratic agencies is the most efficient and equitable institutional arrangement available. For example, construction and operation of infrastructure to generate and distribute electricity may be accomplished most effectively through a centralized bureaucracy. In other instances, a similar analysis would generate recommendations for national government *provision* but *production* by private or other public agencies arranged for by the national government. Thus, though it may be necessary for trunk roads to be constructed and maintained under the control of a national government ministry, the ministry could utilize private contractors to perform the construction and maintenance tasks. In many other cases, however, complete analysis would indicate that a diversity of noncentralized government provision and production arrangements would result in lower intermediate costs and improved overall performance.

THE ROLE OF DONOR AGENCIES

Any discussion of institutional arrangements for building infrastructure in the developing world would be inadequate without reference to the important role played by donor agencies. The activities of these agencies affect the incentives of all participants in infrastructure development. Furthermore, the resulting incentives may well increase the level of rent seeking, corruption, and accountability.

Foreign aid programs have been severely criticized for overinvesting in large, capital-intensive projects, for the use of inappropriate technology, for their pursuit of donor government interests, and for the high levels of corruption that have frequently been associated with donor-financed projects (see, for example, Wall 1973; Rockefeller 1969; Asher 1970; Hayter 1971; and Levinson and de Onis 1970). At times, the criticism presumes conspiratorial motivation, with donor agencies characterized as fronts for a new form of conscious imperialism.

But anyone who has observed infrastructure projects in operation is struck by the number of extremely hard-working, highly motivated individuals in both the host governments and the donor agencies whose principal goal is clearly to improve the well-being of those living in countries receiving foreign aid. Yet, realistic assessments of many projects designed by donor and host government staff repeatedly reveal unintended negative outcomes. Evaluations show that the projects have increased or reinforced the overcentralization of recipient countries' governments, were poorly designed (given local circumstances), and generated inappropriately large debt burdens for the recipient countries.

How is it possible for highly motivated, hard-working people who sincerely want to improve conditions in these recipient countries to be repeatedly involved in the design and implementation of projects that do not accomplish this goal?

This question has been the subject of several careful studies (see Nelson 1968 and Tendler 1975), and we cannot fully address it within the confines of this volume. But focusing on the incentives facing actors in the donor agencies as they relate to public officials and private enterprises in host countries helps explain how undesirable outcomes can be generated. Some of these incentives are present in most large-scale bureaucratic agencies. Others could apply to most foreign aid agencies, bilateral or multilateral. Still others are unique to particular agencies, such as USAID.[10]

USAID continues to face the apparently contradictory problems of creating an enduring constituency in support of foreign assistance while seeking appropriate ways to spend the large amount of foreign aid money mandated by the U.S. Congress. The legislative mandate to allocate a proportion of foreign assistance to purchases of U.S.-made equipment was an important initial source of bias in project designs toward very large and capital-intensive projects. Administratively, it is likely to be easier to oversee the purchase of U.S.-made heavy construction equipment rather than to obtain the waivers necessary to purchase smaller, foreign-made implements that would, nevertheless, be more effective in some Third World environments. But heavy equipment certainly creates a bias toward large-scale projects. As Judith Tendler's account of equipment purchases for a Brazilian highway project demonstrated, incentives that are generated by donor organizations can lead recipient countries themselves to insist on the use of foreign-made, rather than locally manufactured, equipment (see Box 7.2).

The notorious need to spend money that all government agencies face, in which next year's funding depends on the agency's efficiency in spending this year's budget, also contributes to a bias favoring large projects. Projects requiring large expenditures for major capital goods are more likely to be funded than labor-intensive projects using small-scale and locally manufactured equipment. As "economy" measures have been implemented to severely reduce the numbers of agency personnel, the pressure of coping with a gushing pipeline has probably been further increased: Fewer people are now available to oversee the spending of more money. Fear of external criticism about lack of control and corrupt practices also leads donor agencies to favor project funding that appears to give project monitors greater control over what is happening. And this usually means funding a few large projects, rather than several small ones.

BOX 7.2   The Capital-intensive Bias in Development Projects

The design of a $31.5-million highway maintenance equipment project in Brazil poignantly illustrates the potential incentives for donor agencies. The initial proposal included an equipment import list of $35.5 million, which would have produced an equipment-per-mile ratio higher than the average equipment-per-mile ratio in the United States at the time (Tendler 1975:68–69). In early discussions of this project, Brazilian firms made several proposals to reduce by two-thirds the U.S.-made equipment that would be imported for capital-intensive repair strategies and instead substitute equipment that could be purchased locally. Because any shifting of equipment from the import list to the domestic list represented an equivalent drop in the amount of funds available through USAID, mission personnel realized that such a shift to local technology would place a large financial burden on the three southern states of Brazil where the project would be located. The shift represented a real threat to the likelihood of *any* project funding, so major technical questions regarding the basic design of the project were not raised. Tendler summarized some of these missing questions:

> Needless to say, the technical logic of the solution excluded other important considerations. For example, was optimum maintenance a desirable goal in a country with much less capital than the United States, where this standard was formulated? Also, would faltering maintenance divisions in highway departments with a penchant for construction be able to absorb such a massive dose of new equipment and such a spurt in the intensity of their maintenance? Or would some of the abundant equipment be siphoned off into highway construction, as had happened in other maintenance loans, thus reinforcing the vicious circle of construction-without-maintenance? (Tendler 1975:68–69)

According to Tendler, these questions were largely ignored, not because of malicious intent to design a poor project but because all the incentives facing the engineers in both the USAID mission and the relevant government offices led these individuals to focus their attention on equipment. For everyone involved, the more equipment, the better. For the engineers working in the recipient agency, the larger the equipment list, the better the chances for getting financing. And for USAID personnel, the chances for "producing" a given amount of capital transfer would be greater with a larger equipment list. Consequently, the incentives facing all participants ultimately biased projects and reduced their long-run efficiency and sustainability.

Monitoring project performance in order to discourage corruption requires performance criteria that can be easily measured. A preoccupation with monitoring is likely to lead, however, to undue concern for project inputs, while outputs are ignored.[11] This concern may even alter the nature of certain development activities, solely in the hope of being able to measure project effort. For example, in Bangladesh, as we discussed earlier, nearly all observers recognize that successful rural road construction requires that the soil in road embankments be thoroughly compacted. Yet donors supporting road building have limited monitoring activity almost exclusively to measuring the amount of earth moved. This is because it is easy to measure excavated earth but very difficult to measure compaction. The unintended outcome has been that many, many miles of earthen embankments have been constructed over the past decade but that, due to lack of concern for compaction, few of these roads remain passable to vehicles at the end of a single monsoon season.

Similar tendencies favoring indicators of effort that are easy to measure, as well as equipment-intensive projects, are present within large-scale government bureaus. Hence, the incentives for donor and host government personnel are similar and tend to be reinforcing. As a result, the types of projects that receive the most funding by external donors can be better explained by sets of incentives inside both donor and host government agencies that are extremely difficult to overcome, rather than by conspiracy theories.

Fiscal responsibility will always require that institutional arrangements provide adequate oversight to ensure that limited foreign assistance resources are not misspent. To this end, it is unlikely that any one optimal oversight arrangement can ever be crafted. Consequently, there will always be trade-offs between the most desirable project design from the recipients' standpoint and the donors' need to maintain financial oversight.

CONCLUSION

This chapter has focused on what may be the most prevalent institutional arrangement for the provision of large-scale rural infrastructure in the Third World—highly centralized national governments. The analysis suggests that although such arrangements help to reduce some provision and production costs, they also appear to increase others. The provision and production of public infrastructure by a national government may achieve economies of scale in production, overcome free riding, and allow for maximum utilization of scientific knowledge.

But, we argue, analysis that supports the current dominance of national governments is truncated in that it fails to consider the full array of transaction costs and the full range of alternative institutional arrangements. The problems of capturing time and place information and reducing shirking, rent seeking, and corruption, for example, do not receive much attention in analyses of the problem of infrastructure deterioration in developing countries.[12] As long as these problems are not incorporated in analyses and recommendations, projects that generate unintended consequences—high levels of corruption, overinvestment in large-scale projects, and underinvestment in smaller projects and in operations and maintenance—will continue to be planned, financed, and constructed. With the more complete set of intermediate performance measures illustrated here, the unintended consequences of past institutional arrangements for infrastructure development can be seen as expected outcomes, given the incentives of the various participants.

Instead of ignoring the problem of corruption, analyses should point out that civil servants are going to be seriously tempted to accept illegal payments when

- official salaries are steadily eroded by inflation;
- high-quality educational facilities are limited to the major cities, so that officials assigned elsewhere must keep two households in order for their children to get a good education;
- promotion and/or transfer is only tangentially tied to on-the-job performance and strongly tied to connections with political figures;
- no competitors exist to show that a particular activity could be undertaken more efficiently and without corruption;
- it is difficult for citizens or other public officials to gain information about what is happening; and
- civil servants control a service (or contract) that has immense marginal value to the wealthier individuals in their territory.

Similarly, rent-seeking behavior should be expected where there is little connection between collecting taxes and distributing benefits, so that funds in the common treasury are perceived to be someone else's money (and, to a large extent, they actually are, as in those countries receiving large sums of external funds). And it should be expected that facilities designed without substantial inputs by the intended beneficiaries are less likely to be sustained than those that utilize meaningful inputs.

Recognition of these problems does not imply that there are cost-free ways of solving them. Indeed, to reduce the errors associated with a lack of information, resources must be expended to obtain more information. And attempts to reduce the costs associated with one strategic problem—such as free riding—can establish institutional incentives that create opportunities for individuals to engage in other strategic behaviors, such as rent seeking and/or corruption. In other words, trade-offs exist among the intermediate costs we have been discussing. A good solution must guard against excessive spending in one area without investing more resources or creating even worse problems in another.

Given the constrained sets of performance criteria (production economies, access to technical knowledge, and control of free riding) and of institutional arrangements (markets versus national governments) that have been the focus of most past analyses, the presumption that the need for public sector involvement requires a heavy reliance on a national government is understandable. However, when the set of intermediate performance criteria to be examined is widened, some of the trade-offs that exist among performance criteria are revealed. No one institutional arrangement will score higher than all others on all performance criteria. And we have only begun to elucidate the array of institutional arrangements that can be used to govern infrastructure development.

In Chapter 8, we will examine decentralization efforts, particularly the administrative deconcentration approaches that have been used in many countries, to see whether they are able to overcome some of the weaknesses of centralized national government bureaus. We contrast decentralized structures with polycentric structures, which we believe offer a genuine alternative to sole reliance upon the national provision and production of rural infrastructure. We will discuss polycentric principles of organization in Chapter 9.

NOTES

1. The discussion here is consistent with many descriptions of the incentives and behavior of public officials in centralized agencies who are responsible for constructing and operating large-scale irrigation systems (see Ascher and Healy 1990; Wade 1984; Chambers 1980; Coward 1980; Harriss 1984).

2. The recorded production costs of many large-scale irrigation projects are extremely high. Rather than challenge the well-accepted presumption that large-scale agencies will capture economies of scale, we presume that these recorded costs are largely attributable to the higher coordination, information, and strategic expenses associated with this arrangement.

3. In some cases, the opportunities for illegal side-payments are so substantial that individuals may consider the purchase of official positions as an investment (see Wade 1984, 1985; Jagannathan 1987:chapter 8).

4. Whether the promises are made primarily to voters organized in specific

territorial districts or to individuals dispersed throughout the country who share common economic or cultural interests depends on the particular voting rules in use. For this analysis, the point is that some groups will be promised higher levels of benefits than others.

5. In many developing countries, the national government is not chosen in a general election. But the way in which a national government is selected is not central to the analysis and does not affect our conclusions. The officials within a military government—or any other form of nonelected government—still confront the problem of allocating scarce resources to different districts and groups in a society. Their ability to stay in office and improve their position depends on satisfying these relevant groups. And whether officials are elected or not, there are no direct links in fully centralized regimes between the officials' perception of the benefits from a particular project and their perception of the costs.

6. Import duties also have the added effect of protecting domestic producers from external competition and permitting a country to limit use of scarce hard currency.

7. See, for example, the table in Tait (1988:10–14), which lists fifty countries that introduced the VAT primarily during the 1970s and 1980s. The book also contains a full analysis of the reasons for adopting a VAT and issues associated with designing its structure and administration.

8. See Weingast, Shepsle, and Johnson (1981) for an excellent analysis of logrolling mechanisms and Ferejohn (1974) and Mayhew (1974) for empirical evidence about logrolling in the United States.

9. The NIAs in Korea and Taiwan are considered to be among the better performing centralized agencies with regard to both construction and O&M. USAID investments in Korean irrigation projects have resulted in well-engineered projects that are completed close to schedule and are expected to bring increases in crop yields. The investment in large-scale irrigation, as compared to other potential investments, is hard to characterize as efficient, given that the price paid to farmers for producing rice has been highly subsidized. Steinberg et al. (1980:15) concluded that Korea could import at least 50 percent more rice than it could produce domestically with the same expenditure. In Taiwan, farmers have been well organized at several levels and much more involved as key participants in managing irrigation systems than they are in most countries where a national agency plays a major role (see Levine 1980).

10. We are not attempting to single out USAID as the only bilateral donor organization that faces or facilitates these problems. We are, however, better informed about the special conditions that govern foreign assistance administered by USAID.

11. The same is, of course, true in most evaluations of public sector undertakings in developed countries, where (due to the vagueness of public sector outputs and the difficulties of measurement) analysts commonly assess governmental activities by focusing on inputs or expenditures.

12. See U.S. Government Accounting Office (1983), for example. Major exceptions are Ascher and Healy (1990), Chambers (1988), and Repetto (1986).

8

Decentralized Institutional Arrangements

At least since the 1970s, decentralization in various forms has been recommended as a way to reduce the problems, discussed in Chapter 7, that occur when a highly centralized public agency is used to provide and produce infrastructure (see, for example, Bell 1977). The assumption that decentralization is the answer to sustainability problems has been supported by the success some groups have had in creating and maintaining appropriate infrastructure facilities (see Conyers 1983; Cohen et al. 1981; Landau and Eagle 1981). When infrastructure users are involved in decisionmaking, they appear to invest substantial resources both in constructing and maintaining local facilities (see Cernea 1985; Uphoff 1986a). However, not all who have tried to construct decentralized institutions to encourage greater user participation have succeeded (Raby 1991).

The evidence that "overcentralization" of governmental authority has contributed to the difficulties of sustaining investments in infrastructure is convincing. But on the surface, overcentralization is a rather general diagnosis. The dominant prescription for this condition—decentralization—has, in turn, become a generic, all-purpose solution that lacks specificity and grounding in empirical and theoretical analysis. As Landau and Eagle (1981:10) pointed out in their survey of the literature, "Decentralization is presented as a solution to a rather large number of problems." They argued that the claims for the effectiveness of decentralization are just that: claims, not hard facts.

In this chapter, we first review how the concept of decentralization has evolved from a simple dichotomy to a multidimensional concept. Given the complexity and multiple meanings of the term, the precise intention of an infrastructure project involving a decentralization component is never quite certain. In practice, "decentralization" has frequently meant some deconcentration or *temporary* devolution of authority within a bureaucracy to lower-level officials, combined with enhanced opportunities for citizen participation. In the second section of this chapter, we consider in greater detail the likely consequences of the administrative decentralization policies that are so common in the developing world.

Involving both lower-level bureaucrats and citizens more effectively in infrastructure development can be expected to increase the quality of information available to decisionmakers and to enhance the motivation of participants to maintain something that they helped to create. The authority that is reassigned by a national government to lower-level officials in a bureau and to citizens, however, can easily be revoked by the same government. Thus, the benefits of a decentralization program or project may not be lasting.

DECENTRALIZATION EFFORTS

Efforts to decentralize have taken many forms and have a variety of underlying motivations.[1] In many (if not most) cases, institutional reforms have been initiated by the political leadership of centralized national governments with the support of international development assistance organizations. These efforts have been aimed at developing a new partnership between the human resources and energy of communities and the existing political leadership of the national government. The theoretical foundations of these efforts have been drawn from elements of democratic theory that stress the importance of participation by local people in the operation of their own public affairs (see Esman 1980; Uphoff and Esman 1974).

In some areas, the public "demand" for decentralization has been violent. But some of the institutional changes pursued in response to very strong public demands for decentralization were never really expected to yield positive results. National governments reluctantly relinquished power and tried to recover it as soon as possible. The allocation of power and authority was viewed as a zero-sum game, in which authority allocated to local or regional authorities was considered to have been "taken away" from the national level. Therefore, in places like Sudan where the need to decentralize was pressing, recent efforts to decentralize have not produced substantial, long-run improvements (Khalid 1985; Malual 1987; Duany 1992). The viability of a major redistribution of authority depends on the major actors' thorough understanding that all stand to gain in the long term from this redistribution.

Just as the underlying motives for decentralization have differed across settings, so have the types of institutional changes referred to as decentralization. One definition of decentralization exemplifies the variety of institutional changes that are now subsumed under this term.

> [Decentralization] can be defined as the transfer of responsibility for planning, management, and the raising and allocation of resources from the central government and its agencies to field units of central government ministries or agencies, subordinate units or level of government, semi-autonomous public authorities or corporations, area-wide, regional or functional authorities, or nongovernmental private or voluntary organizations. (Rondinelli and Nellis 1986:5)

In the face of such diversity of meaning, considerable effort has been devoted to elucidating the term.

The Evolving Meaning of Decentralization

Several historical reviews of the term *decentralization* provide good accounts of how this word, which once had a well-specified referent, has been applied to a rapidly expanding array of changes in institutional structure (Conyers 1983, 1984; Mawhood 1983; Mawhood and Davey 1980; M. Cohen 1980). The fairly consistent set of institutional changes introduced in the 1950s in preparation for the granting of independence to many African countries (particularly in the former colonies of Great Britain) was the first modern referent for the term in the development literature. This "classic" decentralization, as Mawhood and Davey (1980: 405) described it, was organized around five principles.

1. Local authorities should be institutionally separate from central government and assume responsibility for a significant range of local services (primary education, clinics and preventive health services, community development, and secondary roads being the most common).
2. These authorities should have their own funds and budgets and should raise a substantial part of their revenue through local direct taxation.
3. Local authorities should employ their own qualified staffs, who could be temporarily transferred from the civil service as necessary in the early stages.
4. The authorities would be governed internally by councils, predominantly composed of popularly elected members.
5. Government administrators would withdraw from an executive to an advisory, inspectorial role in relation to local government.

Mawhood (1983:4) expressly referred to these newly created bodies, which often took the form of district or provincial councils, as "local governments." He excluded from his definition of local government both local jurisdictions intended to provide a single service and federal arrangements in which constitutional law provides for national and subnational governments to share many governmental functions and revenues. During the 1950s, *deconcentration* was the term used to refer to institutional changes that shifted the authority to make certain types of decisions from national civil service personnel in the capital to national civil service personnel posted in dispersed locations.

Since the second round of decentralization efforts began in the 1970s, the word has been used in the development literature to refer to many different institutional changes. But because of the proliferation of institutional changes, a precise meaning for the term decentralization no longer exists. The political leadership of developing countries has tended to use the word indiscriminately to refer to any kind of institutional change. Many new initiatives that were called decentralizations did, in fact, involve extensive redistribution of executive authority among the employees of national ministries or bodies closely tied to them (deconcentration), but the reorganizations still tightly constrained the independent legislative, taxing, and spending authority of what Mawhood called local governments.

Because governments had captured the term *decentralization* to describe what were, in many cases, administrative reorganizations, other words were coined by academic observers sensitive to the need to differentiate among different types of institutional changes. *Devolution* was applied to reorganization efforts that approximated "classic" decentralization in that significant amounts of independent legislative and fiscal authority were transferred to subnational governments. In an effort to make further important distinctions, two additional terms to categorize decentralization efforts have been adopted: *delegation*, referring to transfers of authority to public corporations or special authorities outside the regular bureaucratic structure, and *privatization*, referring to transfers of responsibility for public functions to voluntary organizations or private enterprises (Rondinelli and Nellis 1986:5; Rondinelli, McCullough, and Johnson 1987:4).

Multiple Dimensions of Decentralization

Debates about what labels can appropriately be attached to different reform efforts reflect the complex content of the rule changes taking place. Cohen and his colleagues observed that "decentralization is not one thing; nor is it even a series of degrees along a single spectrum or scale. For comprehensibility and utility in policy circles, the overarching abstraction 'decentralization' must be split into a host of separate, occasionally conflicting entities" (S. Cohen et al. 1981:5–6). To discuss decentralization efforts in support of the poor, Leonard and Marshall (1982:30) proposed a typology based on four dimensions that can be represented by a matrix containing 24 subtypes of decentralization. Each institutional change can be located in one of these 24 cells depending on (1) what type of organization is involved at both the intermediate and local level; (2) whether mediating organizations are representative, private, or agencies of the central government; (3) whether governmental bodies are generalist or specialist; and (4) whether representative entities are inclusive or alternative organizations limited to the poor.

Conyers (1985) also emphasized that institutional changes regarded as decentralization vary widely on a number of dimensions, five of which she considered characteristic of all decentralization efforts. These dimensions point to the deeper structure of the institutional changes involved in a decentralization initiative. They are:

- the functional activities over which authority is transferred;
- the type of authority, or powers, which are transferred with respect to each functional activity;
- the level(s) or area(s) to which such authority is transferred;
- the individual, organization or agency to which authority is transferred at each level; and
- the legal or administrative means by which authority is transferred (Conyers 1985:24).

Thus, recent scholarship on decentralization has stressed that the term refers not to phenomena that can be arrayed along a single dimension but rather to many different phenomena that can only be represented by multiple dimensions. Although some of the dimensions addressed by one scholar overlap those selected by another, the specific dimensions have something of an ad hoc character. The reasons an analyst should choose one particular dimension over others are not always clear. These dimensions allow some additional descriptive discrimination, but they do not necessarily help develop a cumulative body of knowledge about how various institutional changes affect the incentives of participants, their resulting actions, and the effects of their cumulated behavior.

The dimensions that Conyers used to elucidate the deeper structure of decentralization efforts seem quite reasonable. But because they are not related to a broader theory that identifies the factors affecting the incentives that individuals in centralized or decentralized institutional arrangements face, they represent simply one of many efforts to specify important dimensions. What is needed, therefore, is a more general set of dimensions closely tied to a body of theory.

DOES ADMINISTRATIVE DECENTRALIZATION IMPROVE THE PERFORMANCE OF CENTRALIZED NATIONAL GOVERNMENTS?

Proposals for administrative decentralization have been a common policy response to the weaknesses associated with highly centralized national governments. Such proposals are generally based on analyses that highlight many of the problems we have discussed. That is, huge sums are invested in infrastructure facilities that are later determined to be poorly suited to the needs of a particular community and/ or are poorly maintained. This occurs because the officials in the best position to know about local circumstances have too little influence in decisionmaking processes within the ministries. In addition, decisions regarding any single infrastructure investment are too far removed from local political processes and therefore do not reflect community preferences. Residents of a community have no means of directly shaping the infrastructure development that takes place in their locality.

These problems have led to proposals that employees should be physically relocated and decisionmaking authority within ministries be rearranged in order to give employees working in regional or subregional offices a larger role in determining the character of infrastructure development and maintenance in their jurisdictions. Scholars commonly refer to these policy initiatives as "deconcentration" because they are intended to lessen the concentration of authority exercised by national government officials working in the capital by transferring it to national government officials in dispersed locations.

In some instances, local representative councils have also been created as advisory bodies for ministry employees. But even if councils have some limited authority in making laws, ministries overseeing local government retain veto power over legislation. Thus, decisionmaking power is not fully "devolved" to local governmental bodies. Because the local councils are not intended to be independent governments with limited law-making or law-enforcing autonomy, structural changes associated with administrative decentralization are essentially changes in the *production side* of the original, centralized national government. Employees are shifted from headquarter locations to field locations within production agencies. The array of intermediate costs and valuative criteria that we developed in Figure 7.1 for a centralized agency could, therefore, still represent the bulk of the costs associated with such decentralized agencies. There are, however, some possible differences that are worth discussing.

The dispersal of administrative offices inevitably places many officials in closer physical contact with residents and local council members of the communities in which infrastructure development will occur. The time and effort required of officials who wish to learn more about local circumstances is thereby reduced. Thus, relative to highly centralized agencies, administrative decentralization may lower the costs of securing relevant time and place information. The question, of course, is whether officials posted in a village will actually collect this information or use it once it is collected. Even if the site of a planned road or irrigation system is nearby, an official assigned to a regional or subregional office must still make some effort to learn about the area. If this official is convinced that local people know nothing of consequence about economic development or if he or she knows what courses of action senior officials strongly prefer, proximity alone may not be enough to encourage the official to obtain information about local conditions.

Administrative reorganization of this type could be expected to improve the performance of officials who are assigned to the same areas in which they were raised and in which their principal economic interests (or those of their families) are located. It would, in this case, behoove the officials to provide infrastructure facilities appropriate for their own needs. Such facilities might or might not be considered appropriate by members of a local advisory council or by most residents of the jurisdiction. But in reality, many developing countries deliberately post employees outside their home areas. This is done to prevent them from using their positions to promote their own or familial economic interests. The policy has not, however, prevented officials who are so inclined from favoring one local group over another in exchange for illegal payments of some kind.

Furthermore, administrative reorganization usually does not substantially alter the career track within ministries. Even though some administrative decentralization initiatives mandate that the personnel performance evaluations of ministry officers are to be conducted by elected officials in the locality where they are posted, the final decisions concerning promotions and transfers are generally made by senior national government officers. And reorganization does not change the fact that, due to a long history of centralized authority, the best schools and hospitals are located in the capital city. Therefore, lower-level officers will still be primarily concerned with how their senior officers assess their performance, rather than with how they are judged locally.

Because local advisory councils rarely have an effective veto over infrastructure decisionmaking, ministry officials need not take their opinions too seriously. One experimental participatory program in the Philippines did, however, give farmers an effective veto on the decisions of central government engineers. Under the program, farmers had to assume responsibility for operating and maintaining a rehabilitated irrigation system after it was constructed but only after they had agreed to do so. Once engineers were rewarded for the rate of successful turnovers completed, farmers gained a much more effective voice (F. Korten 1982:21). But later evaluations revealed that though provisions for sharing authority were successful, they have not been included in other Philippine projects (see Box 8.1).

Even if local councils have some influence over the choice of local infrastructure, financing arrangements under administrative decentralization are generally less effective. The vast proportion, if not all, of the funds used to finance capital infrastructure are derived from the national government. The government is, therefore, normally unwilling to yield power over how these funds are spent, even if statutes permit the local council to play more than an "advisory" role. Even more problematic for the longer-term sustainability of these infrastructure investments is the fact that the national government may then require the local council to operate and maintain the facility without simultaneously giving them the revenue mobilization authority necessary to adequately finance the O&M costs involved. Furthermore, local users, who had little role to play in siting or constructing the project, are likely to feel that the infrastructure and its maintenance are the responsibility of the national government.

Prominent members of a local council with connections to senior officials or political leaders are in a position to make local-level public service employees take their views into account. They may not, however, have the potential development impact on their community in mind when they exert their influence; rather, they may act to advance their own interests or the local interests of their patrons. Thus, patron-client links between public officials at different levels and between local and national leaders—*not* a local consensus—may actually determine the allocation of public funds.

In some cases, ministry technical officers have been posted to local governments at the same time that considerable decisionmaking authority is transferred to these jurisdictions, in an attempt to increase the amount of technical information directly available to the locality. But

BOX 8.1   The Bicol River Basin Development Program

   The Bicol River Basin Development Program, initiated in the Philippines in 1973, was a large-scale, integrated rural development project for building rural infrastructure (roads, irrigation structures, and water supply systems) with broad objectives, including a substantial improvement in the socioeconomic well-being of the basin's population. The Buhi-Lala Project, discussed earlier in Box 3.4, was a Bicol program that was also part of the National Irrigation Agency's experimental participation program. Bicol was expected to establish "a set of institutional innovations calling for decentralized decision making, local people's participation, and a multisectoral and integrated area approach" (Sommer et al. 1982:IV). By 1982, USAID had made two grants and five loans totaling $30.4 million and the government of the Philippines had invested about $75 million in the project (Sommer et al. 1982:IV). An evaluation of the entire Bicol program was conducted in the ninth year of the project, by which time the evaluators determined that a "large staff and institutional infrastructure [had] been put into place and numerous plans and studies [had] been produced" (Sommer et al. 1982:V). The evaluation team noted that the Program Office had become a "coordinator of committees, a receiving point for project reports, and only occasionally a packager of project proposals and solver of problems facing Basin projects. This appears a modest role for a 421-member staff . . . with a 1981 budget of more than $1 million" (Sommer et al. 1982:13).
   The evaluation concluded that "the weak point in the institutional chain is a critical one: The farmers, on whose behalf the whole program is conducted, have not participated in anything but a passive sense. Although participation was a widely heralded part of the original plan, it is only recently that experimental efforts have begun to engage them in activities beyond the various meetings to which they were summoned in the past to hear officials talk of project plans and exhort farmers to help" (Sommer et al. 1982:14). NIA officials appeared to recognize this problem in those project areas under its control and assigned COs (community organizers) to several project areas overtly based on the experimental program described earlier. In several of the areas visited, the evaluation team was impressed with the performance of the COs but ruefully noted that "NIA is already beginning, apparently for budgetary reasons, to reduce the number of its community organizers in some areas of the Bicol" (Sommer et al. 1982:14).[2]
   What is instructive—and sad—about the failure of this program to effectively engage the farmers in Bicol Basin is that the program was developed side by side with the very successful NIA participatory experiment. This leads one to question whether agencies like NIA can learn even from their own experimental projects.

problems have arisen when these more technically astute individuals seize an inordinate amount of power from local decisionmakers and insist on technocratic or bureaucratic solutions without considering the preferences of local citizens. Jenkins and Bird (forthcoming) refer to this type of outcome as "centralized decentralization" and describe events taking place in Madras, India, as an example of this phenomena. Enhancing the capacity of employees in provincial or district offices to plan and implement policy has been the objective of numerous institutional development programs, such as the Provincial Development Assistance Program (PDAP) described in Box 8.2. The history of PDAP reveals that training did initially improve the skills and professional confidence of provincial planning staff members.

No formal evaluations have been made of the longer-term effects of PDAP, but a recent assessment of local government performance suggests that financial management and budgeting practices are weak (Hubbell et al. 1989). Analysts observe that (1) revenue forecasting is rudimentary and often does not consider known factors that will influence the jurisdiction's revenues during the following year; (2) budget officers seldom provide executives with sufficient information for understanding the budget; and (3) many supplemental budgets are prepared each year, suggesting that the budgeting is carried out without any regard for the financial realities the province will face during the fiscal year. Because the position of provincial budget officer is a new one, comparisons of the current budgeting process with the situation at the close of PDAP may be unfair. On the other hand, if provincial budgeting efforts were adequate at the close of the project, there would seem to be little reason to have created this new office. The longer-term effects of the PDAP experience suggest that a skill-enhancement program unaccompanied by changes in the incentives personnel face may have little or no enduring effect on performance.

In contrast, training programs organized in Nepal for members of farmer-managed irrigation systems have been more successful in increasing productivity (see N. Pradhan and Yoder 1989). These training programs are funded by the national government but are actually produced by persons farming in highly successful farmer-managed systems. In this case, the trainees have instructors who share a similar social status and an intimate familiarity with the problems they face. Unlike provincial planning staff trainees in PDAPs, these farmer trainees can hope to effect substantial changes in rules governing their systems in order to enhance productivity after the training program ends. PDAP trainees usually returned to a work environment whose rules they could not hope to alter.

BOX 8.2   The Provincial Development Assistance Program
             in the Philippines

The Provincial Development Assistance Program was a USAID project conducted in the Philippines between 1968 and 1981, ultimately covering twenty-eight provinces (Iglesias 1985). The project provided support for both the construction of specific infrastructure facilities and a considerable amount of technical assistance. PDAP was "based on the assumption that decentralization could not be meaningful unless local governments had the technical and managerial capability to plan and implement local development activities" (Rondinelli 1983:188). The program is an example of an externally supported initiative intended to increase the capacity of provincial governmental organizations to play a larger role in economic development by improving provincial-level planning and management capabilities.

Prior to PDAP, provinces had insufficient technical abilities to permit provincial governors to hold their own against national ministerial line agencies in discussions about the allocation of funds in the national government budget. Thus, training in the use of management tools, especially those related to planning and budgeting, was emphasized in the program. Most of these tools were developed by U.S. consultants working with specialists from various national government agencies (Wunsch 1983:2).

During the initial 1968–1972 phase, the project was directed by a committee of specialists from several national government ministries. Participating provinces were required to establish provincial development staffs (PDSs) to assist the governor in exercising his development functions. When the country was placed under martial law in 1972, responsibility for PDAP was transferred to the Office of the President. A strong executive director took control from the committee, and a full-time PDAP staff was hired to manage the project. Requirements on the use of the planning and budgeting procedures were rigidly enforced. The central PDAP staff also engaged in direct administration of infrastructure projects, rather than assisting provinces in administering them. As Landau et al. (1980:7) noted, "PDAP-Central was building a tightly controlled hierarchical system. We also observed that the sheer number of PDAP [planning and budgeting procedural] requirements overloaded an already impoverished provincial government."

During the final phase of the program, 1976–1980, PDAP went into a period of decline. Responsibility was transferred from the Office of the President to a deputy minister in the Ministry of Local Government and Community Development. A newly created program office was able to retain direct implementation responsibility for only a few special

(continues)

BOX 8.2   (continued)

infrastructure projects. This weakening of the central office permitted provincial officials to take more initiative in decisionmaking, a result that, ironically, was more in line with the original intent of the project.

Evaluators point out that the positive results of PDAP would not have occurred had the program been implemented as planned (Wunsch 1988:13–14). PDAP's design ignored the organizational incentives that were key determinants of its success. The program inadvertently worked because the incentives provided by the special projects encouraged provinces to join the program, which helped them establish provincial planning staffs. Project money, together with new administrative capacity and the desire to get reelected, encouraged provincial governors to act more assertively than before.

At the close of the project, Landau et al. (1980:15) concluded that PDAP and the special projects "have set in motion a process which, if sustained, promises to produce a *de facto* decentralization at the provincial level." The evaluators found that in some, but not all, provinces, the PDAP-trained staff was playing an important role in the annual budget process (Landau et al. 1980:91). This, they argued, had increased the influence a governor could exert in that process and therefore was "a crucial element in strengthening his control over programs at the provincial level" (Landau et al. 1980:93).

In summary, the PDAP approach to supporting decentralization through a deconcentration of decisionmaking capacity was based on the expectation that, by providing additional support for infrastructure improvements, provinces would have incentives to upgrade their administrative capabilities. Over the course of the project, those results were realized because of the diminished control exercised by the project's national administrators over activities at the provincial level. Unfortunately, it does not appear that these improvements resulted in lasting effects, at least in the crucial area of budgeting.

Although some experimental decentralization projects have involved temporary shifts of substantial joint authority to local-level officials and to the citizens involved in a project, most have done little more than transfer personnel from headquarter offices to field locations. If information obtained in the field is not taken more seriously than it was previously, the transfer is unlikely to substantially affect any of the intermediate costs involved in either construction or maintenance of a large-scale irrigation system. Thus, the performance of administratively decentralized agencies is likely to be similar to that of centralized agencies. What is required are major structural changes assuring considerable joint autonomy and responsibility for lower-level officials and the citizens they are servicing.

CONCLUSION

In Chapter 7, we demonstrated that an assessment of the performance of centralized provision arrangements that uses a wider array of valuative criteria reveals important weaknesses in this type of arrangement for infrastructure development. We are certainly not the first or the only analysts to have recognized these difficulties. Governments have often responded by pursuing some form of "decentralization." This chapter has shown that the term decentralization has been used to refer to an extremely wide variety of institutional reorganizations. Perhaps the most common of these has been deconcentration or administrative decentralization, wherein considerable decisionmaking power is retained by national government officials. Although such policies have some potential to decrease transaction costs associated with the highly centralized provision of public infrastructure, many of the institutional changes have not yielded the expected results. In the next chapter, we will consider more substantial changes to highly centralized institutional arrangements.

NOTES

1. The literature on decentralization is extensive. See, for example, Bryant and White (1982, 1984); Esman and Uphoff (1982); Kee (1977); Landau and Eagle (1981); Leonard and Marshall (1982); Montgomery (1981); Rondinelli (1981); Rondinelli and Nellis (1986); Rondinelli, McCullough, and Johnson (1987); and Wunsch (1988).

2. An appendix to the evaluation that focused entirely on the participatory aspects of the Bicol project illuminated some of the possibilities and contradictions of attempting to decentralize within the context of a centralized program. The evaluation did not question the sincerity of NIA officials in trying to change the ways in which they related to farmers. Several references were made to lessons learned from the prior experimental program. The use of COs was positively received by the farmers, and the COs themselves were enthusiastic about their work. Some felt that the technical staff at NIA considered the work of the COs a "nuisance cost" but thought that more doors were opening. One CO indicated that the most rewarding part of her job was in the field, working directly with the farmers. "When in the project office, I get the feeling that the engineers do not really

see any need for our work" (quoted in Sommer et al. 1982:F-8). She further reflected that she felt a little guilty at times because her sympathies were with the farmers: "They are not getting water; the designs are faulty; construction is delayed—and yet I get my salary from NIA, and I want to defend it as well" (quoted in Sommer et al. 1982:F-8). A somewhat more jaded CO expressed her misgivings in the following manner: "We are not doing CO work, we are PR officers for NIA. What we do is sell a project. We often find ourselves in sympathy with the people, but then, we are NIA employees" (quoted in Sommer et al. 1982:F-7).

9

Polycentric Institutional Arrangements

In previous chapters, we have drawn on bodies of theory from institutional economics, public finance, and institutional analysis to derive a set of intermediate performance criteria for institutional arrangements. We considered how likely five stylized types of these arrangements will perform the difficult tasks of developing and sustaining infrastructure. These included the institutions of a pure market, a differentiated market, and a user group, in addition to centralized and administratively decentralized national government bureaus. In this chapter, we will consider a sixth type of arrangement—polycentric, nested governmental institutions—that promises to more completely meet the performance criteria we elaborated in Chapter 5.

Centralized provision arrangements are frequently able to forestall free riding, achieve economies of scale in production, and bring scientific information to bear on decisionmaking. Although most administrative decentralizations have been introduced in order to reduce the cost of acquiring time and place information or the errors due to a lack of this type of information, they typically have not been successful in meeting either goal. Administrative decentralization has also failed, in many instances, to reduce the high costs of strategic behavior—shirking, corruption, and rent seeking, in particular. An analysis of the structure of authority relationships makes it clear why centralized and most decentralized institutional arrangements should be considered unicentric: Decisionmaking authority is organized within a hierarchical chain of command, with a single, ultimate center of authority.

In this chapter, we consider the improvements a noncentral or polycentric institutional structure can provide in reducing strategic and information costs while retaining the advantages of larger-scale production agencies when economies of scale are present. Polycentric or noncentral institutional arrangements distribute circumscribed but independent rule-making and rule-enforcing authority among numerous jurisdictions. All public authorities have official standing, and no individual or group serves as the final, all-purpose authority that stands above the law.

We first consider the concept of polycentricity and how a polycentric institutional arrangement might be expected to lower the costs of acquiring time and place information and to reduce some forms of strategic behavior. We then discuss whether polycentric structures are appropriate and feasible for less-developed countries. Because the relevance of polycentric systems has not been widely recognized by students of development administration and finance, we then address some of the more common reservations about the relevance of polycentric arrangements for developing countries. Finally, we consider the conditions under which privatization might serve as another way to improve the quality of decisionmaking in the development and maintenance of rural infrastructure.

THE CONCEPT OF POLYCENTRICITY

In contrast to the centralized and decentralized structures described in Chapters 7 and 8, a polycentric governing structure offers citizens the opportunity to organize not one but many governing authorities (see V. Ostrom, Tiebout, and Warren 1961; V. Ostrom 1987, 1991). Each government may exercise considerable independent authority to make and enforce rules within a circumscribed scope of authority for a specified geographical area. Every government is, first and foremost, a provision unit. Some provision units may organize their own production bureaus, as when a ministry of transportation establishes a road construction bureau, or they may choose to contract with other public bureaus in a national or subnational jurisdiction or with private firms that produce a particular good or service. The option of choosing from among multiple producers makes it possible to take advantage of diverse economies of scale for one or more of the design, construction, maintenance, and operational services involved in infrastructure development and maintenance.

The nature of the authority exercised by different governments in a polycentric system varies enormously. Some have general-purpose authority and provide a wide array of public services to a community. Others may be special-purpose authorities that do nothing but provide for, operate, and maintain a single irrigation system or road. The varied functions of these governments means that individuals maintain citizenship in several governments simultaneously. Figure 9.1 illustrates

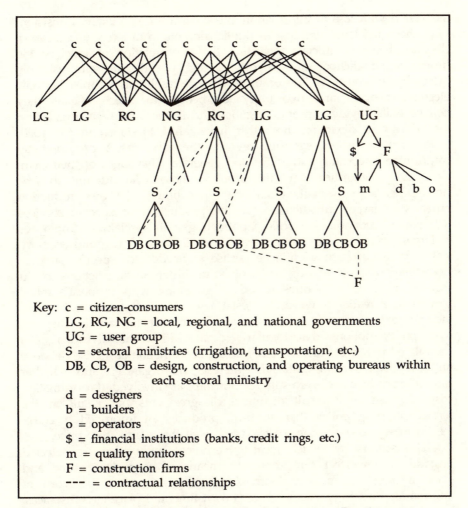

FIGURE 9.1 A Polycentric Arrangement for Infrastructure Development

some of the diverse relationships possible between citizens and governments, as well as among governments themselves (for empirical examples, see Blomquist 1992).

Where individual governments exercise independent authority, officials for each government are selected independently of selection processes in other jurisdictions. An official in one jurisdiction does not function as a superior to officials in other jurisdictions and thus does not control their career paths. Although hierarchical relationships will exist within any one jurisdiction, the long chains of relationships closely associated with loss of information and control are less likely. Consistent with the equal legal standing of public servants in different jurisdictions, disputes between officials regarding the interpretation of laws or the limits of jurisdiction are properly settled outside an administrative hierarchy, in courts of law or other dispute-resolution forums. Periodic elections provide an opportunity for people to select officials they believe will provide appropriate goods and services for their jurisdiction (or at least to discipline those that have failed to do so in the past).

Polycentric orders sacrifice few of the advantages provided by centralized governing authorities and generate advantages of their own. Governing authorities can still penalize those who attempt to free ride. Officials in a small jurisdiction can contract with the production bureaus of larger jurisdictions for the production of specific services that permit economies of scale. Contracting with specialized employees in larger jurisdictions or with private firms is a convenient and economical way to purchase scientific expertise as needed for specific projects. Coordination costs among authorities in different jurisdictions could increase if these authorities refuse to go along with proposals made by others. In reality, however, contestation over different policies between independent units is likely to simply be more open than the disputes over policy options that regularly occur within the divisions of a centralized public bureau. Whether actual coordination costs rise depends on how diverse communities of interests are organized and whether mutually productive or zero-sum relationships are involved. If coordination costs do rise as a result of initial disagreements but result in the refinement of a policy that, in turn, produces an improved outcome, the increased coordination costs could well be worth the price.

The elections by which local government authorities are selected provide an imperfect but important means of aggregating time and place information for decisionmaking. This is because the store of information about a particular voter's own time and place circumstances, in combination with his or her own interests, determines that voter's preference for the policy positions of one candidate or another. Once elected, officials or representatives face strong incentives to keep at least some of their constituents happy in order to secure reelection. Retaining popularity requires that officials keep themselves well informed about changing preferences. By definition, local candidates are also likely to possess a large fund of local time and place information to draw upon in decisionmaking.

Polycentric systems also provide a means of reducing the costs of opportunism. Citizens who wish to remove corrupt or lazy elected officials need not rely on the cooperation of senior administration officials; they can accomplish this themselves through elections or other selection and removal processes. In addition, with more officials operating independently in more jurisdictions, the likelihood that any one of them will monopolize control over important public goods and services is reduced.

Economic Rationale for Polycentricity

Most economists researching and writing about the problems of public sector decentralization are associated with the subdiscipline of public finance. The name that has been given to the subject of their study is "fiscal federalism." This title is somewhat misleading because it implies that these issues are relevant only to a federal system of government. In reality, however, wherever multiple jurisdictions are recognized—even within a unitary system of government—the questions considered here must be addressed. Unlike the political science literature, in which the term *federalism* is reserved for a fairly well-defined approach to the structure of governments, the fiscal federalism literature has adopted a much looser definition, as demonstrated by the following description of economic federal government by Oates: "a public sector with both centralized and decentralized levels of decision-making in which choices made at each level concerning the provision of public services are determined largely by the demands for these services by the residents of (and perhaps others who carry on activities in) the respective jurisdiction" (Oates 1972:17). Oates went on to note that, under this definition, the term *federal* refers equally to systems in which local decisions are based on delegated authority and to systems with constitutionally guaranteed independent authority.

Among the questions that must be addressed under any such polycentric or multitiered system is the assignment of functions to an appropriate level within that system. The traditional public finance approach assigns governments responsibility for three principal functions: allocation, distribution, and stabilization (Musgrave 1959). The last of these functions involves designing strategies for achieving the macro policy goals of economic growth, employment, and price stability. The national government quite naturally pursues these goals because usually only this government controls the monetary, trade, and debt policies that must be consistent with fiscal policies in order to achieve stable economic growth.[1]

Redistribution, particularly at the level of the individual or the household, is also usually considered an appropriate task for national governments, although there is little doubt that the public spending and taxation decisions of smaller units of government affect income distribution. The principal point here is that any attempt by local governments to elicit a major alteration in the distribution of income and wealth is doomed to failure if interjurisdictional mobility can occur. This is because local jurisdictions that attempt to "soak" the wealthy and redistribute this money to the poor are likely to find that the wealthy will flee the locality and that greater numbers of poor individuals will migrate into the area.[2]

The strongest argument in favor of polycentric provision of services is that it increases allocative efficiency. In its simplest form, the argument rests on the expectation that, although the demand for public services differs among individuals, there is likely to be a greater homogeneity of demand within small groups than over broad segments of society. The argument also presumes that if the national government were to provide these services, it would attempt to offer exactly the same levels of services to all areas, regardless of local demand.[3] A countrywide, uniform set of services, however, is likely to result in suboptimal spending in some areas and excessive spending in others. If each locality is allowed to choose (and pay for) the level of services it deems most appropriate, the overall satisfaction in the economy can be enhanced. Hence, a polycentric decisionmaking process can more effectively determine the local demand for these goods and services than can a highly centralized bureaucracy.

Theoretical work in this area, including that by Bish (1971) and Barzel (1969), was summarized by Oates in the following statement of a theorem:

> For a public good—the consumption of which is defined over geographical subsets of the total population, and for which the costs of providing each level of output of the good in each jurisdiction are the same for the central or the respective local government—it will always be more efficient (or at least as efficient) for local governments to provide the Pareto-efficient levels of output for their respective jurisdictions than for the central government to provide any specified and uniform level of output across all jurisdictions. (Oates 1972:17)

The same arguments lead to the theoretical conclusion that different districts, probably of different sizes, should be established for each of the many types of services provided by the public sector. That is, rather than have a single local government provide fire protection, street services, recreation, and education, separate fire, street, recreation, and education districts should be established to provide each service. The boundaries of each district should be drawn in a way that minimizes the variability of demands within the district and increases the variability of demands across districts.

Another advantage of separate provision organizations is that officials of each would be able to focus their attention on arranging for and monitoring maintenance and use activities for that organization alone. When officials are responsible primarily for one, rather than many, infrastructure facilities, they may be far more tenacious in protecting the past investments of their organization. When responsibility for the provision and maintenance of many different goods and services is assigned to a single set of officials, the temptation to increase the flow of immediate services to clients by deferring future maintenance activities may be difficult to resist.

The number of single-purpose (or even multipurpose) local governments that can be created within a particular area is limited by transaction costs. Allocative efficiency requires a flow of information about preferences between citizens and local government decisionmakers. The efforts citizens must make to select, monitor, and communicate with decision-makers is not, however, costless. Indeed, ensuring high-quality information flows can be extremely costly. Hence, there is a trade-off between the economic efficiency achieved by many small, single-purpose districts and the technical efficiency of larger, multipurpose jurisdictions. As stated by Bish (1971:53): "While every aggregation will reduce an individual's ability to articulate his own particular preference on each of the issues involved, combining some functions in the same unit should result in sufficient savings in decision-making costs to more than offset the loss of precise demand stipulation."

Operating together, the price system and competition ensure that private markets yield efficient allocations of private goods. The mechanism(s) by which polycentric governments can produce efficient allocations is more complex. In Tiebout's (1956) pioneering work in this area, mobility was the mechanism that guaranteed that public service outcomes closely matched individual preferences. Essentially, the Tiebout model assumes that different localities each offer their residents a different taxing and spending package. If mobility is costless and if perfect information is available, persons and firms will move to a locality in which their preferences are best served, in the same way that consumers will spend their incomes on different goods and services, depending on their willingness and ability to do so. The basic Tiebout model was extended by V. Ostrom, Tiebout, and Warren (1961) to include the possibility of separating provision from production and allowing provision units to contract for production with their own or private production enterprises. Allowing for some competition on the production side enhances the potential efficacy of "exit" as a strategy available to citizens (V. Ostrom and E. Ostrom 1977).[4]

There are, of course, some major limitations to the Tiebout model. Just as information is costly, so is mobility. Most property owners who wish to move from one jurisdiction to another must first find someone to buy their property (and replace them as taxpayers in this jurisdiction) before they can afford to leave. Furthermore, the production of some services by one district provides benefits that spill over onto those residing in neighboring districts. For example, a sewer treatment system is likely to affect persons and firms outside the service district itself, particularly those downstream. If each locality is permitted to choose independently (and is forced to pay for) the level of sewage treatment services it considers optimal, downstream communities are likely to find themselves flooded with poorly treated wastewater. From the perspective of the entire population, the aggregate level of sewage treatment services will be suboptimal.[5]

Finally, although mobility may help to bring about an efficient outcome, it may also have a detrimental effect. As more people enter a jurisdiction to take advantage of the attractive set of services being provided, the costs of providing these services may increase and must be borne by those already located there. That is, if more people enter to take advantage of a good school system, costs per pupil may rise as additional classroom space, more teachers, and other education inputs must be acquired. Such congestion costs may exceed the efficiency gains from the polycentric decisionmaking process, resulting in a net decline in welfare.[6] The conceptual solution to the problem is to charge new immigrants the full marginal costs of the services they are enjoying; however, estimating such costs and devising a workable system to capture them is not a trivial task.

THE POSSIBILITY OF POLYCENTRICITY IN DEVELOPING COUNTRIES

Among observers of development efforts over the past quarter century, Goran Hyden (1980, 1983) is noteworthy for the significance he assigned the role currently being played in developing countries by indigenous social and economic organizations, including family and ethnic groups. One objective of the constitutions of centralized regimes has been to replace particularistic loyalties with national loyalty. Even though there are, in fact, multiple centers of ethnic loyalty in developing countries, only infrequently do the jurisdictions to which these loyalties attach overlap. And few, if any, of the leaders recognized as legitimate in each center are authorized officials. Such situations provide individuals with the experience *not* of polycentricity as we use it here but of imperfect imperial control. Even within imperial systems, however, one finds ethnic groups (the Masai and the Nuer, for example) and special-purpose groups (like the zanjeras) that provide individual members with the experience of a polycentric governing system. The basis for cautious optimism about the potential value of fully authorized polycentric institutional arrangements in developing countries stems from the productive manner in which the underlying principles of polycentric organization are already operating there.

Sources of Polycentricity

A search through the development literature for institutions that have successfully supported productive, legal collective activity over long periods of time frequently leads to local indigenous institutions (Curtis 1991; D. Korten 1980, 1986; D. Korten and Alfonso 1983; Uphoff 1982, 1986b). Some of these institutions are officially recognized as having independent, though circumscribed, authority to make and enforce local rules. But many indigenous institutions remain almost invisible to national government officials (and to many academics); others are strictly outlawed. Invisible institutions, however, frequently provide substantial public services. For example, the "informal economy" was an invisible part of most developing countries until quite recently, when careful observers began to realize that a substantial portion of the economic activity in Eastern Europe and developing countries was conducted by unlicensed firms (see de Soto 1989; Jagannathan 1987; Jenkins 1988). For the most part, unauthorized indigenous institutions constitute the "informal polity" that governs the informal economy (see Box 9.1). The cost of the informality is some degree of inefficiency, due to the lack of a fully open factor market. Further, "justice" in an informal polity can take on more sinister forms, as the Sicilian Mafias have (see Sabetti 1984).

Indigenous institutions are frequently small in size and are therefore able to provide services for members on either a voluntary or involuntary basis, using social and moral pressure to enforce rules that limit free riding. Some, however, also make use of authorized or unauthorized police powers to enforce payment of fines for failing to contribute to the group effort. And some effectively organize larger-scale group efforts. In countries as diverse as Indonesia, Nepal, Japan, Taiwan, and the Philippines, large-scale irrigation works have been constructed and maintained over long periods of time by indigenous institutions

BOX 9.1 Informal Judicial Authority in Peru

Research conducted by the Peruvian Institute for Liberty and Democracy (ILD), founded by Hernando de Soto, has succeeded not only in documenting the nature and extent of the informal economy in Peru but also in understanding the informal polity that makes and enforces the rules that shape that informal economy. One type of informal polity is the settlers' association that organizes the illegal invasion and settlement of undeveloped land in urban areas. In his 1989 work, de Soto described the nature of the informal judiciary that interprets the rules by which the settlers' associations order affairs in newly created settlements.

Informal organizations are responsible for administering justice on their own account and do so essentially in two areas of jurisdiction: land disputes and criminal offenses. Jurisdiction over land disputes is largely a response to the absence of official intervention. Over the years, the formal judicial system, overwhelmed by numerous problems, has tended to ignore individual disputes over land in informal settlements. A number of provisions have thus transferred jurisdiction over these disputes from the judiciary to the government bureaucracy. However, the bureaucracy has been overtaken by the initiative of settlement residents and forced to formalize decisions adopted by informal organizations or to intervene only at a very late stage in the dispute. There have even been cases where unresolved disputes have been taken informally to justices of the peace for arbitration, instead of to the competent government authorities. These justices of the peace tend to rely on extralegal norms to resolve the disputes, since it is the extralegal system which is the socially relevant one and there is often no formal law on which to rely.

All of this has encouraged the development of informal justice to resolve disputes over land. The leadership and the general assembly of the informal [settlers'] organization function as courts of the first and second instances, respectively, and resolve disputes over competing rights, breaches of sales contracts or tenancy agreements, boundary lines, and even family disputes about who owns the land. However, according to the ILD's calculations, 13 percent of the lots recognized in informal settlements are in litigation— evidence that the lack of coercive authority reduces the effectiveness of this system of justice.

Since informal organizations have to preserve law and order, they inevitably develop practical criteria for administering justice in criminal matters also. If an offense is committed, for instance, both accused and plaintiffs are allowed to appear, the accused

---

BOX 9.1 (continued)

defend themselves, certain evidence is allowed (including the testimony of residents, to which great value is attached), and a jury consisting of heads of families settles the case. On the other hand, the Peruvian judicial system does without juries and prefers the professional administration of justice, keeping alive a long-standing prejudice that the average Peruvian lacks the education in civics and the responsibility to decide whether an accused is innocent or guilty.

A number of penalties are invoked, depending on the nature of the offense. The penalties for ordinary criminals are beating, forced nudity, or expulsion, the last of which is enforced by members of the settlement who evict the culprits from their lot. If they resist and the expulsion cannot be carried out, it is customary to allow a new member to settle on the free areas of the lot so that sooner or later the outcasts lose all or part of their expectative property right.

Homicide is usually dealt with by handing the culprit over to the police, unless the nature of the crime triggers a lynching. Raping a child is often punished by death. Rapists, referred to as "monsters" in popular speech, are usually lynched if they fall into settlers' hands. When the police discover the body, they learn little or nothing from the residents and generally limit themselves to taking the body to the morgue, in an unusual tacit recognition of the informal system of justice. All the punishments are governed by custom, however—there are no written penal regulations in informal settlements. (de Soto 1989:28–29)

(Lando 1979; P. Pradhan 1983; Beardsley, Hall, and Ward 1959; Pasternak 1972; and Bacdayan 1974).[7] Box 9.2 describes a polycentric institutional arrangement created by farmers to govern the construction, operation, and maintenance of the Chhattis Mauja irrigation system, which supports approximately 25,000 people settled on 3,500 hectares of land.

In regimes where indigenous institutions have no legal standing, many smaller institutions are able to survive unnoticed or unchallenged. Such idiosyncratic factors as a forbidding environment (for Botswana's Bushmen) or a particularly ferocious reputation (for East Africa's Masai and Nuer) provide some degree of autonomy for acephalous groups (those organized on nonhierarchical, polycentric principles) caught up in centralized systems. The problems of information and control loss endemic in hierarchically organized systems would also suggest that small organizations could develop and flourish in such environments.

BOX 9.2   Chhattis Mauja: A Large-scale, Farmer-managed
Irrigation System

Of an estimated 943,000 hectares of irrigated land in Nepal, nearly 600,000 hectares are irrigated by systems built, operated, and maintained exclusively by the farmers who cultivate the land (Rana 1991). Many of the farmer-managed systems are small in size and utilize ingenious but primitive technology. In contrast, Chhattis Mauja (Thirty-six Villages) is a large-scale, gravity-flow, farmer-managed system, which was originally constructed in the middle of the nineteenth century. Despite its primitive technology, the original system not only has survived but has expanded in size. It now irrigates almost 3,500 hectares of land farmed by approximately 25,000 people in 54 villages. The system is located just south of the town of Butwal, where the Tinau River falls precipitously from the hills to the plains of southern Nepal.

Although Chhattis Mauja is more than twice as large as the Philippine Zanjera Danum described in Box 4.1, the array of organizations that govern the development, operation, and maintenance of the systems are similar. The Chhattis Mauja system consists of two principal parts: (1) diversion works and a main canal 25 kilometers in length (from 3.6 to 9.7 meters in width) and (2) a simple network of secondary and tertiary canals serving land associated with each village and fed by outlets from the main canal. This physical system is operated by a four-tier organization (Rana 1991). At the first level, residents of each village annually elect a chairperson and members of a committee who set rules about the distribution of water and the organization of maintenance work on the village canals, as well as collect fines and resolve intravillage disputes. Each of nine regional committees are composed of the chairs from six villages, one of whom is selected to serve as regional chair. Members of the regional committee coordinate the work of the residents of six small villages on the diversion structure and the main canal and adjudicate intervillage disputes. The central committee for the entire system is composed primarily of regional chairs. A chair and vice chair for the central committee are elected every two years at a general assembly of the entire system. This chair and five other people draw very modest salaries for part-time work during the monsoon season. These five include an appointed secretary, two *meth mukhtiyars* ("supervisors" of maintenance and repair work on the main canal and diversion dam), and two messengers. Some villages also compensate their chair and a *mukhtiyar*, who operate the portion of the system serving the village. The central committee acts as an appeals court for disputes and organizes the development, operation, and maintenance of the main canal and diversion structure. The chair of the central committee also represents Chhattis Mauja on

BOX 9.2 (continued)

the Tinau Committee, the institution at the fourth level of organization that controls the distribution of water among five irrigation systems fed by the Tinau River. The Tinau Committee monitors the length of the five diversion dams in the Tinau to ensure that all systems get their fair share of the river's water.

The fact that the diversion structures and canals are made of stone, mud, and tree branches has meant that the farmers of Chhattis Mauja could independently build and maintain their own system with simple tools and local materials. This also means, however, that users must contribute an extraordinary amount of labor every year to maintain the system. Each year in May and June, farmer-representatives from the entire system rebuild the diversion structure in the Tinau so that it can withstand the swift river currents produced by the monsoon rains and excavate large amounts of silt, gravel, and boulders deposited in the main canal by the previous year's flows. A mukhtiyar from each village assigns work and keeps records of villagers present at each work session. At any time during the monsoon season, boulders carried by the current can sweep away part or all of the diversion structure, requiring that large amounts of labor be mobilized on an emergency basis in order to save the one rice crop that can be supported in this area.

Critical to the system's operational success is a distribution of the costs (labor) and benefits (water) that is perceived locally as being fair. Each village contributes laborers (*kulara*) and construction materials according to the number of water shares (also called kulara) assigned to it. Water shares are calculated according to the size of the landholding and the location of the village in the system. Normally, no water is available for tail-end villages during the dry season. Thus, these villages contribute significantly less labor than head-end villages (Rana 1991). Careful records of landholdings are kept by the village and central committee, as well as records of days worked by each farmer. Villages are fined if they provide too few laborers or do not accomplish their share of the work. Records for 1988 show that about 7,600 person-days were spent in desilting the main canal and another 7,300 person-days in cleaning the branch and field canals. On average, about 760 persons were working each day of main canal desilting. Although the 1988 monsoon deposited less sediment in the canals than is left in an average year, about 20,000 tons of silt and rock were removed from the main canal alone (Yoder 1992:62). In addition, about 16,000 person-days of labor for emergency repairs were reported for the 1988–89 period (Yoder 1992: 66). Chhattis Mauja illustrates the capabilities of self-organized, nested, polycentric systems to govern and manage relatively large-scale irrigation systems.

Wade (1988) documented one case in which the leaders of an Indian village, constitutionally authorized to exercise very limited taxing, spending, and police powers, have illegally purchased (through bribes) the right to exercise much more extensive authority from local government officials. With this authority, village leaders currently govern an irrigation system and provide a wide range of public services that are well tailored to local needs. Unauthorized institutions like these include provisions to ensure accountability to village residents. But indigenous institutions characterized by large size, significant revenue-mobilizing capacity, or active partisan political participation eventually attract the attention of government authorities, who may attempt to remove local leaders whom they discover acting ultra vires, that is, beyond legal authority (see Sawyer 1988 for a recent example from Liberia).

Extensive empirical evidence in studies of local indigenous institutions provides clear proof, if any were needed, that the self-organizing capabilities of people can survive and occasionally even flourish under repressive regimes (see Wade 1988 and cases contained in Bromley 1992; Berkes 1989; V. Ostrom, Feeny, and Picht 1988; McCay and Acheson 1987). The developmental impact of the social capital these organizational skills represent will remain tragically constrained or will be amplified exponentially throughout the entire population of each country, depending on the success experienced in (1) limiting the authority of institutions representing larger communities of interest and (2) finding ways of structuring complementary, rather than predatory, relationships between organizations that serve larger communities of interest and these smaller organizations. All countries must be able to organize public authorities to address problems with widely varying effects. Several large, comparative studies of local organization found that complementary relationships between authorities representing both small and larger communities were important to the successful operation of the smaller units (Leonard and Marshall 1982:6; Uphoff and Esman 1974:25).

The results of Roger Stone's recent study of the impact of nongovernmental organizations (NGOs) on sustainable development is highly congruent with our analysis of the importance of local institutions as well as larger-scale organizations. Stone stressed that help from the outside—particularly scientific knowledge—is frequently essential to complement the indigenous knowledge of local peoples. He also argued that a "formidable obstacle to change is the absence of effective community institutions in place" (Stone 1992:199). He pointed out that as "decades of grass-roots experience have demonstrated and early returns from the ecodevelopment sector have confirmed, progress is most likely if local citizens are full partners. Top-down planning seldom flourishes in the field" (Stone 1992:201).

Principles Versus Blueprints

The principles by which indigenous institutions are structured constitute an important source of "social capital" that could be tapped in the design of new institutions in developing countries. The term *capital* is used in this context in its broadest sense, referring to those goods or ideas with which something else can be created or established. Thus, the social capital of a particular community is the body of shared knowledge about how to organize people in a productive manner. Some traditional or indigenous social organizations in developing countries utilize strictly hierarchical principles that are inconsistent with democratic government and productive human interaction. But there are numerous examples of polities that are acephalous or lacking a single leader. The principles underlying those nonhierarchical institutions offer a genuine alternative to political systems that rely exclusively on hierarchical decisionmaking arrangements. We consider these underlying principles to be a more general form of social capital than the specific rules used within any particular indigenous institution.

Although a shared knowledge of the specific rules used within an indigenous institution—the "blueprint" of that institution—is essential for its survival over time, a knowledge of the underlying principles used in the design or evolution of these specific rules is likely to be more helpful to others facing similar problems in different circumstances. General principles may be transferable to other settings and used by many communities to craft particular institutions that meet their needs. Because the way rules affect the incentives of participants depends on very specific attributes of the goods involved and on the cultural and physical environment of a particular community, the specific rules developed in one indigenous institution may not work in the same way elsewhere. Thus, the blueprint may not be transferable.

At the end of his book, *Community Resource Management: Lessons from the Zanjera* (1982), Robert Siy summarized what he believes are the underlying design principles of the indigenous institution he studied, the zanjera (see Box 4.2). Siy also contended that it is an institution's design principles that are transferable, not the highly specific blueprints that constitute any particular indigenous institution. Siy identified the following zanjera design principles:

- In order to discourage "free riding," *it is necessary to develop incentives and sanctions to promote long term participation and involvement in group tasks.* (p. 153; author's emphasis)
- It appears that organizations can best gain and maintain the commitment of members to the work of the organization if *individual*

obligation can be *assigned in proportion to the benefits derived by each member from the group activity or project.* In other words, each members' share of total costs should correspond to his actual share of total benefits. (p. 155; author's emphasis)

- In selecting the appropriate method of estimating individual benefits, several issues should be considered: the validity of the indicator in members' eyes, the capability of the organization to collect the information accurately and reliably, and the simplicity of the indicator. (p. 155)

- The next step is to determine a procedure for assigning and assessing members' contributions. . . . The important condition is that, in contexts where the organizational demands on labor and material resources vary from year to year, provisions must be made to have those resources available for use when the situation requires, regardless of the specific method which accomplishes this. (p. 156)

- An irrigation organization should be considered as a going concern, as an institution with a clearly defined purpose and function. . . . It is, therefore, important for such groups to be able to generate the resources which they require for their continued operations. These resource requirements include not only the direct inputs for providing the good or service that the group offers but also the resources required to enforce agreements, procedures and regulations. (p. 162)

- A major lesson is that particular organizational principles are practicable and appropriate only within certain types of physical arrangements. For example, maximal decentralization is not feasible within a system that requires close coordination between each sub-unit (as when water is rotated along a main canal or lateral). (p. 167)

These principles are consistent with the theoretical approach taken in this volume and are general lessons that can be transferred to other settings.[8]

SOME COMMON CONCERNS ABOUT POLYCENTRIC ARRANGEMENTS

Although the ability of polycentric systems to constrain the national political leadership and empower the more attractive local organizations appeals to academics and development professionals, many have expressed serious reservations about the value of polycentric arrangements, particularly in developing countries. These reservations are rooted in concerns about several governance and finance issues. Consequently, we address four specific concerns about governing a polycentric system: how a coherent body of law can be maintained in a system of multiple independent lawmakers, how a legal system that protects minorities and the poor within the smaller jurisdictions can be established by larger jurisdictions, how an adequate administrative capability can be achieved by many governments in countries where literacy levels are still low, and how service responsibilities can be rationally assigned to different tiers of government.

We then turn to a discussion of financial issues and consider the assignment of revenue instruments. Related financial issues of concern here include questions of whether interjurisdictional equity can be achieved in a polycentric system where jurisdictions vary in their natural or artifactual endowments and how the recurrent costs of multiple local governments can be contained.

Governance Issues

At least since the time of Napoleon, the process of modernizing a country has been commonly associated with empowering a group of well-educated, highly motivated individuals to guide the affairs of subordinate jurisdictions. This presumably provides the means for organizing a competent administration, interested in conveying new ideas to poorly educated people about preventing disease or increasing agricultural output while protecting them from autocratic, hereditary leaders who may prefer to keep their followers dependent and subservient. The idea of conferring some amount of independent law-making and law-enforcing authority on many single- or multipurpose governments generates fears of legal chaos. Would this not lead to the promulgation of incompatible rules administered by incompetent local officials who continue to exploit local populations? Proponents of polycentric organizations must be able to respond to these concerns.

How Can the Coherence of Law Be Maintained? If many groups within a single country are authorized to make regulations concerning broad or narrow aspects of public policy, will the law eventually become a jumble of incompatible rules? Certainly, the willingness of individuals to invest in any economy requires fairly high levels of predictability—the capacity to anticipate the behavior of others. Predictability, in turn, depends on the likelihood that rules governing behavior are widely understood and effectively enforced.

In fact, many developing countries still recognize one or more bodies of traditional and religious law and maintain special court systems with jurisdiction over conflicts in these arenas. These countries already have a limited type of polycentric system in operation—a fact that should make the threat of incoherence appear less likely.

Although conflict among laws arises in existing, genuinely polycentric federal systems, coherence in the law is achieved. This is accomplished by a judicial system consisting of multiple levels of courts, all recognizing the principle of a hierarchy of law. This principle states that local laws are valid only if they are consistent with regional or subregional law that is, in turn, consistent with the fundamental law of the land, as expressed in the country's constitution. Apparent inconsistencies in the laws of two jurisdictions are evaluated in the context of a court proceeding. The court may be approached by either public officials or citizens interested in upholding provisions of a regional law, or by citizens who have been injured by the enforcement of a local law. Defenders of the local law must prove that the inconsistency does not exist or that the provision of the regional law is inconsistent with the country's constitution. The losing party may appeal through a hierarchy of courts via an appeals process that offers the losing party further hearings in courts whose personnel are chosen from different jurisdictions by different criteria and are therefore further removed from any local prejudices that may have biased the judgment of a local court.

Extending greater authority to more groups to make rules about a greater variety of problems would be likely to increase the number of conflicts of law that would have to be resolved in this way. The increased costs of greater investment in the dispute resolution services of a polity must be considered, however, in the context of the potential for increased productivity in the economy made possible by a body of law that is better fitted to the particular problems that individuals face.

How Can a General Rule of Law Be Maintained? Perhaps the most serious reservation about devolving independent taxing and spending authority to a subnational jurisdiction or a special-purpose authority concerns the issue of how local authorities can be held accountable for their actions. The independent selection of local officials by election or other means is inconsistent with the removal of these officials by administrative action on the part of national government officials. Indeed, provisions for the dismissal of local officials by administrative action make a mockery of the electoral process. But if officials of larger jurisdictions cannot discipline local officials as they would junior officers, how is it possible to ensure that the locally elected officials of smaller jurisdictions will faithfully enforce the law of the larger jurisdictions?

One means of penalizing elected officials who ignore rules established for all citizens is for local residents to remove them from office (using recall or some other provision) or to fail to reelect them. This mechanism may not be helpful, however, if it is a minority group in the smaller jurisdiction that is suffering from the illegal behavior of a local official.

In the U.S. and Swiss federal systems, the courts are the major control mechanisms. The officials of larger jurisdictions may bring suit in court against officials of a smaller jurisdiction who have failed to enforce a law established by the larger body. An individual who believes he or she has been harmed by a local official's unwillingness to enforce a law of the larger jurisdiction may also bring suit against this official in court.[9] An important advantage of a system of local government organized on such principles is that it produces a structure of incentives that places local executive authorities in a "double bind." The necessity of facing voters in future elections causes them to be attentive to the concerns of local people; the threat of a court suit encourages local executives to take note of the law of the larger jurisdictions of which their community is a part.

The zanjera irrigation systems demonstrate how rules that are derived from several organizational levels can be integrated and enforced. An initial contract is negotiated by the set of previously landless farmers who wish to acquire atar shares. This contract specifies the mutual obligations of all farmers to each other and to the owner of the land. Although general sets of principles (as described above in the quote from Robert Siy's work) are followed in drafting this type of contract, each contract specifies the particular rules and obligations of an individual system and the way in which that system will be governed. Conflicts between farmers or between farmers and their elected officials are first handled within a zanjera. If the conflict is not resolved at this level and if the zanjera is a member of a federation, the conflict next goes to the federal council for discussion and potential resolution. If a satisfactory resolution is not reached at this level and the conflict pertains to legal rights specified in their contract, participants can take the matter to the Philippine court system. In fact, conflicts between zanjeras over their respective water rights have frequently been turned over to the formal court system for resolution (Cruz, Cornista, and Dayan 1986). In such a nested-rule system, regulations at a lower level that are not consistent with those of a higher level are eventually eliminated. Still, there is a considerable diversity of lower-level rules that are fully consistent with the rules of larger jurisdictions.

One would expect to find dispute resolution mechanisms playing an important part in controlling political officials in any polycentric system. But concerns about the ability of the poor to operate control mechanisms in any political system are important (see Leonard and Marshall 1982) and underscore the need to keep the costs of access to dispute resolution mechanisms low. In developing countries that have maintained a customary court system separate from courts that hear cases based on statutory law, the jurisdiction of most of these customary courts is limited to family law and petty criminal questions. Containing the costs of access to courts with jurisdiction over public officials requires that all courts maintain simplified procedures.

How Can Competent Administration Be Developed? The subnational administrations of virtually all developing countries are inefficient and unresponsive to the residents of the jurisdictions in which they operate. In many countries, government offices at all levels lack a sufficient number of highly trained personnel. And the ranks of people with postsecondary educations are still slim. Given this situation, would it not seriously compromise even the inadequate quality of the current administrations to create additional subnational governments and devolve to them larger amounts of decisionmaking authority? Although the problems of overcentralization are widely acknowledged, the problems of actually organizing an alternative administrative structure are not inconsequential. We do not question the importance of maintaining adequate administrative capability in smaller general- or special-purpose jurisdictions. We do, however, question the soundness of the theory that district or provincial personnel are currently inefficient primarily because they have had so little professional training. We argue, instead, that considerably more administrative talent exists in local governments than is commonly recognized.

Enhancing the capacity of employees in provincial or district offices to plan and implement policy has been the objective of numerous institutional development programs, such as the PDAP described in Box 8.2. Evidence appears to indicate, however, that a program designed to improve skill levels may have little or no long-term effect on performance if it is unaccompanied by changes in the incentives personnel face. The history of PDAP reveals that training initially improved the skill levels and sense of professional confidence of provincial planning staff members. A more recent review, however, indicated that, over time, the skills acquired by administrators seem to have atrophied through nonuse (see Hubbell et al. 1989). Certainly, the level of initiative shown by provincial governors during the latter stages of PDAP has not been maintained. The more enduring effects of this program therefore suggest that simply increasing staff skill levels may not be sufficient to increase the productivity of provincial governments. In contrast, the farmer-to-farmer training program in Nepal has been quite successful in increasing productivity (see N. Pradhan and Yoder 1989).

Careful attention to incentives is evident in the organization of the accounting systems used by the illegal Indian village governments described by Wade (1988) and the zanjeras irrigation systems in the Philippines (see Siy 1982). In one Indian village where the mutual suspicions of two factions threatened the viability of the government, two treasurers were appointed with responsibility over a portion of the net monetary income from "taxes" and fines. Each man kept a separate book that was examined by the other at predetermined times when their accounts were entered into the principal account book for the village. The secretaries of each zanjera kept careful records of attendance on workdays and the monetary and in-kind contributions of each member. Once a year, a "settling-up meeting" was held, at which persons owing outstanding fines for missed workdays were expected to pay in full. The meeting was followed by a feast. The secretaries' simple accounting books could be examined at any time to ensure their honesty.

Evaluations of human capital endowments that rely almost exclusively on the formal educational qualifications of a population have quite appropriately emphasized the importance of continued heavy investment in education. But they also dramatically underestimate the extent and the nature of the existing human capital endowment in developing countries. Good administrators need information that is not taught in schools. The tragic consequences of the unfortunate choices made by well-meaning officials who lacked good local time and place information and access to local scientific information demonstrate the inadequacy of assessing qualifications solely on the possession of certificates. Indeed, an exclusive reliance on certificates has disqualified many potential public service candidates who have extensive experience with the specific problems facing local populations. The capacity of communities to independently finance, build, and staff schools (the *Harambee* schools of Kenya are well-known examples) and to organize private courts regarded as fairer than official courts (see Box 9.1) points to the existence of an important reservoir of skills that is not currently being recognized or utilized in public administration.

The issue of shortages in trained manpower in local governments also implicitly assumes that the public sector must produce all the goods and services that are to be provided publicly. Such an assumption ignores the tremendous potential for private sector production, which may be capable of overcoming labor shortages while simultaneously helping to increase efficiency. We will provide a more general overview of possible linkages between the private and public sectors in a later section of this chapter.

How Can Service Responsibilities Be Assigned Rationally? Where there are multiple tiers of government available to provide public services for the express purpose of overcoming the inefficiencies of private sector allocation, the question of what services each tier might most effectively provide persists. The simplest general rule states that the group of people experiencing a problem should pay for the public good or service provided to resolve that problem. Because the effects of problems vary, applying this general principle for assigning service responsibilities can be expected to result in many overlapping public jurisdictions of varying sizes. In most developing countries, central governments have assigned sweeping responsibilities for the provision of services to themselves and so have severely limited the number of governments exercising independent taxing and spending authority (see Box 9.3).

If there are significant spillovers of benefits and/or costs associated with the provision of a good or service, the existing assignment of responsibilities for providing this good or service may be inappropriate. If substantial benefits of services are enjoyed by people outside a jurisdiction but only residents of that jurisdiction bear the burden of paying for them, then a small jurisdiction is likely to provide an inefficiently low level of service (from the perspective of the entire society). An example of such a spillover would be sewage processing. When a village or, worse, a city dumps raw sewage into a river, downstream water users are burdened with additional costs for purifying the water in spite of the fact that they played no role in the earlier decision to pollute the river. This is, of course, a form of a "market failure" or externality—in this instance, a spatial externality.

To internalize such externalities, several policy approaches are feasible. One alternative is to expand the size of the appropriate provision jurisdiction by reassigning the responsibility for sewage processing to a wider jurisdiction, for example, a district or province rather than the village. Where substantial spatial externalities are likely to accrue from a particular infrastructure service or where there are substantial economies of scale due to the attributes of the infrastructure in question (such as the construction of a major multipurpose dam), provision decisions may be most appropriately assigned to a larger government jurisdiction.

Relying only on the national government or other, larger jurisdictions is not, however, the only alternative. Two other methods for encouraging provision of particular services are mandates and intergovernmental grants. Central or even regional governments like provinces or states may mandate that particular services be provided by local governments, primarily due to the broader base of benefits that such services may yield. For example, central governments may mandate that local

BOX 9.3 Many Problems, Many Publics, but Not
Enough Governments

In a recent report to USAID's Africa Bureau, James Thomson (1991) argued that the economic and political crises currently facing the nine countries served by a consortium of donors known as the Comité Inter-état de Lutte Contre la Sécheresse au Sahel can be explained by (1) too much intervention by central governments in economic activities and (2) too few governments to intelligently address genuinely public problems.

The Sahelian populations face many problems, which they must overcome to develop, or at least avoid losing further ground. These problems occur in different sectors. They vary in size, and therefore involve "publics"—those people affected by a problem— of greater or lesser size.

Some problems are best handled by the private sector, that is, individual households, single entrepreneurs, small and large firms. . . . Food grain production and distribution in CILSS countries is one sector where private activities, subject only to limited governmental controls, offer efficient means to resolve the distribution problems involved in making sure that everyone gets enough to eat. Since 1985, CILSS governments have modified policies extensively to recognize this.

Another large set of problems do require collective regulation or action *by some government(s)* for resolution. Land use and renewable resources management are two examples. Other services of public utility also fit this category. In all of these areas, the problems that create "publics" differ in character over time and from place to place.

To illustrate this point, five comparisons are noted below:

- problems of primary education in a pastoral production system on the desert edge differ radically from those posed by university education in a major city;
- keeping the peace in an agricultural village in rural Bambara country involves a much smaller scale problem and much less need for information and coordination of activities than does arranging for national security within the CILSS countries;
- managing river flows in the Niger basin involves a different scale of organization and action than does the effort to manage the watershed of a minor Niger tributary populated

(continues)

BOX 9.3 (continued)

  by people from only two different ethnic groups with a
  common production system;

• organizing management and exploitation of a common bush
  area used by people from five villages in two different
  cantons raises issues different from those posed by an effort
  to introduce soil conservation measures on lands controlled
  by a single quarter in a Mossi village; and

• facilitating the movement of transhumant Wodaabe Fulbe
  through Nigerian agricultural lands poses issues different
  from those raised by efforts to preserve or revive a land
  use management scheme in a Serer village.

All of these public problems require some degree of collective
action, by some government(s). The government(s) in question
need not always be the national Government. For many problems,
national government involvement guarantees inefficiency or even
stalemate. Soil conservation in a Mossi quarter and land use
management in a Serer village are examples of this sort. By
contrast, other problems on this short list will be best resolved
by national government action, for example, provision of nation
security or university education. Yet others, such as management
of stream flows in the Niger River, probably require inter-state
compacts implemented by special agencies. Finally, some of these
problems, for instance the movements of transhumant Wodaabe
Fulbe north and south [through] Nigerian farming communities,
may be best handled by sub-national governments, or by a series
of special districts that can encourage ad hoc arrangements between
village regimes and Wodaabe groups. While examples could be
multiplied for other services of public utility, the point is clear:
the character and range of problems faced by Sahelians do not
argue for a single exclusive Government, organized in a series
of administrative echelons. The existence of semi-autonomous urban
communities in most CILSS states confirms that national governments
formally recognize this point.

  These examples imply that the west sahelian region is severely
"under-governed." To obtain services of public utility necessary
to make sustained development possible, people need far more
governments than they now have, scaled to conform to the geographic
domains of problems of vastly different sizes. (Thomson 1991:8–
9; author's emphasis)

governments treat raw sewage before it is dumped into a river or stream. Or they may mandate that local governments provide all youngsters with a minimum of education because, once grown, these same youth may move to other parts of the country where their education will ensure that they are productive members of the labor force and literate voters.

Intergovernmental grants constitute another method whereby central governments may "encourage" local governments to provide a higher level of services. For instance, a central government may offer to fund all or nearly all of a sewage treatment plant, or it may agree to finance the bulk of all elementary education spending. As discussed a bit further in the following subsection, a possible disadvantage of intergovernmental grants to encourage spending is that they may simply be used to substitute for locally mobilized resources, with no substantial net effects on spending.

Either the mandate or the grant approach to multitier public service provision may, however, give rise to principal-agent problems (Ferris and Winkler 1991). Both a mandate and a grant make the higher tier the principal that must attempt to ensure that the lower-tier agent provides services. Where there are information asymmetries between these tiers of government and where the preferences of local and national jurisdictions differ, neither mandates nor grants may be able to achieve outcomes that are efficient from the perspective of those living in a society. In any event, policies concerning the service responsibilities of polycentric governments must recognize the potentials for principal-agent problems.

Finally, the network features of at least some infrastructure facilities are also often highly relevant to the assignment of service responsibilities in a polycentric institutional arrangement. A system of roads is a very good example of such a network. The amounts and types of traffic carried by different roads differ radically. Some local roads serve only those living nearby; others carry traffic between villages and regional centers. And highways facilitate the movement of people and goods between different parts of a country. In such instances, it is reasonable to assign responsibility for different types of roads to different jurisdictions; indeed, many countries do exactly that. Bangladesh, for example, assigns responsibility for farm-to-market roads, secondary roads, and main highways to local *upazila* (subdistrict) councils, *zila* (district) councils, and the national Roads and Highways Department, respectively.

At the same time, unless considerable autonomy is given to each level within a multitier system, the full range of benefits of polycentricity will not necessarily be realized. For example, numerous directives from central ministries requiring that uniform methods be used to provide and produce road services are inconsistent with independent efforts to provide roads in different jurisdictions. In addition, central ministries often continue to exercise considerable authority as the controllers of block grant funds and as the contracting parties with the international donors who provide much road development funding. Again, this negates the apparent polycentric arrangement of service responsibilities.

Finance Issues

Some strong reservations about polycentric institutional arrangements are rooted in the perception that such arrangements yield serious inequities and inefficiencies. In this section, we address these concerns by initially discussing the question of assignment of revenue sources, which is, of course, closely linked to the previous discussion of service responsibility assignments: Indeed, unless service responsibility assignments are made with some thought to revenue assignments, problems with polycentric governance arrangements are extremely likely to occur. In addition, we consider ways that many local governments could be financed in low-income countries and how equity questions may be best addressed.

How Can Revenue Instruments Be Assigned Rationally? In the discussion of issues associated with resource mobilization in Chapter 4, both user fees and taxes were mentioned as possible revenue instruments. We noted there that when nonpayers cannot easily be excluded, user fees must give way to some form of taxation if adequate resources are to be mobilized. There are, of course, numerous alternative tax instruments available, but not all are equally appropriate for the different levels of polycentric polity.

The issue of how best to assign taxes across multiple tiers of government has been addressed by a number of analysts (Musgrave 1983; McClure 1983; Brennan and Buchanan 1983). Although the review by Growenewegen (1990) suggested that there is less than unanimous agreement on the issue, Musgrave (1983) postulated several general principals for tax assignment in a federation that serve as a useful starting point. These principals, listed below, relate directly to the set of functional objectives for government activities mentioned earlier—allocation, distribution, and stabilization.

1. Taxes designed for economic stabilization and redistribution should be national.

2. Nonbenefit taxes on highly mobile tax bases should be national because they can induce artificial distortions in the spatial allocation of economic activity.
3. Taxes on bases that are distributed highly unequally across regions (for example, taxes on deposits of natural resources) should be imposed by a national government to avoid excessive inequities.
4. User taxes and fees, as well as taxes on immobile resources such as land and capital, are particularly appropriate for smaller local units of government.

Of particular importance in developing countries, the costs of administering taxes fairly (including the costs of ensuring compliance) must also be considered in the tax assignment decision. Though, again, the evidence is not fully established, there may be economies of scale in the collection of some types of taxes. Poorer local communities tend to rely extensively on labor mobilization, and, in these cases, smaller jurisdictions most probably face the lowest resource mobilization cost.

An important implication of these normative aspects of tax assignments is that they generally lead to considerable centralization of tax revenues. At a more pragmatic level, central governments in most developing countries often reserve for themselves the most productive and elastic tax sources.[10] Furthermore, it is common for central governments to greatly limit the amount of local government autonomy in levying taxes. Again, the implication is that central governments generally control the bulk of all tax revenues that are collected. If multiple, noncentral governments are to have the wherewithal to pay for the services discussed earlier, they will likely be heavily dependent on fiscal transfers from the central government. This carries an added risk of increased rent-seeking behavior and dispersal of funds to favored localities based on criteria other than those stated in legislation.

A full consideration of issues regarding the design of intergovernmental grant systems is far beyond the scope of this volume.[11] Nevertheless, it is useful to recognize that grant finance can create perverse incentives for public officials. The principal-agent problem associated with intergovernmental grants has already been noted. Similarly, because grant funds may be viewed as essentially costless to recipient jurisdictions, less care may be exercised in effectively spending these funds than if resources are mobilized locally. The implications for infrastructure sustainability can be particularly problematic, especially if grants are earmarked for capital construction and cannot be used for maintenance. The relatively lower "cost" of capital construction grants can encourage localities to expand capital spending without regard for their ability to operate and maintain the facilities they build. Similarly, where grants are available for recurrent spending on personnel but cannot be used for nonlabor expenditures on materials and supplies, imbalance between labor and nonlabor expenditures on the operation and maintenance of capital may result. Finally and perhaps most crucial to the general issue of availability of resources for sustaining rural infrastructure by many local governments, transfers can discourage recipient governments from mobilizing resources of their own.

How Can a Developing Country Afford Many Local Governments? From the vantage point of people familiar with the current accounts deficits of highly centralized political systems, proposals that would recognize communities of interest as local governments can appear to be a recipe for public bankruptcy. Such proposals are particularly frightening if one assumes that people serving in all these local governments might claim roughly similar salaries and benefits, as well as similar working conditions. Creating a host of local governments would, in fact, require an increase in the numbers of elected officials, but the financial implications of this are less disturbing if the issue of funding local government is approached using different assumptions.

First, changes in the constitution or statute law that would enable communities to form both special and multipurpose governments need not require that all of them do so. It should be possible for villages to continue to contract with larger district or provincial jurisdictions for services for which economies of scale exist.

But if funds for salaries of local government officials are made available, why would any village choose *not* to form its own multipurpose government and pay its officials the wages paid by other local governments? To fail to do so would be to deny local people the income from those salaries, as well as the added benefits of well-tailored public services. Undoubtedly, the number of communities that decide they want a local government would multiply beyond all reason unless it was accepted that the salaries and working conditions of public service need not be the same for all those working in every jurisdiction, even jurisdictions of the same size. The duties of officials in small village jurisdictions, for example, often are intermittent and might easily be handled on a part-time or voluntary basis. Moreover, these officials do not need elaborate office complexes in order to carry out their business effectively; elaborate offices not only are expensive but also produce the wrong incentives in a developing country attempting to establish control over public officials. At present, traditional headmen in Botswana carry on substantial amounts of dispute resolution and resource governance activities that are crucial to the survival of their communities with no offices nor any salary (see Odell 1985).

Similar circumstances exist in many developing countries where local authorities, some of whom are hereditary leaders, have been stripped of their authority by colonial or independent governments.

If communities are to reach responsible conclusions about establishing local governments, deliberations about how many governments should be created and how much will be spent on these governments must take place in light of a budget constraint. The principles guiding the calculation of this budget assume considerable significance. Revenue transfers can be used to redistribute tax revenues collected by a central government, but this source of revenue must be considered secondary to the financial support a community provides for creating the services it enjoys. In such a context, citizens can decide how many officials they need and how much they want to pay them, understanding that money spent on administrative salaries leaves less for the materials needed to build infrastructure.

What About Equity? Polycentric systems have been dismissed by some analysts because high levels of local autonomy over taxing and spending are assumed to produce high levels of inequality due to regional differences in income or resource base. Differences in taxable income are assumed to result in unequal access to tax-supported public goods and services.

Such resource-based differences may, in fact, produce no differences in the levels of services produced in two jurisdictions if the productivity of the poorer jurisdiction is much higher than that of the wealthier jurisdiction or if its residents choose to tax themselves more heavily. As was mentioned in Chapter 6, empirical studies in developing countries have consistently shown that wealthier groups tend to profit disproportionately from subsidized government services. One careful study in Côte d'Ivoire showed that, in this highly centralized polity, civil servants had much easier access to services than did ordinary citizens (M. Cohen 1974).

In general, equity problems in federal systems have been approached in two ways (ACIR 1987:13). One has been to manipulate the boundaries of local government units in order to include a heterogeneous population. Thus, tax contributions of varying amounts can be pooled and redistributed within the unit itself.[12] A second approach has been to rely on overlapping units to pool revenue on a larger scale and redistribute resources to units considered disadvantaged according to some set of criteria. But any effort to redistribute resources represents a departure from the criterion of fiscal equivalence. And arranging boundaries to encompass a deliberately heterogeneous community is also inconsistent with fiscal equivalence and may kill any inclination among residents to cooperate. "Getting what you pay for and paying for what you get" is also a principle of equity, albeit not redistributive equity. The alternative approach—relying on redistribution by overlapping jurisdictions—attempts to combine the principle of fiscal equivalence, as a first-order criterion of organization, with redistributional equity, as a second-order criterion. Redistribution is undertaken only when the first-order criterion generates unacceptable patterns of resource distribution. The simple adoption of a noncentral institutional arrangement does not guarantee that the different jurisdictions will always be able to reach a mutually agreeable settlement about the distribution of resources (see Hinchliffe 1980).

PRIVATIZATION AS A FORM OF DECENTRALIZATION

Like the term *decentralization, privatization* has been used to refer to different institutional arrangements for the provision and production of public goods. The generality of the concept is made clear in the following definition: "Privatization is the act of reducing the role of government, or increasing the role of the private sector, in an activity or in the ownership of assets" (Savas 1987:3). The term has been used to refer to arrangements in which:

- public funds are used to pay part or all of the cost for goods produced and delivered by a private firm or a nonprofit organization—known as contracting out;
- private firms produce and sell services formerly provided or produced by public authorities (see Roth 1987);
- public funds are used to pay for goods or services provided for a public authority by a private firm—another form of contracting out;
- public corporations are created to produce goods like electric power, which are paid for by consumers (sometimes at rates that are subsidized by public monies); and
- publicly supervised cooperatives or other groups are authorized to produce a service that is paid for by consumers (sometimes at rates that are subsidized by public monies).

As Savas (1987:58–59) pointed out, using this term to refer to such an array of institutional forms is misleading (and has, therefore, generated considerable misunderstanding) because, in most cases of privatization, public authorities continue to play an important role of some kind. When public authorities pay in full or in part for the production of a good, collective action by legislative and executive authorities is necessary to decide (1) which goods are to be paid for from the public treasury, (2) how much of the public budget is to be devoted to the production costs of a given good, (3) how the necessary revenue is to be raised, and (4) what criteria are to be applied to the production of the good. In addition, public officials must be available to oversee the contracting process, monitor the production process and audit the expenditure of public funds, and evaluate the final product to determine whether the contract terms have been fulfilled.

The principal reason for contracting out the actual production of public goods is to increase the efficiency with which they are produced. Contracting mechanisms provide a means of capturing the advantages of market competition in the production of public goods, with contracts awarded on the basis of bids, as well as on some estimation of dependability. Private firms operating in a competitive market situation are assumed to have a greater incentive to keep costs low than does a public bureau that is the only authorized producer of particular services. Again, appropriate mechanisms must be in place to ensure that such contracts are enforced.

Public Concessions as a Buttress for Centralization

No necessary connection exists between privatization initiatives and the distribution of authority in a polity; either highly centralized or non-central political systems can carry out extensive privatization. Privatization can also be achieved by either democratic or authoritarian regimes.

Various types of privatization (such as contracting out) can be expected to produce quite different outcomes, depending on the nature of the political system in which they occur (Donahue 1989). Contracting out in a highly centralized polity probably will not increase efficiency in the production of public goods because, in a highly centralized political system, the executive authorities who award contracts and monitor performance are difficult to control (Sawyer 1992). Competition between prospective contractors therefore will likely be minimal, and government contracts become lucrative awards to cronies whose production efficiency is likely to be as low or lower than that of a public producer. Similarly, the ownership of natural resources by the government provides political leaders with lucrative concessions to award to foreign or domestic firms. Awardees, in turn, can be expected to support the tenure of the leadership at the apex of authority.

Monopolies Versus Competitive Markets

The concentration of political and economic authority that characterized the traditional political institutions of many developing countries has been preserved or increased since colonial control ended. This means that many ideologically capitalist economies maintain no competitive markets, and few of these capitalist economies support a dependable capital market or a stable currency. The extensive control of central government authorities over access to import licenses and foreign currency ensures that only the politically well-connected are able to get the materials necessary to maintain a productive enterprise of any complexity. De Soto (1989) referred to these as mercantilist economies.

In such an environment, privatization efforts that involve the sale of public corporations frequently result in neither a wider distribution of control over valuable assets nor an increase in productive efficiency. Sales of large businesses often end up transferring the ownership of public firms to people who hold political office or who are closely connected to others who do. This occurs because, in the absence of a dependable capital market, only the wealthy and well-connected can expect to purchase such enterprises. And political authority can be used to protect the new private enterprise from competitive pressures.

High concentrations of executive authority also often mean that the judiciary has little independence. In such circumstances, the security of the rights in property of less well-connected people is uncertain. In the absence of a stable currency, a capital market, and an independent judiciary, competitive markets are untenable.

Privatization Is Not a Panacea

The point of this argument is to warn against wholesale efforts to privatize the production of publicly provided services in developing countries without first considering the overall consequences. Indeed, we are skeptical of *any* institutional option that is accepted as a panacea for a wide variety of problems.[13] Privatization of production activities, though likely to increase production efficiency, does *not* solve the wide array of provision problems. Although additional research is needed, a combination of polycentric provision and privatized production may prove to be an efficient approach in many developing countries. With polycentric provision, there are multiple consumers of services, rather than a single, centralized agency with monopsonistic power that can quite easily be abused. Privatization of production can, in at least some instances, provide for competition that, again, will foster increased production efficiency. Efforts to explore the options available for organizing production, however, should be conducted systematically within the special environment of each developing country.

CONCLUSION

Consistent with the work of other scholars interested in development, we see indigenous institutions as an important source of social capital for forming effective noncentral (or polycentric), public-private, institutional arrangements within which sustainable infrastructure can be developed. Indigenous institutions represent what a community knows about how to get things accomplished that require a collective effort. In many developing countries and in Eastern Europe, the successful effort to eliminate this social capital has created a substantial lacuna in effective organization. Where indigenous institutions are still working effectively to construct, operate, and maintain rural infrastructures, it is important to study the design principles that create a structure of incentives leading to sustainable infrastructure because this information is transferable to other populations with similar infrastructure concerns. Earlier efforts to devise optimal blue-prints consisting of the specific rules with which to organize a public sector activity have produced little transferable knowledge.

We have introduced polycentric, or noncentral, organization as a distinctly different way of distributing decisionmaking authority. Hierarchical principles have a place in organizing public sector activities. But noncentral principles also have much to contribute to the provision and production of sustainable facilities. This assertion is reinforced by documented evidence of noncentral principles operating in some of the more effectively governed irrigation systems, such as the zanjeras.

We have also examined some common reservations about the applicability of noncentral institutional arrangements for developing countries. This discussion emphasized the crucial role played by an independent system of forums for dispute resolution in maintaining both the coherence of law and a rule of law in a noncentral polity. Together, the rule of a hierarchy of law and a hierarchy of courts selected by independent jurisdictions can resolve contra-dictory law in the absence of a single, ultimate center of law-making authority. Independent courts are also the key to ensuring that a general law can be maintained throughout a country, even though law enforcers are not subject to the administrative control of a central authority.

Although further training will be needed to improve systems of public administration, training without improved incentives for administrators is not likely to yield increased productivity. Current administrative organization also generally fails to take full advantage of existing manpower resources in developing countries.

Polycentric organization is often criticized for fostering both inefficiency and inequity. Our discussion has highlighted the allocative efficiencies associated with a primary reliance on the rule of fiscal equivalence—a rule that does not exclude the possibility of redistributing revenues if a polity finds the outcomes of strict adherence to fiscal equivalence unacceptable. A primary reliance on the principle of fiscal equivalence also guards against the creation of unnecessary governments in a polity in which groups are free to form governments to carry out joint projects.

A view of the development and maintenance of public facilities that is not narrowly confined to the public sector has led us to examine public-private industry structures as one form of polycentric organization. The privatization of the production of public facilities, in which genuine competition is maintained among producers, can enhance efficiency substantially, but it should not be considered as a panacea for all the ills of overcentralization. The independence of the adjudication services provided in any polity is critically important to maintaining competition among producers. In addition, public sector actors play a crucial role in funding, contracting, and monitoring, even when production is organized privately. How well these functions are carried out strongly influences the sustainability of the public facilities produced.

NOTES

1. Analysts debating the stabilizing and destabilizing effects of subnational governments have produced a vast literature. This subject is well beyond the scope of our interests here.

2. Again, analysts doing tax and expenditure "incidence" research have studied the redistributive effects of local fiscal actions (Bish 1971). This work is important because general local revenue instruments can impose differential burdens on persons with different incomes and wealth. Likewise, expenditures may affect different segments of a local society quite differently and therefore will likely have differential distributional effects. Nevertheless, redistribution as a broad policy goal is not generally viewed as an appropriate local government activity. For an argument to the contrary, see Pauly (1973), who argued that some local redistributional efforts are reasonable, just as the provision of local public services is.

3. In fact, it is quite unlikely that uniform service levels would result from central government provision of services. Substantial evidence from the United States shows that within large local governments, there is considerable variation in service levels across subareas within the same jurisdiction. In education, for example, studies have shown that the quality of education is better in higher-income areas of central cities than in poorer neighborhoods (Sexton 1961; Mandel 1975; Owen 1972; Berk and Hartmann 1971; Katzman 1978). Similarly, police have been unable to keep crime rates approximately equal across different neighborhoods, nor do they allocate services equally across neighborhoods (Weicher 1971; Mladenka and Hill 1978; E. Ostrom 1983). In general, studies of delivery patterns within jurisdictions have found wide variation, with some patterns favoring the rich, some favoring the poor, and many others that favor neither group (Boyle and Jacobs 1982; Levy, Meltsner, and Wildavsky 1974; Lineberry 1977).

4. Paul (1992) also utilizes the concept of exit in a recent paper on accountability. Drawing heavily on concepts originally developed by Albert Hirschman (1970), Paul argues that "the public's use of 'exit' (competing sources of supply) or 'voice' (participation/protest to induce service providers to perform) will enhance public accountability in a given situation when it is consistent with the characteristics of the services and of the publics involved. . . . It is further argued that public service accountability will be sustained only when the 'hierarchical control' (HC) over service providers is reinforced by the public's willingness and ability to use exit or to use voice" (Paul 1992:4).

5. We recognize that alterations in the "rules" might result in an optimal outcome, even in the context of decentralized service provision; for example, rules that required sewer outlets from a community to be placed upstream from water inlets would force each community to internalize the externalities associated with suboptimally treated sewage.

6. This concept has been analyzed under the general heading of the theory of clubs, in which a small group may find it advantageous to add members in order to decrease each individual's share of total costs but, after some point, may wish to limit membership if the congestion costs associated with new members outweigh the benefits of spreading the fixed costs of running the club over a larger number of members (see Buchanan 1965).

7. Robert C. Hunt (1988:349) examined the hypothesis that "no large canal irrigation system ought to be able to function if managed only by farmers" and after reviewing many empirical studies, concluded, "Yet they do, and very successfully."

8. See E. Ostrom (1990) for a further discussion of design principles derived from a much larger set of cases.

9. In the Anglo-American jurisprudence tradition, an individual may secure a court order that would force an official to act or refrain from acting, even before proving that he or she has been harmed by the official's actions. If an individual can convince a judge that the official's expected action or inaction will produce harm that cannot be adequately compensated for after the fact, the judge can issue a writ of mandamus, directing the official

to act, or a writ of injunction, directing the official to refrain from acting, until a full hearing of the issue can be held.

10. An elastic tax source is one for which revenues grow (or decline) in response to increases (or decreases) in economic activity without any need for explicit policy changes in the tax rates or definition of the tax base.

11. The public finance literature on intergovernmental fiscal relations and grant systems is voluminous, but the bulk of that literature is directed at more industrialized nations. For some background information on intergovernmental grants with special reference to developing countries, see Bird (1978) or Schroeder (1988).

12. However, as noted earlier, even in the United States, the redistributions may not benefit the poor.

13. Skepticism concerning decentralization as a panacea is also strongly articulated by Gow and VanSant (1985:109).

10

Implications of an Institutional Approach to Sustainable Development

In Chapter 1, we identified the two central questions that we planned to address in this volume. Each is of substantial importance to understanding the problems being faced in developing countries:

Why has so much rural infrastructure been unsustainable?
What can be done about it?

Because of its difficulty, we have devoted most of the volume to addressing the first question. On the surface, one can provide a simple answer by stating that the tragic overinvestment in unsustainable infrastructure has a *single* underlying cause—the set of incentives confronting multiple actors involved in the design, finance, construction, operation, maintenance, and use of infrastructure in developing countries. The wrong incentive is also the simple answer to the puzzle we introduced in the first chapter—why the post-war development responses differed so substantially in Western Europe as contrasted to developing countries. But as one digs deeper into the problem, that answer is correct but too facile. Many different and interacting factors affect any particular set of incentives. Further, the specific incentives that lead to unsustainable infrastructure differ from one country to another and even from one project or program to another within countries.

Thus, instead of providing one answer to the first question, we have presented a *mode of analysis* that can be used to address the question of why has a particular rural infrastructure facility been unsustainable wherever that facility may have been built. The mode of analysis involves a paradigmatic shift for those who have been schooled in the traditional approaches to public administration (V. Ostrom 1989; Wunsch 1991). Instead of presuming that creating one central authority is necessary for solving public sector problems, other

213

possibilities can be explored. This mode of analysis can be used by scholars, citizens, government officials, donors, and others to (1) identify the complex set of incentives that exist in any particular setting, (2) locate the subsets of incentives that enhance or detract from the likelihood of sustainable infrastructure, (3) search for factors relating to the provision and production of the infrastructure in this setting that affect incentives, and (4) recommend rule changes likely to yield a new set of incentives more consistent with improving infrastructure sustainability.

We recognize that once perverse incentives infiltrate all aspects of infrastructure development, achieving any genuine change is difficult. Rarely can simple changes be made that will significantly improve a system. Major institutional changes are, however, needed to create a macropolitical system conducive to sustaining infrastructure and development efforts in general. The officials and citizens of the countries, who desperately need appropriate, sustainable infrastructure, should be the ones to analyze these problems so that reforms undertaken are better suited to their particular physical and social environment.[1] As we have stressed throughout this volume, changes in formal procedures may be no more than ideas written on paper, with no impact on the ways that individuals interact with one another. Even worse, such changes may have counterintuitive results when implemented in one setting as contrasted to others. Thus, more important than any specific recommendation that we might make is the recognition that motivating individuals to take a long-term perspective and the interests of a wide diversity of unknown individuals into account when making choices is among the more difficult tasks that practitioners face. There are no quick fixes and no simple solutions.

Providing sustainable infrastructure is, however, a key step toward achieving higher levels of sustainable economic development. When designed, financed, constructed, operated, maintained, and used in a sustainable manner, rural infrastructure—roads, water systems, power generation and transmission facilities, community buildings, and irrigation systems—enhance the life prospects, productivity, and income of the people in developing countries. Investments in infrastructure entail allocating resources that could otherwise be spent on immediate consumption goods (food, medicine, clothing, and so forth) or on other capital investments (such as construction of urban housing or manufacturing establishments). In resource-poor countries, the waste of resources that occurs when investments in infrastructure projects are not sustained is particularly devastating.

As discussed earlier in this volume, massive expenditures have been allocated during the past forty years to construct rural infrastructure projects throughout the developing world. Some of these investments have enhanced productivity, but many have not been sustainable. This dissipation of needed capital has disappointed donors, host governments, development scholars, and the intended beneficiaries of these investments. In recent years, donors have begun to require that host governments commit themselves in advance to bearing the recurrent costs associated with donor-assisted infrastructure projects. But these paper requirements have been ineffective instruments for improving the likelihood of infrastructure maintenance. Securing credible commitments from officials has proven extraordinarily difficult.

Thus, multiple causes, deeper than a simple disregard for the maintenance requirements in international aid contracts, are responsible for the failure to invest in recurrent costs of maintaining infrastructure. Further, as we have emphasized throughout, no single change in an international aid contract or any other formal rule change will be sufficient to alter the dynamics that continue to be reproduced. The blueprints for action that work in one setting will not necessarily work in another. Rather, we need a different approach to the analysis of this problem—an approach from which many different blueprints for action are likely to emerge. Consequently, we will provide a brief synopsis of the mode of analysis presented in this volume.

THE PROPOSED ANALYTICAL APPROACH

In Chapter 1, we make a simple assumption:

Individuals who are expected to invest resources (including their own time and labor) in the maintenance of rural infrastructure must perceive that the benefits they obtain exceed the costs of the resources they devote to this task.

In application, this means, for example, that lower-level public officials who are expected to brave the mud and dust to monitor the work of road contractors will not exert much effort (or any effort at all) unless the rewards received—in terms of pay, status, and benefits from the infrastructure—are greater than the cost of shirking or not contributing at all (including any sanctions that can be imposed). Similarly, farmers served by a government-owned irrigation system cannot be expected to organize themselves to operate a rotation system and clean canals unless the benefits they receive from this activity (including more and predictable water) exceed their costs. Contracts between donor agencies and host governments that do not eventually change the benefit-cost calculations of those who are expected to do the day-to-day work will have little effect on infrastructure sustenance.

The mere existence of aggregate benefits that exceed aggregate costs is not, however, enough to elicit individual efforts at a sufficient level to obtain these benefits. This is particularly true when individuals may obtain some portion of the benefits produced without expending much individual effort. The free-rider problem is now well accepted as a characteristic of many situations in which individuals can withhold contributions toward the production of joint benefits but cannot be excluded from enjoying the benefits once they are provided. If all potential beneficiaries follow the free-rider strategy, everyone receives fewer net benefits overall.

We are certainly not the first to notice the pervasiveness of free riding in the provision of infrastructure and other types of public or common-pool resource goods and services. Prior analyses have focused on free riding and two additional problems: (1) the lower costs that may be achieved when projects are constructed by enterprises that can realize substantial economies of scale and (2) the need for technical expertise in the design and construction of major infrastructure projects. We consider all three of these problems in our analysis.

As we pointed out in Chapter 7, however, truncated analyses, focusing exclusively on these three problems, frequently have been used to support policy recommendations to "strengthen" national-level government institutions in developing countries. Such strengthening is often interpreted as training civil servants in technical and managerial skills and helping to increase the power of the national government in relation to competing interests. The purported consequences of such policy reforms have included enhanced design and construction technologies, improved agency budgeting and managerial skills, and firmer commitments to fund the recurrent costs of operation and maintenance.[2] But in practice, such policies help increase the power of centralized national governments in relation to competing interests without making much impact on the sustainability of rural infrastructure.[3] Indeed, increasing the power of national governments over other legitimate voices in a polity actually *reduces* the difficulty of gaining credible commitments from such governments on almost any front.

Reforms based on truncated analyses frequently produce counter-productive outcomes. Among these is the potential for rent seeking that occurs as soon as the free-rider problem is solved through coerced financial contributions to a common, public treasury. Once taxes are imposed, they become a fixed cost for everyone, except those who are willing to risk exposure and punishment for pursuing illegal tax avoidance strategies. Individual net benefits can be legally enhanced, however, by lobbying for special entitlements or other forms of disproportionate benefits supported by the common treasury. Wealthy and powerful individuals or groups are likely to have the resources necessary to influence the allocation of public funds and obtain economic rents from large-scale infrastructure projects. Thus, highly concentrated benefits can be generated—benefits that far exceed the costs of rent-seeking activities. And the resulting costs are spread across many individuals who are less motivated—and usually less able—to prevent the disproportionate allocation of government funds and entitlements.

Elected officials and higher-level civil servants may also participate in these activities with or without conscious awareness of the consequences. Elected officials in all countries seek ways to obtain benefits for their constituents that are likely to generate further electoral support. For national officials, getting the potholes fixed in a local road does not significantly increase their probabilities of being reelected. But getting potholes fixed or a water supply system repaired can be very important for locally elected officials. For civil servants, particularly those trained as engineers, professional status and promotions within the service come through work in constructing large-scale civil projects. Extralegal opportunities for income are sometimes also present. For these reasons, we urge that the principles of polycentric governance systems be seriously studied for their applicability in developing countries.[4]

The problem is exacerbated by an absence of institutional arrangements that facilitate and encourage beneficiaries of localized, rural infrastructure to find ways of financing, constructing, operating, and maintaining their own projects. If few legal instruments exist to enable individuals to make credible and enforceable commitments to finance the construction and maintenance of a local infrastructure, potential beneficiaries must seek support from a larger governmental unit for facilities that have only local benefits. Furthermore, when everyone else in a country is so obviously seeking national government support, beneficiaries are apt to feel that the national leaders should provide certain kinds of infrastructure even though their benefits are highly localized: If these types of infrastructure have been provided by the national government elsewhere, local beneficiaries may argue, why not here?

Incentives to engage in rent seeking exist in all countries with large, public treasuries. These incentives are compounded in many developing countries by two factors: (1) the availability of large sums of donor assistance devoted to infrastructure development[5] and (2) the absence of local and regional, general-purpose or special-purpose governments to whom beneficiaries can express local preferences and aggregate resources related to infrastructure.

Another intermediate performance criterion that we have stressed is the availability of local time and place information to complement the technical information needed to design many infrastructure projects. Those designed without extensive knowledge of physical and hydrological site characteristics and without serious discussions with users about constraints and patterns of use rarely operate well once constructed and are far more costly to maintain.

GENERAL POLICY IMPLICATIONS OF OUR APPROACH

In Chapters 7, 8, and 9, we presented detailed analyses using fourteen intermediate performance criteria for evaluating the production and provision of infrastructure. These criteria reflected the transaction costs associated with coordinating the actions of multiple actors in situations in which they have less than perfect information and can be expected to engage in strategic behavior. We strongly recommend that analyses of particular infrastructure issues in specific settings consider the full array of relevant characteristics of goods described in Chapter 4, as well as all the intermediate and overall performance criteria described in Chapter 5 and applied in Chapters 7 through 9.

However, by considering only six additional criteria along with the three criteria stressed in Chapter 7's discussion of a truncated analysis (scientific information, economies of scale, and free riding), we can suggest particular policies to improve the sustainability of rural infrastructure. Specifically:

- to the already perceived need for gaining *scientific knowledge,* we add a recognition of the importance of blending time and place information in provision and production;
- to the already perceived benefits of gaining *economies of scale* in production, we add a recognition of the problems of controlling shirking and corruption in production and the importance of monitoring and reward structures; and
- to the recognized potential for *free riding,* we add a recognition of the additional strategic behaviors of rent seeking and corruption in provision.

Given the additional transactions costs, when the design, construction, operation, and maintenance of infrastructure are predominantly organized within a single, national government and largely financed by external funds, we can predict with some confidence the following results:

- overinvestment in poorly designed and poorly constructed large-scale infrastructure facilities;
- underinvestment in the operation and maintenance of these facilities;
- rapid deterioration of infrastructure; and
- excessive investment in repair and rehabilitation of previously constructed facilities.

Although this might be perceived as a relatively grim picture—and in many ways, it is—it is also a picture with working parts. Once the working parts are identified, the chances for change and improvement are enhanced considerably.

An understanding of this logic also helps explain why the temporary deconcentration of authority from national bureaucratic offices to regional offices and the creation of user groups that lack sufficient autonomy are not likely to have a strong, long-term impact. Some officials may recognize that such deconcentration results in more effectively designed, constructed, and operated infrastructure. But such changes are also likely to create additional burdens for lower-level civil servants, to diminish these individuals' opportunities to enhance income through corrupt practices, and to reduce the powers of most senior bureaucrats. Thus, when a project is completed, the bureaucrats are unlikely to wish to retain these institutional changes.[6] And if the beneficiaries of the changes—primarily the users of the infrastructure—have little voice in the matter, such institutional changes have little chance of survival. This is even more likely if the user groups created and supported by national governments under these programs are not formally recognized and given the right to mobilize their own resources. Consequently, they will even have trouble surviving once the source of their support is withdrawn, let alone actively opposing a return to earlier practices.

The most successful decentralization projects, as we learned in Chapter 8, do have positive (albeit sometimes short-lived) effects that are quite consistent with the theoretical argument developed here. Projects are better designed and constructed at lower costs when well-trained engineers must seriously consider the ideas and local knowledge of users. Projects are better maintained when users are able to mobilize high levels of resources to perform operation and maintenance activities themselves. When the users must pay the costs of constructing or rehabilitating a facility, they are highly motivated to keep original costs as low as possible and to monitor the activities of producers to avoid corrupt practices. Users are also highly motivated to devise formulas that fairly distribute the costs of design and construction, as well as operation and maintenance activities. Keeping an open set of books that everyone can inspect ensures that no one will get away with free riding and that public officials will be held accountable. Furthermore, mobilizing labor and materials, rather than cash, makes it far more difficult for public resources to be diverted to private ends.

Designing institutions that motivate all the actors in infrastructure development to keep transformation, coordination, and information costs down, while trying to counteract potential strategic behaviors, is a substantial challenge. We do not see a way, however, that the challenge can be avoided if sustainable development is to be achieved. The evolution of polycentric provision and production arrangements, adapted to local experiences and circumstances, is a long-term strategy well worth serious consideration. Enabling potential beneficiaries of infrastructure and other types of public goods to organize themselves into special-purpose enterprises, with circumscribed governmental authority at local and regional levels, is essential if the needed resource mobilization is to be accomplished without the immediate threat of massive rent seeking that is involved when large funds are clustered in national, general-purpose treasuries. Some level of autonomy is needed if citizens and officials are to treat these units of government as their own and to allocate the resources they mobilize with considerable care and thought.

If production enterprises of varying size are also established over time, smaller governments can select larger enterprises with diverse skills and expensive, specialized equipment to handle certain aspects of infrastructure design and construction; at the same time, they can decide to retain full responsibility for operation and maintenance themselves. Devising appropriate rules to regulate use of facilities in order to reduce the rate of deterioration can also be accomplished more effectively by those who have seen firsthand the adverse consequences of destructive patterns of use.

Developing polycentric governance systems is not something that can or should be done primarily from the outside. Of course, outsiders can contribute in a number of highly constructive ways. The scientific knowledge and infusion of external resources that many NGOs bring to grass-roots development work (particularly in those projects where outsiders stay long enough to become effective partners with local residents) can frequently be catalysts that enable local residents to break out of past practices and find new opportunities. Such grass-root local projects become part of the social capital for the future. But a political order that is genuinely polycentric should be designed primarily by those who must make it work over the long haul. The repeated failures of efforts to import the U.S. Constitution to other countries teach us that it is not the blueprint of a particular constitutional document that matters. Rather, a successful polycentric constitution is one where there is a common understanding of polycentric design principles. In this volume, we recommend institutional reforms that are consistent with a polycentric system of governance, not as purveyors of a new quick fix but as analysts suggesting an alternative way to organize the public sector that is fundamentally different from that used in project designs in the past.

Our confidence in the applicability of this approach derives from evidence of polycentricity working productively in developing countries. As "discovered" by de Soto (1989) in Peru, a vigorous, constructive, informal public sector exists in many developing countries. Organizational principles similar to those involved in building polycentric systems are found in dispute resolution mechanisms and other informal public institutions. Many indigenous institutions that have proven highly success-ful over time also are organized using polycentric principles. But because institutions are typically designed to cope with a particular array of circumstances, it is not always possible or advisable to preserve indigenous institutions, unchanged, over long periods of time. Where circumstances or the nature of the task they must perform change, these institutions must also change. What is critically important about indigenous institutions that did or still do provide ways of effectively managing difficult tasks are the underlying principles by which they were organized.

Many indigenous irrigation institutions use a variety of mechanisms to assign obligations to members in proportion to the benefits they receive, to measure benefits in a way that is considered valid by participants, and to reduce free riding by monitoring the contributions of farmers (E. Ostrom 1992). As change occurs (with the construction of more permanent diversion works in an irrigation system, for example), some of the tasks people must perform will change. Institutional mech-anisms created to avoid free riding in maintaining a brush dam must, however, still be adapted to prevent free riding in maintaining a concrete dam. Farmers who are familiar with how their institutions work now can use these principles as a foundation for new institutional arrangements that reflect the changed circumstances. All too frequently, however, irrigation development projects that are intended to involve farmers instead create "user group organizations" imposed by official organizers who travel from site to site. Although the membership of the user group organizations and farmer organizations like the zanjeras is the same (that is, local farmers), the major difference between these groups is that the former are created and managed by national government officials whereas the latter are self-organized and self-governed. No explanation of institutional arrangements given in a user group organizational meeting that lasts, at most, a few hours can convey the same depth of understanding of how to make an institution work that can equal what members of the zanjeras have derived from their own experience with rule forming and reforming over time.

External advisers can provide more effective assistance by learning how some of the better-operating groups have solved the problems that many face. The International Irrigation Management Institute in Nepal, for example, has held a number of meetings on irrigation practices and institutions. Some of these feature reports by scholars concerning the operation of different types of systems and what lessons can be learned from them (see, for example, N. Pradhan and Yoder 1989); some involve site visits by farmers to some of the more success-fully managed local irrigation systems; others are seminars at which farmers exchange information about how they cope with various prob-lems. The more successful farmer organizations become the model for others to study, rather than some abstract, printed charter.

One criticism of relying on effective local institutions to handle various aspects of sustainable development suggests that the operation of these institutions may improve the lives of only a relatively few people. As Roger Stone (1992:205) recounted the criticisms, "The question that many development professionals now ask is not whether the micro-programs can work; it is whether their principles and methodologies can be effectively applied to *nations*. It is all very well, they argue, for a tiny staff working in a far corner to do a good job meeting a limited objective for a small number of community beneficiaries" (author's emphasis). Stone noted that many grass-root agencies are sensitive to such criticisms and are searching for ways to "scale up" their activities and achieve both respectability among development bureaucracies and a broader "impact." Stone (1992:211) then asked whether the need to scale up is as important as the need for larger-scale governments and donor agencies to scale down. "Is it feasible, then, for the big lenders and donors—the foundations and large govern-ment or semipublic agencies—to slice up their programs into little segments to accentuate these values. . . . Can they scale themselves down? Can they themselves achieve flexibility any more readily than the little programs can achieve sustainable growth?" The answer given by many development professionals is No because this would require massive increases in the costs of projects.

Stone (1992:212) argued, on the other hand, that if many large agencies were to "relinquish field activities to the new clusters of smaller national and international nongovernmental organizations" and strive instead to create the kinds of environments where NGOs and indigenous institutions are able to flourish and be held accountable, outcomes could be significantly improved. This position is quite similar to ours. Indigenous institutions and smaller-scale NGOs may form a foundation for the evolution of a locally adapted polycentric system. The implementation of such a system also requires the design of other encompassing institutions by public officials and citizens. No polycentric system can be very productive without monitoring, sanctioning, and conflict resolution mechanisms that enable individuals to enter into enforceable agreements. Without assurance that others involved in an agreement will perform as agreed, many potentially beneficial ways of organizing infrastructure development must be foregone. Certainly, in any long-term undertaking, conflicts arise. But without fair and low-cost conflict resolution mechanisms, unresolved disputes fester and increase the likelihood that individuals will refuse to join in maintenance activities.[7] Thus, any effort to increase the diversity of provision and production units must also consider ways to enhance conflict resolution mechanisms—both at a local level and among major providers and producers of infrastructure services.

Indigenous institutions in developing countries often evolved during an era in which most relationships were not monetized. Moreover, there were well-developed ways to constrain the authority of leaders regarding the use of communal labor. These constraints were relatively easy to maintain because farmers could simply refuse to work on projects that were not defined as legitimate communal efforts. But where monetized relationships have since developed rapidly, indigenous institutions have no effective mechanisms for ensuring the financial accountability of local officials: It is, after all, much easier to pocket money or use it for private purposes than to reassign a neighbor from maintaining a road or irrigation system to building a private house. Devising new rules on the appropriate use of funds is a challenge confronting participants in many indigenous institutions. External advisers can provide information about options that have proven successful in other settings.

IMMEDIATE POLICY IMPLICATIONS OF OUR APPROACH

Are there no shorter-term strategies that national governments and donor agencies could adopt to enhance the likelihood that appropriate infrastructure, once constructed, would be maintained? Although we offer some proposals that could be implemented immediately, they necessarily consist of general principles rather than specific designs. In applying these general principles, planners must take into account the specific attributes of (1) the infrastructure involved, (2) the individuals who are likely to be beneficiaries and their resources, and (3) the governance system within which a project is located.

In analyzing what can be done to improve the performance of infrastructure projects, we must first consider the type of joint use that is involved. As we discussed in Chapter 4, all infrastructure are jointly used to some extent by a set of beneficiaries. Of course, individuals directly consume the services (for example, the transportation service or the water) generated by an infrastructure rather than the infrastructure itself, but they do so jointly. Gradually, individuals also wear out the facility itself. It is therefore important to identify the users of an infrastructure and determine how large a set they comprise, how localized they are, and how homogeneous their preferences, assets, patterns of use, and general ways of life are. It is also important to examine how subtractable the flow of services is, given the patterns of use that exist.

Many types of rural infrastructure facilities can be distinguished by using the attributes that we defined and described in Chapter 4. As an illustration of how these attributes can be used in specific types of policy analysis, let us distinguish two quite different types of rural infrastructure using the attributes discussed in Chapter 4 that relate to the problems of joint use. First, let us focus on a facility used by an identifiable, localized group that obtains substantial and highly salient benefits from that facility. Second, we will focus on a facility used by a larger and more dispersed population, many members of which do not experience (in the short-term) any substantial, readily identifiable improvement in their lives from an improvement of that facility. An example of the first type of facility is a small-scale irrigation system or a rural water supply system; an example of the second is the main trunk of a national highway system or some of its heavily traveled branches. Central government officials and donors can adopt more stringent project design principles in the first case than in the second.

Sustaining Small-scale Infrastructure

Consider the general approach that could be used to design small-scale irrigation projects in a developing country.[8] We advise donors and national governments interested in enhancing investments in sustainable, small-scale irrigation projects to invest in the financing and construction of infrastructure projects *only* when there is firm evidence that those who are supposed to benefit from a facility

1. are aware of the potential benefits they will receive
2. recognize that these benefits will not fully materialize unless facilities are maintained
3. have made a *firm commitment* to maintain the facility over time
4. have the organizational and financial capabilities to keep this commitment
5. do not expect to receive resources for rehabilitating the facility if they fail to maintain it.

This can be accomplished by investing in infrastructure projects that meet the following conditions:

1. The direct beneficiaries are willing to invest some of their own resources up front.
2. The direct beneficiaries are willing to pay back a substantial portion of the capital costs (perhaps at subsidized interest and over a long time, if necessary) and to undertake maintenance.
3. The direct beneficiaries are assured that they can:
   • participate in designing the project
   • monitor the quality of the work performed
   • examine the accounts that form the basis for their financial responsibilities
   • protect established water rights
   • hold contractors accountable for inferior workmanship that is discovered after the system is in operation.
4. The granting agency is assured that:
   • farmers' commitments to repay costs will be enforced by appropriate legal action, if necessary
   • farmers have an effective organization with demonstrated capabilities to mobilize resources, allocate benefits and duties, and resolve local conflicts.
5. All donors and the host government are firmly committed to these principles and will not provide funds to bail out those beneficiaries who fail to perform their responsibilities.[9]

Individuals who are willing to make initial investments to obtain capital goods demonstrate their own recognition of future benefits. Furthermore, the higher the proportion of the capital investment that beneficiaries are willing to repay, the higher the likelihood that these beneficiaries are not seeking rents but rather are attempting to make economically sound investments to enhance productivity. If the infrastructure is really going to increase the well-being of the supposed beneficiaries, they will have increased resources to devote to repayment in the future. Furthermore, if they know that they have to repay capital costs, the beneficiaries are likely to insist (if they have the institutional autonomy to do so) that the project has a high likelihood of producing net benefits in the future. Under these conditions, donor or national government funds are thus enhancing projects that the beneficiaries believe are of real value.

This means that direct beneficiaries or their representatives must be involved in the design and financial planning of an infrastructure producing highly localized benefits and that they must have the right to say no to a project that they do not think worthwhile. If they cannot say no, they cannot make a commitment that is considered binding because they can always assert that they were forced to agree. In addition, to make enforceable commitments, the beneficiaries need to be

- organized in a legally recognized form prior to the creation of financial and construction arrangements; beneficiaries can then participate in the design and financing of the project, as well as in the approval of a contract to eventually assume ownership of the facility and responsibility for its maintenance
- confident that government officials are also making enforceable contracts—that beneficiaries can hold public officials accountable, as well as being held accountable themselves
- assured that future conflicts over contract enforcement will be resolved fairly and that impartial conflict resolution arenas exist if needed.

The policy implications of our analysis in regard to small-scale infrastructure projects are relatively straightforward:

- encourage the beneficiaries to organize themselves into provision units that can mobilize resources to acquire ownership of small-scale infrastructure over time and assume full responsibility for operation and maintenance
- invest in general institutional facilities that enhance the capabilities of such provision units.

Some readers may respond that we are simply recommending privatization. Such an observation, however, does not capture the essence of our analysis. Strictly private provision involves individuals or family units interacting with firms to finance, design, construct, operate, and maintain a facility. In Chapter 6, we examined both simple and differentiated market arrangements involved in an investment in housing. Such arrangements can appropriately be called private or market arrangements. However, if a simple or differentiated market is to function efficiently or fairly, there must be clearly demarcated property rights, fair and low-cost court systems, and effective police systems to enforce these rights. Thus, *public* institutions play a crucial role in the operation of markets in the so-called private sector.

When groups of beneficiaries organize to provide a joint benefit by assuming mutual obligations for resource mobilization and for joint decisionmaking, some type of governing authority must be created to ensure that these mutual obligations are met. Such an authority is often created even if the organization technically remains a private, rather than a public, one. The zanjeras are an example of a provision unit that is legally recognized as a private corporation. If, however, we were to list the powers of the officers of the zanjeras to mobilize resources and sanction people for noncompliance with rules, the list of powers would closely resemble those of many organizations, such as special districts in the United States, that are formally recognized as public governmental units.

Sustaining Large-scale Infrastructure

The task of enhancing investments in facilities like roads that yield benefits to a set of less easily identifiable beneficiaries scattered over a larger spatial area is much more difficult. It is further complicated by the fact that the benefits generated by the road that are enjoyed by any one individual are often quite small relative to the benefits enjoyed by the set of all road users. Even when the principal beneficiaries are local residents, the incremental benefit of decreased transportation costs for a single user may be small enough to substantially weaken the individual's incentives to contribute to road improvement efforts. Under these circumstances, it is difficult to rely on efforts by individual or small groups of consumers to maintain a road.

Our advice to donors and national governments facing such conditions is similar to that given earlier: Opportunities to assist in such an investment should be foregone until there is firm evidence that the intended beneficiaries will contribute substantially toward the costs of developing and maintaining this investment. However, in this instance, it is much harder to specify a set of principles that should guide project design. There are several reasons for this.

When the beneficiaries of a road project form a large, relatively amorphous group, mobilizing and allocating resources to forestall free riding is extremely difficult. The relatively small observable benefits currently enjoyed by local residents as a result of maintenance efforts may make it difficult to rely on contributions of in-kind resources to finance maintenance. Instead, monetary resource mobilization instruments are likely to be necessary. But monetary instruments commonly entail considerably greater opportunities for rent-seeking activities and the possibility of corruption. Furthermore, the services generated by rural roads are such that charges directly linking payment with benefits received may well be impossible to implement; instead, broader resource mobilization tools must be used. In such cases, the degree of accountability that can be exercised by beneficiaries over service provision is minimal.

This suggests that increased accountability of the actors involved in the provision and production of road services is a key to improved sustainability. In this regard, we concur fully with Harral and Faiz (1988:32) in their review of road deterioration in developing countries, where they concluded that "inadequate maintenance in developing countries has various causes, but only institutional failure can explain the extent of the inadequacy. At the heart of this failure is the absence of public accountability. All activities to strengthen institutions, enhance incentives, and improve the internal workings of road agencies should be judged by their ability to increase accountability."

We do not presume to have *the* solution to the accountability problem, but we do believe that the approach to institutional analysis proposed in this volume is suggestive. At the heart of any institutional reform must be a concern for increasing the competitiveness of both providers and producers and ensuring that commitments are credible.

First, with respect to the provision of facilities like roads, provision units should be organized in ways that facilitate the communication of preferences between users and providers. Multiple provision units for different types of roads (for example, localized units for minor collector roads primarily serving local residents, larger units for roads connecting market centers, and even larger units for regional highways) permit more efficient preference aggregation.

Again, decisions on funding infrastructure investments should be contingent on the up-front investments by users who are also required to repay at least some portion of the capital costs. But the requirement to repay loans implies, as well, that the provision units must have some general revenue-raising powers of their own. At the local level, such revenues can be mobilized by using local fees and taxes that reflect the benefits received from having passable roads—property-based levies or local marketing fees, for instance. Where roads are provided by regional or national authorities and predominantly serve motorized vehicles, indirect taxes associated with vehicle inputs such as petroleum and tires are more likely to be feasible. Where such taxes are already imposed by national governments, tax sharing based simply on use-level differences, such as vehicle miles based on accurate traffic counts, may be most appropriate. Again, specific mobilization techniques must be tailored to the particular situation.

Although local or regional road provision units must have revenues available to arrange for road services, their commitments must be credible as well. If local units soon learn that deteriorated roads will be replaced through additional grant or loan funds even if they have not maintained them, maintenance is unlikely to be done. This means that the national government must hold them to their commitments; at the same time, the national government must also be credible in its commitment (if made) to transfer revenues to local jurisdictions.

Finally, on the provision side, those who are using and paying for the infrastructure (for example, through indirect taxes on vehicle use-related activities) must have the wherewithal to communicate their preferences to the providers and to hold the providers accountable for their decisions. This requires an open decisionmaking process at all levels in which taxpayers realize that they are contributing resources to support road services and have some ability to influence decisions that affect the quality of those services. Interest groups such as bus and truck owners' associations and even towns or villages served by regional roads must therefore be given the opportunity to voice their preferences in allocation decisions. When multiple groups are allowed to participate in open arenas to determine outcomes and when multiple jurisdictions control decisions about their own revenues for roads, the ability of any single group to secure rents can be limited. Similarly, when public sector decisionmakers are forced to compete for their positions, the quantity and quality of services can be expected to rise as these decisionmakers respond in ways designed to increase their likelihood of remaining in power.

Competition and the ability to enter into credible commitments are also necessary for effective production of road construction and maintenance services. Again, production contracts are only likely to result in well-built facilities if producers can be held accountable both directly by provision units and as directly as possible by users. Although competition can be facilitated by multiple private producers, nothing should preclude public bodies or private voluntary organizations from also engaging in the competitive process. Thus, for example, one road provision jurisdiction may contract with another to produce particular construction or maintenance services. Some provision jurisdictions may appropriately resemble a special-purpose jurisdiction, such as a bridge authority, where capital is invested in a particular facility and tolls are collected to repay capital costs and finance recurrent costs. The key is that the process is genuinely competitive; the exact legal structure of all units that participate in the surface transportation industry is less important.

The preceding chapters also suggest, however, that the competitive process will work efficiently only if contracts between providers and producers give both parties equal access to independent dispute adjudication services. Contractors must be unequivocally informed that failure to carry out the promised work will result in penalties that will harm them both in the present and in the future (through decreased likelihood of winning subsequent contracts). Public decisionmakers must also recognize that actions on their part that impede the ability of contractors to carry out the promised tasks effectively will also make them liable for some type of penalty or punishment, as determined by an independent judicial body.

Because the results of inadequate construction or maintenance may not show up for a long time, one institutional device that deserves greater attention is some form of independent insurer that derives small payments from all contractors or even from provision units. In the event of system failures that can be traced to contractor negligence, the insurance company would be held liable. Such an arrangement creates a third body that would find monitoring road service production in its own best interest; it could also act as an independent source of information in helping adjudicate contractual disputes. Thus, as we have emphasized throughout this volume, careful crafting of appropriate institutional arrangements that provide an opportunity for actors to ensure their own best interests can produce results that serve the best interests of all.

CONCLUSION

Analysts agree that simple market arrangements, without any opportunity for public provision, will fail to provide adequate rural infrastructure. In addition, we conclude here that simple hierarchical arrangements, without local public provision, will also fail. The costs associated with market failure are different from those associated with bureaucratic failure, but the end result is much the same: inadequate infrastructure that impedes development.

We know from empirical observation that it is possible for individuals to devise complex institutional arrangements that are highly successful in counteracting perverse incentives in infrastructure provision and production. Successful institutional arrangements take into account specific provision and production problems in a particular economic, technological, and cultural setting. Rarely, however, can such arrangements be characterized simply as part of "the market" or "the state." Nor is there a single blueprint that can be used to construct successful institutions for maintaining all types of rural infrastructure in all settings. We can assert, however, that successful institutional arrangements are usually complex rather than simple and that polycentric institutions that perform relatively well for some types of rural infrastructure have not been successfully fitted into a simple typology.

No single institutional arrangement, regardless of how complex or simple it is, can solve the problems of unsustainable infrastructure without incurring substantial costs. When we refer to institutional arrangements that counteract perverse incentives, we do not mean to suggest that perverse incentives are eliminated. Successful institutions for sustaining rural infrastructure will continue to incur some combination of transformation, coordination, information, and strategic costs. Even in an idealized model of an institution that ignores transaction costs, some fault can be found with relatively successful institutional arrangements because their operation will have been influenced by these costs. What is most relevant from an analytical and policy perspective is a realistic appraisal of the entire array of costs associated with alternative institutional arrangements. The preceding chapters have illustrated the nature and source of these costs and have shown how they can guide analysts and policymakers in their quest for institutional reforms that lead to improved sustainability of the rural infrastructure in developing countries.

The method of analysis that we have pursued in this book to analyze the effects of diverse policies related to infrastructure investment does not presume determinate causes of human behavior. Many physical, cultural, and institutional factors combine to create particular mixes of incentives facing multiple actors in complex settings. Rather, we recommend that those involved in policymaking related to infrastructure design, construction, operation, maintenance, and use recognize that crafting appropriate institutions to encourage long-term sustainability is as important a task as is good engineering design. We hope we have given those who must craft their own institutions to match their own circumstances some useful tools of analysis to aid them in their difficult but essential task.

NOTES

1. Recent findings from the Harvard Project on American Indian Economic Development are quite instructive in this regard. In light of extensive research

on many Indian reservations in the United States, Cornell and Kalt (1990) argued that the development of self-governing institutions that are well matched to traditional cultural views and to the problems involved is a necessary condition for enhancing economic development. They stressed that a variety of institutional forms work relatively well but that those that lack means to constrain executive and legislative authority are not linked to successful development efforts. "But the check is not blank. The theory of institutions set forth above would suggest that successful tribes have institutions that not only provide a match between cultural norms and formal structures; they also are adequate to the task at hand. 'Matched' solutions that fail adequately to constrain the powers and behaviors of those that govern will only further undermine the possibilities of politically, socially, and economically successful development" (Cornell and Kalt 1990:28). See also Cornell and Kalt (1992).

2. The U.S. Government Accounting Office, for example, made the following recommendations for solving the recurrent cost problem:

> We believe AID should strengthen the project planning, loan agreement, and . . . certification process as a serious mechanism for establishing recipient country capability, willingness, and commitment to operation and maintenance. To do this AID, in conjunction with other donors, should work with recipient countries to:
>
> • build necessary institutional capability through O&M projects (management, technical training, and equipment maintenance);
> • estimate annual life-of-system O&M costs, including personnel, training, and equipment requirements;
> • establish O&M funding sources with the ultimate objective of recipient countries, including system users, assuming all O&M costs; and
> • provide necessary monitoring and early warning of O&M shortfalls. (U.S. Government Accounting Office 1983:21–22)

3. Obviously, investments in training civil servants in technical and managerial skills can be of long-term value in developing human capital. We consider training a potentially worthwhile investment. Our concern is with the focus on strengthening the power of national institutions rather than strengthening the capabilities of national, regional, and local agencies, as well as those of courts, interagency arrangements, and private associations.

4. Elected officials rarely expect to be in office as long as the expected life-of-system for most infrastructures facilities in their jurisdictions and will usually derive more personal benefits by constructing new facilities, rather than maintaining old ones. Locally elected officials, however, frequently rely on the same infrastructure as the people they serve do. They can also be voted out of office for indifference to maintenance and repair issues, and they must face angry constituents on a daily basis.

5. These large sums are readily available as a result of perverse incentives that operate inside many donor agencies. These incentives are generated

by performance evaluation criteria that reward officers, in part, on the basis of their ability to design projects that absorb large amounts of money. Donor agencies regard these criteria as necessary evils if they must comply with legislative mandates to spend the large sums appropriated for foreign assistance.

6. Although failing to retain these institutional changes may appear unfortunate in the immediate context, the experience may provide an educational benefit for participants that will prove of value in the long term. When future opportunities for institutional reform again arise, the lessons learned from previous experiments with institutional change may ultimately help create institutions that are both productive and enduring.

7. Water allocation disputes, for example, can undermine mutual trust and willingness to cooperate in regard to maintenance activities.

8. This general approach is also presented in E. Ostrom (1992).

9. In light of the imperative that donor agency officers "move money" and the temptations of rent seeking for government officials, this is a particularly difficult commitment for donors and host governments to make. It may require the major donors to work with the host government on a joint funding strategy. And both donors and host governments may want to provide funds in case of major disasters to help rebuild structures destroyed by earthquakes, floods, or avalanches. This form of "insurance" does not destroy incentives to perform routine maintenance unless the definition of a natural disaster is interpreted too broadly.

References

Aaron, Henry J. 1990. "Comments on 'Why is Infrastructure Important,'" in Alicia H. Munnell, ed., *Is There a Shortfall in Public Capital Investment?* Pp. 51–63. Boston, Mass.: Federal Reserve Bank of Boston.

Abeywickrema, Nanda. 1986. "Government Policy on Participatory Irrigation Management," in *Proceedings of the Workshop on Participatory Management in Sri Lanka's Irrigation Schemes.* Pp. 17–28. Digana Village, Sri Lanka: International Irrigation Management Institute.

Adelman, Irma, and Erik Thorbecke. 1989. "Special Issue on the Role of Institutions in Economic Development." *World Development* 17(9): 1317–1498.

ACIR (Ronald J. Oakerson). 1987. *The Organization of Local Public Economies.* Washington, D.C.: Advisory Commission on Intergovernmental Relations.

———. (Ronald J. Oakerson, Roger B. Parks, and Henry A. Bell). 1988. *Metropolitan Organization: The St. Louis Case.* Washington, D.C.: Advisory Commission on Intergovernmental Relations.

Ahmed, Raisuddin, and Mahabub Hossain. 1988. *Infrastructure and Development of the Rural Economy of Bangladesh.* Report to USAID, Dhaka. Washington, D.C.: International Food Policy Research Institute.

Akerlof, George A. 1970. "The Market for 'Lemons': Quality Uncertainty and the Market Mechanism." *Quarterly Journal of Economics* 84(3) (Aug.): 488–500.

Akin, John, Nancy Birdsall, and David de Ferranti. 1987. *Financing Health Services in Developing Countries.* Washington, D.C.: World Bank.

Alchian, Armen A. 1950. "Uncertainty, Evolution, and Economic Theory." *Journal of Political Economy* 58(3) (June): 211–221.

Alchian, Armen A., and Harold Demsetz. 1972. "Production, Information and Economic Organization." *American Economic Review* 62(5) (Dec.): 777–795.

Anderson, G. William, and Charles G. Vandervoort. 1982. *Rural Roads Evaluation Summary Report.* Program Evaluation Report no. 5. Washington, D.C.: U.S. Agency for International Development.

Anderson, James E. 1974. *Public Policy-making.* New York: Praeger.

Arnold, Steven H. 1989. "Sustainable Development: A Solution to the Development Puzzle?" *Development* 2(3): 21–25.

Arrow, Kenneth J. 1951. *Social Choice and Individual Values.* 2d ed. New York: John Wiley.

Aschauer, David Alan. 1990. *Public Investment and Private Sector Growth: The Economic Benefits of Reducing America's "Third Deficit."* Washington, D.C.: Economic Policy Institute.

Ascher, William, and Robert Healy. 1990. *Natural Resource Policymaking in Developing Countries: Environment, Economic Growth, and Income Distribution.* Durham, N.C.: Duke University Press.

Asher, Robert E. 1970. *Development Assistance in the Seventies: Alternatives for the United States.* Washington, D.C.: Department of State.

Azabon, Mongi, and Jeffrey B. Nugent. 1989. "Tax Farming: Anachronism or Optimal Contract? (An Illustration with Respect to Tunisia's Weekly Markets)," in Mustapha K. Nabli and Jeffrey B. Nugent, eds., *The New Institutional Economics and Development: Theory and Applications to Tunisia.* Pp. 178–199. Amsterdam: North Holland.

Bacdayan, Albert S. 1974. "Securing Water for Drying Rice Terraces: Irrigation, Community Organization, and Expanding Social Relationships in a Western Bontoc Group, Philippines." *Ethnology* 13: 247–260.

Bagadion, Benjamin, and Frances F. Korten. 1985. "Developing Irrigators' Organizations: A Learning Process Approach to a Participatory Irrigation Program," in Michael M. Cernea, ed., *Putting People First: Sociological Variables in Rural Development.* Pp. 52–90. New York: Oxford University Press.

Bahl, Roy W. 1984. "Intergovernmental Grants in Bangladesh." Occasional Paper no. 87. Syracuse, N.Y.: Syracuse University, Metropolitan Studies Program.

Bain, Joe S. 1959. *Industrial Organization.* New York: John Wiley.

Barbier, Edward B. 1987. "The Concept of Sustainable Economic Development." *Environmental Conservation* 14(2): 101–110.

Barker, Randolph, E. Walter Coward, Jr., Gilbert Levine, and Leslie E. Small. 1984. *Irrigation Development in Asia: Past Trends and Future Directions.* Ithaca, N.Y.: Cornell University Press.

Barzel, Yoram. 1969. "Two Propositions on the Optimum Level of Producing Collective Goods." *Public Choice* 6 (Spring): 31–37.

———. 1982. "Measurement Cost and the Organization of Markets." *Journal of Law and Economics* 25(1) (Apr.): 27–28.

Bauer, P. T. 1984. "Remembrance of Studies Past: Retracing First Steps," in Gerald M. Meier and Dudley Seers, eds., *Pioneers in Development.* Pp. 25–43. New York: Oxford University Press.

Beardsley, R. K., J. Hall, and R. E. Ward. 1959. *Village Japan.* Chicago, Ill.: University of Chicago Press.

Beenhakker, Henri L. 1987. *Rural Transportation Services: A Guide to Their Planning and Implementation.* Boulder, Colo.: Westview Press.

Bell, Daniel. 1977. "The Future World Disorder." *Foreign Policy* 23 (Summer): 134–135.

Benjamin, Paul. 1989. "Local Organization for Development in Nepal." Ph.D. diss., University of North Carolina, Chapel Hill.

Ben-Porath, Yoram. 1980. "The F-Connection: Families, Friends and Firms, and Organizations of Exchange." *Population and Development Review* 6(1) (Mar.): 1–31.

Berg, Robert J., Carleen Gardner, Michael M. Horowitz, Palmer Stearns, and Charles Vandervoort. 1980. *Jamaica Feeder Roads: An Evaluation.* Project Impact Evaluation no. 11. Washington, D.C.: U.S. Agency for International Development.

Berk, Richard A., and Alice Hartmann. 1971. "Race and District Differences in Per Pupil Staffing Expenditures in Chicago Elementary Schools, 1970–1971." Evanston, Ill.: Northwestern University, Center for Urban Affairs.

Berkes, Fikret, ed. 1989. *Common Property Resources: Ecology and Community-based Sustainable Development*. London: Belhaven Press.

Bigelow, Ross E., and Lisa Chiles. 1980. *Tunisia: CARE Water Projects*. Project Impact Evaluation no. 10. Washington, D.C.: U.S. Agency for International Development.

Biggs, S. D. 1980. "Informal R&D." *Ceres* 13(4): 23–26.

Biggs, S. D., and E. J. Clay. 1981. "Sources of Innovation in Agricultural Technology." *World Development* 9(4): 321–336.

Bird, Richard. 1978. *Intergovernmental Fiscal Relations in Developing Countries*. Staff Paper no. 304. Washington, D.C.: World Bank.

Bish, Robert L. 1971. *The Public Economy of Metropolitan Areas*. Chicago, Ill.: Rand McNally/Markham.

Black, Jan Knippers. 1991. *Development in Theory and Practice: Bridging the Gap*. Boulder, Colo.: Westview Press.

Blomquist, William. 1992. *Dividing the Waters: Governing Groundwater in Southern California*. San Francisco, Calif.: Institute for Contemporary Studies Press.

Blomquist, William, and Elinor Ostrom. 1985. "Institutional Capacity and the Resolution of a Commons Dilemma." *Policy Studies Review* 5(2) (Nov.): 383–393.

Boyle, J., and D. Jacobs. 1982. "The Intra-City Distribution of Services: A Multivariate Analysis." *American Political Science Review* 76(2) (June): 371–379.

Brennan, Geoffrey, and James Buchanan. 1983. "Normative Tax Theory for a Federal Polity: Some Public Choice Preliminaries," in Charles E. McLure, ed., *Tax Assignment in Federal Countries*. Pp. 52–65. Canberra: Australian National University Press.

Breton, Albert, and Ronald Wintrobe. 1982. *The Logic of Bureaucratic Conduct: An Economic Analysis of Competition, Exchange, and Efficiency in Private and Public Organizations*. Cambridge: Cambridge University Press.

Brinkerhoff, Derick W., and Arthur A. Goldsmith. 1990. *Institutional Sustainability in Agricultural and Rural Development: A Global Perspective*. New York: Praeger.

Brokensha, David W., D. M. Warren, and Oswald Werner, eds. 1980. *Indigenous Knowledge Systems and Development*. Lanham, Md.: University Press of America.

Bromley, Daniel W. 1992. *Making the Commons Work: Theory, Practice, and Policy*. San Francisco, Calif.: Institute for Contemporary Studies Press.

Bryant, Coralie. 1991. "Sustainability Revisited: States, Institutions, and Economic Performance." Paper presented at the Annual Meeting of the American Society for Public Administration, Washington, D.C., March 23–27.

Bryant, Coralie, and Louise G. White. 1982. *Managing Development in the Third World*. Boulder, Colo.: Westview Press.

———. 1984. *Managing Rural Development with Small Farmer Participation*. West Hartford, Conn.: Kumarian Press.

Buchanan, James M. 1960. *Fiscal Theory and Political Economy*. Chapel Hill: University of North Carolina Press.

———. 1965. "An Economic Theory of Clubs." *Economica* 32(125) (Feb.): 1–14.

———. 1970. "Public Goods and Public Bads," in John P. Crecine, ed., *Financing the Metropolis*. Pp. 51–71. Beverly Hills, Calif.: Sage.

Buchanan, James M., and Gordon Tullock. 1962. *The Calculus of Consent*. Ann Arbor: University of Michigan Press.

Buchanan, James M., Robert D. Tollison, and Gordon Tullock, eds. 1980. *Toward a Theory of the Rent-Seeking Society*. College Station: Texas A&M University Press.

Bumgarner, Mary, Jorge Martinez-Vazquez, and David Sjoquist. 1989. "Municipal Capital Maintenance and Fiscal Distress." Working Paper. Atlanta: Georgia State University, Department of Economics.

Buzzard, Shirley. 1987. *Development Assistance and Health Programs: Issues of Sustainability*. AID Program Evaluation Discussion Paper no. 23. Washington, D.C.: U.S. Agency for International Development.

Campbell, D. T. 1974. "Downward Causation in Hierarchically Organized Biological Systems," in F. J. Ayala and T. G. Dobzhansky, eds., *Studies in the Philosophy of Biology: Reduction and Related Problems*. Pp. 179–186. Berkeley: University of California Press.

Carruthers, Ian. 1988. "Irrigation Under Threat: A Warning Brief for Irrigation Enthusiasts." *IIMI Review* 2(1) (Apr.): 8–11, 24–25.

Cernea, Michael M. 1984. "Can Local Participation Help Development? Mexico's PIDER Program Shows It Can Improve the Selection and Execution of Local Development Projects." *Finance and Development* 21(4): 41–44.

———., ed. 1985. *Putting People First: Sociological Variables in Rural Development*. New York: Oxford University Press.

———. 1987. "Farmer Organization and Institution Building for Sustainable Development." *Regional Development Dialogue* 8(2): 1–24.

Chamberlin, John. 1974. "Provision of Collective Goods as a Function of Group Size." *American Political Science Review* 68(2) (June): 707–716.

Chambers, Robert. 1975. *Water Management and Paddy Production in the Dry Zone of Sri Lanka*. Colombo, Sri Lanka: Agrarian Research and Training Institute.

———. 1979. *Rural Development: Whose Knowledge Counts?* IDS Bulletin (Brighton) 10(2) (Jan.).

———. 1980. "Basic Concepts in the Organization of Irrigation," in E. Walter Coward, Jr., ed., *Irrigation and Agricultural Development in Asia: Perspectives from the Social Sciences*. Pp. 28–50. Ithaca, N.Y.: Cornell University Press.

———. 1988. *Managing Canal Irrigation: Practical Analysis from South Asia*. Cambridge: Cambridge University Press.

Chauhan, Sumi Krishna, with Zhang Bihua, K. Gopalakrishnan, Lala Rukh Hussain, Ajoa Yeboah–Afari, and Francisco Leal. 1983. *Who Puts the Water in the Taps? Community Participation in Third World Drinking Water, Sanitation and Health*. Washington, D.C.: International Institute for Environment and Development.

Cheung, Steven N.S. 1983. "The Contractual Nature of the Firm." *Journal of Law and Economics* 26(1) (Apr.): 1–21.

Chubb, John E., and Terry M. Moe. 1990. *Politics, Markets, and America's Schools.* Washington, D.C.: Brookings.

Coase, Ronald H. 1937. "The Nature of the Firm." *Economica* 4(16) (Nov.): 386–405.

Cohen, Michael A. 1974. *Urban Policy and Political Conflict in Africa: A Study of the Ivory Coast.* Chicago, Ill.: University of Chicago Press.

———. 1980. "Francophone Africa," in Donald C. Rowat, ed., *International Handbook on Local Government Reorganization.* Pp. 415–422. Westport, Conn.: Greenwood Press.

Cohen, S. S., J. W. Dyckman, E. Schoenberger, and C. R. Downs. 1981. *Decentralization: A Framework for Policy Analysis.* Berkeley: University of California, Institute of International Studies, Project on Managing Decentralization.

Colmey, John. 1988. "Irrigated Non-Rice Crops: Asia's Untapped Resource." *IIMI Review* 2(1) (Apr.): 3–7.

Commons, John R. 1959. *Legal Foundations of Capitalism.* Madison: University of Wisconsin Press.

Connerley, Edwin, David Gephart, Larry Schroeder, and Louis Siegel. 1989a. *Bangladesh: Feeder Roads Maintenance and Improvement Project Evaluation.* Decentralization: Finance and Management Project Report. Burlington, Vt.: Associates in Rural Development.

Connerley, Edwin, Iben Nathan, Larry Schroeder, et al. 1989b. *Bangladesh Rural and Feeder Roads Sector Assessment.* Decentralization: Finance and Management Project Report. Burlington, Vt.: Associates in Rural Development.

Conyers, Diana. 1983. "Decentralization: The Latest Fashion in Development Administration." *Public Administration and Development* 3(2) (Apr.–June): 97–109.

———. 1984. "Decentralization and Development: A Review of the Literature." *Public Administration and Development* 4(2) (Apr.–June): 187–197.

———. 1985. "Decentralization: A Framework for Discussion," in Hasnat Abdul Hye, ed., *Decentralization, Local Government Institutions and Resource Mobilisation.* Pp. 22–42. Comilla: Bangladesh Academy for Rural Development.

Corey, A. T. 1986. "Control of Water Within Farm Turnouts in Sri Lanka," in *Proceedings of a Workshop on Water Management in Sri Lanka.* Pp. 25–30. Documentation Series no. 10. Colombo, Sri Lanka: Agrarian Research and Training Institute.

Cornell, Stephen, and Joseph P. Kalt. 1990. "Where's the Glue? Institutional Bases of American Indian Economic Development." Working Paper. Cambridge, Mass.: Harvard Project on American Indian Economic Development.

———. 1992. "Culture and Institutions as Public Goods: American Indian Economic Development as a Problem of Collective Action," in Terry L. Anderson, ed., *Property Rights and Indian Economies.* Pp. 215–252. Lanham, Md.: Rowman & Littlefield.

Cornes, Richard, and Todd Sandler. 1986. *The Theory of Externalities, Public Goods, and Club Goods.* Cambridge: Cambridge University Press.

Coward, E. Walter, Jr. 1979. "Principles of Social Organization in an Indigenous Irrigation System." *Human Organization* 38(1) (Spring): 28–36.

————., ed. 1980. *Irrigation and Agricultural Development in Asia: Perspectives from the Social Sciences.* Ithaca, N.Y.: Cornell University Press.

————. 1985. "Technical and Social Change in Currently Irrigated Regions: Rules, Roles, and Rehabilitation," in Michael M. Cernea, ed., *Putting People First: Sociological Variables in Rural Development.* Pp. 27–52. New York: Oxford University Press.

Crosson, P. R. 1975. "Institutional Obstacles to Expansion of World Food Production." *Science* 188(4188) (May): 519–524.

Cruz, Maria Concepcion J., Luzviminda B. Cornista, and Diogenes C. Dayan. 1986. *Legal and Institutional Issues of Irrigation Water Rights in the Philippines.* Laguna: University of the Philippines at Los Baños, Agrarian Reform Institute.

Curtis, Donald. 1991. *Beyond Government: Organizations for Common Benefit.* London: Macmillan.

Datta, Sama K., and Jeffrey B. Nugent. 1989. "Transaction Cost Economics and Contractual Choice: Theory and Evidence," in Mustapha K. Nabli and Jeffrey B. Nugent, eds., *The New Institutional Economics and Development: Theory and Applications to Tunisia.* Pp. 1–59. Amsterdam: North Holland.

Davis, Gina, and Elinor Ostrom. 1991. "A Public Economy Approach to Education: Choice and Co-Production." *International Political Science Review* 12(4) (Oct.): 313–335.

de Silva, Chandra Richard. 1987. *Sri Lanka: A History.* New Delhi: Vikas.

de Soto, Hernando. 1989. *The Other Path: The Invisible Revolution in the Third World.* New York: Harper & Row.

Development Research Group. 1986. *Rapti Rural Area Development Project: Medium Irrigation Appraisal Study Report.* Lalitpur, Nepal: Development Research Group.

Dickerson, O. D. 1959. *Health Insurance.* Homewood, Ill.: Irwin.

Dildine, Larry, and Fred Massey. 1974. "Dynamic Model of Private Incentives to Housing Maintenance." *Southern Economics Journal* (40)4 (Apr.): 631–639.

Donahue, John D. 1989. *The Privatization Decision: Public Ends, Private Means.* New York: Basic Books.

Dosi, Giovanni, and Massimo Egidi. 1987. "Substantive and Procedural Uncertainty: An Exploration of Economic Behaviours in Complex and Changing Environments." Paper prepared for the International Workshop on Programmable Automation and New Work Modes, Paris, April 2–4.

Downs, Anthony. 1967. *Inside Bureaucracy.* Boston, Mass.: Little, Brown.

Duany, Wal. 1992. "Neither Palaces nor Prisons: The Constitution of Order Among the Nuer." Ph.D. diss., Indiana University, Bloomington.

Eberts, Randall W. 1989. "Some Empirical Evidence on the Linkage between Public Infrastructure and Local Economic Development." Working Paper. Cleveland, Ohio: Federal Reserve Bank of Cleveland.

Ekeh, Peter P. 1975. "Colonialism and the Two Publics in Africa: A Theoretical Statement." *Comparative Studies in Society and History* 17: 91–112.

Esman, Milton J. 1980. "Development Assistance in Public Administration: Requiem or Renewal?" *Public Administration Review* 40(5) (Sept./Oct.): 426–431.

Esman, Milton J., and Norman T. Uphoff. 1982. *Local Organization and Rural Development: The State of the Art.* Special Series on Rural Local Organization no. 7. Ithaca, N.Y.: Cornell University, Center for International Studies, Rural Development Committee.

――――. 1984. *Local Organizations: Intermediaries in Rural Development.* Ithaca, N.Y.: Cornell University Press.

Ferejohn, John. 1974. *Pork Barrel Politics: Rivers and Harbors Legislation, 1947–1968.* Stanford, Calif.: Stanford University Press.

Ferris, James M., and Donald R. Winkler. 1991. "Agency Theory and Intergovernmental Relationships," in Remy Prud'homme, ed., *Public Finance with Several Levels of Government.* Pp. 155–166. The Hague: Foundation Journal Public Finance.

Friedman, Lee S. 1984. *Microeconomic Policy Analysis.* New York: McGraw-Hill.

Frohlich, Norman, and Joe A. Oppenheimer. 1971. "I Get By with a Little Help from My Friends." *World Politics* 23 (Oct.): 104–120.

――――. 1974. "The Carrot and the Stick: Optimal Program Mixes for Entrepreneurial Political Leaders." *Public Choice* 19 (Fall): 43–61.

Frohlich, Norman, Joe A. Oppenheimer, and Oran Young. 1971. *Political Leadership and Collective Goods.* Princeton, N.J.: Princeton University Press.

Gearheart, Robert A. 1990. *Community-based Maintenance and Cost Recovery of Piped Rural Water Schemes: Malawi.* Field Report no. 309. Washington, D.C.: U.S. Agency for International Development, Water and Sanitation for Health Project.

Glennie, Colin. 1983. *Village Water Supply in the Decade.* New York: John Wiley.

Gow, David D., and Jerry VanSant. 1985. "Decentralization and Participation: Concepts in Need of Implementation Strategies," in Elliott R. Morss and David D. Gow, eds., *Implementing Rural Development Projects: Lessons from AID and World Bank Experiences.* Pp. 107–147. Boulder, Colo.: Westview Press.

Growenewegen, Peter. 1990. "Taxation and Decentralization: A Reconsideration of the Costs and Benefits of a Decentralized Tax System," in Robert J. Bennett, ed., *Decentralization, Local Governments, and Markets: Toward a Post-Welfare Agenda.* Pp. 87–115. Oxford: Clarendon Press.

GTZ (Deutsche Gesellschaft fuer Technische Zusammenarbeit/Nepal). 1991. *Dhading Local Roads Programme Status Report.* Kathmandu, Nepal: GTZ.

Guyer, Jane I. 1991. "Representation Without Taxation: An Essay on Democracy in Rural Nigeria, 1952–1990." Working Papers in African Studies no. 152. Boston, Mass.: Boston University, African Studies Center.

Haggblade, Steven, Peter Hazell, and James Brown. 1989. "Farm-Nonfarm Linkages in Rural Sub–Saharan Africa." *World Development* 17 (Aug.): 1173–1201.

Haratani, Joseph, Ana Maria Viveros-Long, and Ana Maria Becerra Marzano de Gonzales. 1981. *Peru: The CARE Water and Health Services Project.* Project Impact Evaluation no. 24. Washington, D.C.: U.S. Agency for International Development.

Hardin, Russell. 1982. *Collective Action.* Baltimore, Md.: Johns Hopkins University Press.

Harral, Clell G. 1987. "The Road Deterioration Problem in Developing Countries." *World Highways* 38(3) (Apr./May): 1, 4–5.

Harral, Clell G., and Asif Faiz. 1988. *Road Deterioration in Developing Countries: Causes and Remedies.* Washington, D.C.: World Bank.

Harris, Milton, and Artur Raviv. 1978. "Some Results on Incentive Contracts with Applications to Education and Employment, Health Insurance, and Law Enforcement." *American Economic Review* 68(1) (Mar.): 20–30.

Harriss, J. C. 1977. "Problems of Water Management in Hambantota District," in B. H. Farmer, ed., *Green Revolution? Technology and Change in Rice Growing Areas of Tamil Nadu and Sri Lanka.* Pp. 364–376. New York: Macmillan.

———. 1984. "Social Organisation and Irrigation: Ideology, Planning and Practice in Sri Lanka's Settlement Schemes," in T. P. Bayliss-Smith and S. Wanmali, eds., *Understanding Green Revolutions.* Pp. 315–338. Cambridge: Cambridge University Press.

Hayter, Teresa. 1971. *Aid as Imperialism.* Baltimore, Md.: Penguin.

Hazell, Peter B.R., and Alisa Roell. 1983. "Rural Growth Linkages: Household Expenditure Patterns in Malaysia and Nigeria." Research Report no. 41. Washington, D.C.: International Food Policy Research Institute.

Heller, Peter. 1974. "Public Investment with Recurrent Cost Constraint." *Quarterly Journal of Economics* 88(2) (May): 251–277.

———. 1979. "The Underfinancing of Recurrent Development Costs." *Finance and Development* (16)1 (Mar.): 38–41.

Hesselberg, J. 1986. "Lack of Maintenance of Irrigation Facilities: Experiences from Southern Sri Lanka," in Irene Norlund, Sven Cederroth, and Ingela Gerdin, eds., *Rice Societies.* Pp. 72–80. London: Curzon Press.

Heston, Alan, H. Hasnain, S. Z. Hussain, and R. N. Khan. 1985. "The Economics of Camel Transport in Pakistan." *Economic Development and Cultural Change* 34(1) (Oct.): 121–141.

Hill, Catharine B., and Katundu M. Mtawali. 1989. "Malawi: Lessons from the Gravity-Fed Piped Water Supply," in *Successful Development in Africa: Case Studies of Projects, Programs, and Policies.* EDI Development Policy Case Series, Analytical Case Studies no. 1. Pp. 57–78. Washington, D.C.: World Bank, Economic Development Institute.

Hinchliffe, K. 1980. "Conflicts Between National Aims in Papua New Guinea: The Case of Decentralization and Equality." *Economic Development and Culture Change* 28(4) (July): 819–836.

Hirschman, Albert. 1970. *Exit, Voice and Loyalty.* Cambridge, Mass.: Harvard University Press.

Honadle, George, and Jerry VanSant. 1985. *Implementation for Sustainability: Lessons from Integrated Rural Development.* West Hartford, Conn.: Kumarian Press.

Horton, Robin. 1967. "African Traditional Thought and Western Science." *Africa* 37(1) (Jan.): 50–71, and (2) (Apr.): 155–187.

Hubbell, Kenneth, Denise Pineda, Norman Ramos, Cesar Saldana, and James T. Thomson. 1989. *Philippines Local Fiscal Integrity Analysis Report.*

Decentralization: Finance and Management Project Report. Burlington, Vt.: Associates in Rural Development.

Hunt, Robert C. 1988. "Size and the Structure of Authority in Canal Irrigation Systems." *Journal of Anthropological Research* 44(4) (Winter): 335–355.

Huntington, Samuel P., and Myron Weiner, eds. 1987. *Understanding Political Development.* Boston, Mass.: Little, Brown.

Hyden, Goran. 1980. *Beyond Ujamaa in Tanzania: Underdevelopment and an Uncaptured Peasantry.* Berkeley: University of California Press.

———. 1983. *No Shortcuts to Progress: African Development Management in Perspective.* Berkeley: University of California Press.

Iglesias, Gabriel U. 1985. "The Provincial Development Assistance Project; Strengthening Local Capability in the Philippines," in G. Shabbir Cheema, ed., *Rural Development in Asia: Case Studies on Programme Implementation.* Pp. 42–66. New Delhi: Sterling Publishers.

Illo, Jeanne Frances I., and Maria Elena Chiong-Javier. 1983. *Organizing Farmers for Irrigation Management: The Buhi-Lalo Experience.* Naga City, Philippines: Research and Service Center.

IIMI. 1988. "Farmers' Panel Discussion," in IIMI, ed., *Irrigation Management in Nepal: Research Papers from a National Seminar.* Pp. 130–134. Kathmandu, Nepal: International Irrigation Management Institute.

International Labour Organization. 1979. *Appropriate Transport Facilities for the Rural Sector in Developing Countries.* Geneva: ILO, World Employment Programme.

———. 1982. *The Maintenance of Rural Access Roads in Kenya: A Discussion Paper.* Geneva: ILO, World Employment Programme.

Jackson, Robert H., and Carl G. Rosberg. 1982. *Personal Rule in Black Africa.* Berkeley: University of California Press.

Jagannathan, N. Vijay. 1987. *Informal Markets in Developing Countries.* New York: Oxford University Press.

Jayawardene, Jayantha. 1986. "The Training of Mahaweli Turnout Group Leaders," in *Participatory Management in Sri Lanka's Irrigation Schemes.* Pp. 77–85. Digana Village, Sri Lanka: International Irrigation Management Institute.

Jenkins, Jerry, ed. 1988. *Beyond the Informal Sector: Including the Excluded in Developing Countries.* San Francisco, Calif.: Institute for Contemporary Studies Press.

Jenkins, Jerry, and Richard M. Bird. "Expanding Consent in the Delivery and Finance of Urban Services," in Jerry Jenkins and David Sisk, eds., *Development by Consent.* San Francisco, Calif.: Institute for Contemporary Studies Press, forthcoming.

Jenkins-Smith, Hank C. 1991. "Alternative Theories of the Policy Process: Reflections on a Research Strategy for the Study of Nuclear Waste Policy." *PS: Political Science and Politics* 24 (June): 157–166.

Jones, Charles O. 1970. *An Introduction to the Study of Public Policy.* Belmont, Calif.: Wadsworth.

Jorgenson, Dale W., John J. McCall, and Roy Radner. 1967. *Optimal Replacement Policy.* Chicago, Ill.: Rand McNally.

Kampsax International, A/S. 1986. "National Highway Maintenance Study: Final Report." Vol. 1. Working Paper. Islamabad: Kampsax International.

Katzman, M. T. 1978. "The Quality of Municipal Services, Central City Decline and Middle-Class Flight." Research Report R78–1. Cambridge, Mass.: Harvard University, Department of City and Regional Planning.

Kee, Woo Sik. 1977. "Fiscal Decentralization and Economic Development." *Public Finance Quarterly* 5(1) (Jan.): 79–97.

Khalid, Mansour. 1985. *Nimeiri and the Revolution of Dis-May.* London: KPI.

Kiser, Larry L., and Elinor Ostrom. 1982. "The Three Worlds of Action: A Metatheoretical Synthesis of Institutional Approaches," in Elinor Ostrom, ed., *Strategies of Political Inquiry.* Pp. 179–222. Beverly Hills, Calif.: Sage.

Knight, Frank. 1921. *Risk, Uncertainty, and Profit.* Boston, Mass.: Houghton Mifflin.

Korten, David C. 1980. "Community Organization and Rural Development: A Learning Process Approach." *Public Administration Review* 40(5) (Sept./ Oct.): 480–511.

———., ed. 1986. *Community Management: Asian Experiences and Perspectives.* West Hartford, Conn.: Kumarian Press.

———. 1991. "Sustainable Development." *World Policy Journal* 9(1): 157–190.

Korten, David C., and Filipe B. Alfonso. 1983. *Bureaucracy and the Poor: Closing the Gap.* West Hartford, Conn.: Kumarian Press.

Korten, Frances F. 1982. *Building National Capacity to Develop Water Users' Associations: Experience from the Philippines.* Washington, D.C.: World Bank, Agricultural and Rural Development Department.

———. 1985. "A Participatory Approach to Irrigation Development in the Philippines," in Jean Claude Garcia-Zamor, ed., *Public Participation in Development Planning and Management: Cases from Africa and Asia.* Pp. 179–186. Boulder, Colo.: Westview Press.

Krueger, Anne O. 1974. "The Political Economy of the Rent-Seeking Society." *American Economic Review* 64: 291–301.

Landa, Janet T. 1981. "A Theory of the Ethnically Homogeneous Middleman Group: An Institutional Alternative to Contract Law." *Journal of Legal Studies* 10(2) (June): 349–362.

———. 1988. "Underground Economies: Generic or *Sui Generis?*" in Jerry Jenkins, ed., *Beyond the Informal Sector: Including the Excluded in Developing Countries.* Pp. 75–103. San Francisco, Calif.: Institute for Contemporary Studies Press.

Landau, Martin, and Eva Eagle. 1981. *On the Concept of Decentralization.* Berkeley: University of California, Institute of International Studies.

Landau, Martin, Suchitra Punyaratabandhu-Bhakdi, Ledivina Carino, Rolando Tungpalan, and James Wunsch. 1980. "Final Report: Provincial Development Assistance Program—Philippines." Working Paper. Berkeley: University of California Institute of International Studies, Project on Managing Decentralization.

Lando, Richard Paul. 1979. "The Gift of Land: Irrigation and Social Structure in a Toba Batak Village." Ph.D diss., University of California, Riverside.

Lee, Barbara. 1989. "Organizational Economics: Links to Developing Country Problems." Paper presented at the Conference on Institutional Development and the World Bank, Washington, D.C., December 14–15.

Leibenstein, Harvey. 1983. "Property Rights and X-Efficiency: Comment." *American Economic Review* 83: 831–842.

Lele, Sharachchandra M. 1991. "Sustainable Development: A Critical Review." *World Development* 19(6): 607–621.

Leonard, David K. 1984. "The Political Realities of African Management." Working Paper no. 18. Binghamton, N.Y.: Institute for Development Anthropology.

Leonard, David K., and Dale Rogers Marshall, eds. 1982. *Institutions of Rural Development for the Poor: Decentralization and Organizational Linkages*. Berkeley, Calif.: Institute for International Studies.

Levi, Margaret. 1988. *Of Rule and Revenue*. Berkeley: University of California Press.

Levine, Gilbert. 1980. "The Relationship of Design, Operation and Management," in E. Walter Coward, Jr., ed., *Irrigation and Agricultural Development in Asia: Perspectives from the Social Sciences*. Pp. 51–62. Ithaca, N.Y.: Cornell University Press.

Levinson, Jerome, and Juan de Onis. 1970. *The Alliance That Lost Its Way*. Chicago, Ill.: Quadrangle Books.

Levy, Frank S., Arnold J. Meltsner, and Aaron Wildavksy. 1974. *Urban Outcomes: Schools, Streets, and Libraries*. Berkeley: University of California Press.

Liebenow, J. Gus. 1981. *Malawi: Clean Water for the Rural Poor*. American Universities Field Staff Report no. 40. Hanover, N.H.: The Wheelhouse.

Lineberry, Robert L. 1977. *Equality and Urban Policy: The Distribution of Municipal Public Services*. Beverly Hills, Calif.: Sage.

Lipsey, R. G., and K. Lancaster. 1956. "The General Theory of the Second Best." *Review of Economic Studies* 24(1): 11–32.

Loveman, Brian. 1973. "The Logic of Political Corruption." Working Paper. Bloomington: Indiana University, Workshop in Political Theory and Policy Analysis.

Malone, Thomas W. 1987. "Modeling Coordination in Organizations and Markets." *Management Science* 33(10) (Oct.): 1317–1332.

Malual, Bona. 1987. "The Roots of the Current Contention," in Francis Deng and Gifford Prosser, eds., *The Search for Peace and Unity in the Sudan*. Pp. 9–14. Washington, D.C.: The Wilson Center Press.

Mandel, A. S. 1975. *Resource Distribution Inside School Districts*. Lexington, Mass.: D. C. Heath.

Marglin, Stephen A. 1974. "What Do Bosses Do? The Origins and Functions of Hierarchy in Capitalist Production." *The Review of Radical Political Economics* 6(2) (Summer): 60–112.

Marschak, Jacob. 1972. *Economic Theory of Teams*. New Haven, Conn.: Yale University Press.

Martin, Edward, and Robert Yoder. 1983. "Review of Farmer-managed Irrigation in Nepal," in *Water Management in Nepal: Proceedings of the Seminar on Water Management Issues, July 31–August 2*. Pp. 82–91. Kathmandu, Nepal: Ministry of Agriculture, Agricultural Projects Services Centre, and the Agricultural Development Council.

Mawhood, Philip. 1983. "Decentralization: The Concept and the Practice," in Philip Mawhood, ed., *Local Government in the Third World*. Pp. 1–24. New York: John Wiley.

Mawhood, Philip, and Ken Davey. 1980. "Anglophone Africa," in Donald C. Rowat, ed., *International Handbook on Local Government Reorganization*. Pp. 404–414. Westport, Conn.: Greenwood Press.

Mayhew, David. 1974. *Congress: The Electoral Connection*. New Haven, Conn.: Yale University Press.

McCay, Bonnie J., and James M. Acheson, eds. 1987. *The Question of the Commons: The Culture and Ecology of Communal Resources*. Tucson: University of Arizona Press.

McClure, Charles E. 1983. "Introduction," in Charles E. McLure, ed., *Tax Assignment in Federal Countries*. Pp. XII–XIX. Canberra: Australian National University Press.

McCullough, James S., and Thomas H. Steubner. 1985. "Project Inception Report: Management Support for Town Panchayats Project." Kathmandu, Nepal: His Majesty's Government of Nepal, Ministry of Panchayat and Local Development.

McGowan, Rick, Dawam Rahardjo, and Nick Ritchie. 1991. *Rural Water Supply and Sanitation in Indonesia: Midterm Evaluation Report for CARE/Indonesia's Community Self-Financing of Water and Sanitation Systems Project*. Burlington, Vt.: Associates in Rural Development.

McGuire, Martin. 1974. "Group Size, Homogeneity, and the Aggregate Provision of a Pure Public Good Under Cournot Behavior." *Public Choice* 18(2): 107–126.

McKelvey, Richard D. 1976. "Intransitivities in Multidimensional Voting Models and Some Implications for Agenda Control." *Journal of Economic Theory* 12(3) (June): 472–482.

Mellor, John W. 1976. *The New Economics of Growth: A Strategy for India and the Developing World*. Ithaca, N.Y.: Cornell University Press.

Mellor, John W., and Bruce F. Johnston. 1984. "The World Food Equation: Interrelations Among Development, Employment and Food Consumption." *Journal of Economic Literature* 22 (June): 524–531.

Mellor, John W., and Uma J. Lele. 1973. "Growth Linkages of the New Food Grain Technologies." *Indian Journal of Agricultural Economics* 18 (Jan.-Mar.): 35–55.

Mitnick, Barry M. 1974. "The Theory of Agency: The Concept of Fiduciary Rationality and Some Consequences." Ph.D. diss., University of Pennsylvania.

———. 1980. *The Political Economy of Regulation: Creating, Designing, and Removing Regulatory Forms*. New York: Columbia University Press.

Mladenka, Kenneth, and Kim Q. Hill. 1978. "The Distribution of Urban Police Services." *Journal of Politics* 40(1) (Feb.): 112–133.

Moe, Terry. 1984. "The New Economics of Organization." *American Journal of Political Science* 28(4) (Nov.): 739–777.

Montgomery, John D. 1981. "On the Decentralization of Integrated Rural Development Activities." Working Paper. Cambridge, Mass.: Harvard University, Institute for International Development.

Moran, Emilio F. 1992. "Deforestation in the Brazilian Amazon." Occasional Paper no. 10, Series on Environment and Development. Bloomington: Indiana University, Indiana Center on Global Change and World Peace.

Morss, Elliot R., and Victoria A. Morss. 1982. *U.S. Foreign Aid: An Assessment of New and Traditional Development Strategies.* Boulder, Colo.: Westview Press.

Munnell, Alicia H., ed. 1990. *Is There a Shortfall in Public Capital Investment?* Boston, Mass.: Federal Reserve Bank of Boston.

Musgrave, Richard A. 1959. *The Theory of Public Finance.* New York: McGraw-Hill.

———. 1983. "Who Should Tax, Where, and What?" in Charles E. McLure, ed., *Tax Assignment in Federal Countries.* Pp. 2–19. Canberra: Australian National University Press.

Nabli, Mustapha K., and Jeffrey B. Nugent. 1989. "The New Institutional Economics and Its Applicability to Development." *World Development* 17(9): 1333–1347.

National Research Council. 1981. *Labor-Based Construction and Maintenance of Low-Volume Roads.* Transportation Technology Support for Developing Countries: Synthesis 3. Washington, D.C.: National Academy of Sciences, Transportation Research Board.

Nelson, John M. 1968. *Aid Influence and Foreign Policy.* New York: Macmillan.

Newberry, David M. 1989. "Cost Recovery from Optimally Designed Roads." *Economica* 56 (May): 165–185.

Niskanen, William A. 1971. *Bureaucracy and Representative Government.* Chicago, Ill.: Aldine-Atherton.

North, Douglass C. 1985. "Institutions, Transactions Costs and Economic Growth." Working Paper. St. Louis, Mo.: Washington University, School of Business and Center in Political Economy.

———. 1986. "The New Institutional Economics." *Journal of Institutional Economics* 142(1) (Mar.): 230–237.

———. 1990. *Institutions, Institutional Change and Economic Performance.* New York: Cambridge University Press.

Nugent, Jeffrey B. 1985. "The Old-Age Security Motive for Fertility." *Population and Development Review* 11 (Mar.): 75–97.

Oates, Wallace. 1972. *Fiscal Federalism.* New York: Harcourt, Brace, Jovanovich.

Odell, Malcolm. 1985. "Local Government: Traditional and Modern Roles of the Village Kgotla," in Louis A. Picard, ed., *The Evolution of Modern Botswana.* Pp. 61–83. Lincoln: University of Nebraska Press.

Okun, Arthur M. 1975. *Equality and Efficiency: The Big Tradeoff.* Washington, D.C.: The Brookings Institution.

Olson, Mancur. 1965. *The Logic of Collective Action.* Cambridge, Mass.: Harvard University Press.

———. 1969. "The Principle of 'Fiscal Equivalence': The Division of Responsibilities among Different Levels of Government." *American Economic Review* 59(2) (May): 479–487.

Ostrom, Elinor. 1983. "Equity as a Performance Issue in Urban Policing," in Gordon P. Whitaker and Charles D. Phillips, eds., *Evaluating Performance of Criminal Justice Agencies.* Pp. 99–125. Beverly Hills, Calif.: Sage.

———. 1985. "Are Successful Efforts to Manage Common-pool Problems a Challenge to the Theories of Garrett Hardin and Mancur Olson?" Working paper. Bloomington: Indiana University, Workshop in Political Theory and Policy Analysis.

———. 1986. "A Method of Institutional Analysis," in Franz-Xaver Kaufmann, Giandomenico Majone, and Vincent Ostrom, eds., *Guidance, Control, and Evaluation in the Public Sector*. Pp. 459–475. Berlin and New York: de Gruyter.

———. 1990. *Governing the Commons: The Evolution of Institutions for Collective Action*. New York: Cambridge University Press.

———. 1992. *Crafting Institutions for Self-Governing Irrigation Systems*. San Francisco, Calif.: Institute for Contemporary Studies Press.

Ostrom, Elinor, Roger B. Parks, and Gordon P. Whitaker. 1974. "Defining and Measuring Structural Variations in Interorganizational Arrangements." *Publius* 4 (Fall): 87–108.

———. 1978. *Patterns of Metropolitan Policing*. Cambridge, Mass.: Ballinger.

Ostrom, Vincent. 1986. "A Fallabilist's Approach to Norms and Criteria of Choice," in Franz-Xaver Kaufmann, Giandomenico Majone, and Vincent Ostrom, eds., *Guidance, Control, and Evaluation in the Public Sector*. Pp. 229–249. Berlin and New York: de Gruyter.

———. 1987. *The Political Theory of a Compound Republic: Designing the American Experiment*. 2d ed. Lincoln, Neb.: University of Nebraska Press.

———. 1989. *The Intellectual Crisis in American Public Administration*. 2d ed. Tuscaloosa: University of Alabama Press.

———. 1991. *The Meaning of American Federalism: Constituting a Self-Governing Society*. San Francisco, Calif.: Institute for Contemporary Studies Press.

Ostrom, Vincent, and Elinor Ostrom. 1977. "Public Goods and Public Choices," in E. S. Savas, ed., *Alternatives for Delivering Public Services: Toward Improved Performance*. Pp. 7–49. Boulder, Colo.: Westview Press.

Ostrom, Vincent, Robert Bish, and Elinor Ostrom. 1988. *Local Government in the United States*. San Francisco, Calif.: Institute for Contemporary Studies Press.

Ostrom, Vincent, David Feeny, and Hartmut Picht, eds. 1988. *Rethinking Institutional Analysis and Development: Issues, Alternatives, and Choices*. San Francisco, Calif.: Institute for Contemporary Studies Press.

Ostrom, Vincent, Charles M. Tiebout, and Robert Warren. 1961. "The Organization of Government in Metropolitan Areas: A Theoretical Inquiry." *American Political Science Review* 55(4) (Dec.): 831–842.

Otsuka, Keijiro, Masao Kikuchi, and Yujiro Hayami. 1986. "Community and Market in Contract Choice: The Jeepney in the Philippines." *Economic Development and Cultural Change* 34(2) (Jan.): 279–298.

Owen, J. D. 1972. "The Distribution of Education Resources in Large American Cities." *Journal of Human Resources* 7 (Winter): 26–38.

Pasternak, Burton. 1972. *Kinship and Community in Two Chinese Villages*. Stanford, Calif.: Stanford University Press.

Paul, Samuel. 1992. *Strengthening Public Service Accountability: A Conceptual Framework*. Discussion Paper no. 136. Washington, D.C.: World Bank.

Pauly, M. V. 1973. "Income Redistribution as a Local Public Good." *Journal of Public Economics* 2(1) (Feb.):35–58.

Pearce, David, Edward Barbier, and Anil Markandya. 1990. *Sustainable Development: Economics and Environment in the Third World*. Hants, England: Edward Elgar.

Perera, J. 1986. "The Gal Oya Farmer Organization Programme: A Learning Process?" in *Proceedings of the Workshop on Participatory Management in Sri Lanka's Irrigation Schemes*. Pp. 86–110. Digana Village, Sri Lanka: International Irrigation Management Institute.

Pipes, Richard. 1974. *Russia Under the Old Regime*. New York: Scribner.

Plott, Charles R. 1967. "A Notion of Equilibrium and Its Possibility Under Majority Rule." *American Economic Review* 57(4) (Sept.): 787–806.

Pohl, Gerhard, and Dubravko Mihaljek. 1992. "Project Evaluation and Uncertainty in Practice: A Statistical Analysis of Rate-of-Return Divergencies of 1,015 World Bank Projects." *The World Bank Economic Review* 6(2) (May): 255–277.

Pollak, Robert A. 1985. "A Transaction Cost Approach to Families and Households." *Journal of Economic Literature* 23(2) (June): 581–608.

Popkin, Samuel L. 1979. *The Rational Peasant*. Berkeley: University of California Press.

———. 1981. "Public Choice and Rural Development—Free Riders, Lemons, and Institutional Design," in Clifford S. Russell and Norman K. Nicholson, eds., *Public Choice and Rural Development*. Pp. 43–80. Baltimore, Md.: Johns Hopkins University Press.

Powell, John D. 1970. "Peasant Society and Clientelistic Politics." *American Political Science Review* 64(2) (June): 411–425.

Pradhan, Naresh C., and Robert Yoder. 1989. "Improving Irrigation System Management Through Farmer-to-Farmer Training: Examples from Nepal." IIMI Working Paper no. 12. Colombo, Sri Lanka: International Irrigation Management Institute.

Pradhan, Prachanda. 1980. *Local Institutions and People's Participation in Rural Public Works in Nepal*. Special Series on Rural Local Organizations no. 4. Ithaca, N.Y.: Cornell University, Rural Development Committee.

———. 1983. "Community-Managed Irrigation Systems Case Study Chhatis Mauja Irrigation System," in *Water Management in Nepal: Proceedings of the Seminar on Water Management Issues Held in Kathmandu 31 July to 2 August*. Pp. 218–242. Kathmandu, Nepal: Agricultural Projects Service Centre, Agricultural Development Council.

———. 1984. "Chhatis Mauja Irrigation System: Community Response on Resource Management." Kathmandu, Nepal: Development Research and Communication Group.

Prebisch, Raul. 1970. *Change and Development: Latin America's Great Task*. Washington, D.C.: Inter-American Development Bank.

Raby, Namika. 1991. "Participatory Management in Large Irrigation Systems: Issues for Consideration." *World Development* 19(12): 1767–1776.

Radnitzky, Gerard. 1987. "Cost-Benefit Thinking in the Methodology of Research: The 'Economic Approach' Applied to Key Problems of the Philosophy of Science," in Gerard Radnitzky and Peter Bernholz, eds., *Economic Imperialism: The Economic Approach Applied Outside the Field of Economics*. Pp. 283–334. New York: Paragon House.

Ramakrishnan, Subramaniam. 1985. "Recurrent Agricultural Expenditures in Kenya," in John Howell, ed., *Recurrent Costs and Agricultural Development*. Pp. 113–127. London: Overseas Development Institute.

Rana, Jitendra. 1991. "A Case Study of the Chhattis Mauja Irrigation System in Nepal," in IIMI, ed., *Performance Measurement in Farmer-managed Irrigation Systems: The Third International Workshop of the FMIS Network.* Pp. 26-I-XI. Kathmandu, Nepal: International Irrigation Management Institute.

Rashid, Salim. 1981. "Public Utilities in Egalitarian LDCs: The Role of Bribery in Achieving Pareto Efficiency." *Kyklos* 34(3): 448–460.

Redclift, M. 1987. *Sustainable Development: Exploring the Contradictions.* New York: Methuen.

Repetto, Robert. 1986. *Skimming the Water: Rent-Seeking and the Performance of Public Irrigation Systems.* Research Report no. 41. Washington, D.C.: World Resources Institute.

———. 1987. "Population, Resources, Environment: An Uncertain Future." *Population Bulletin* 42(2) (July): 1–43.

Richards, Paul. 1985. *Indigenous Agricultural Revolution: Ecology and Food Production in West Africa.* Boulder, Colo.: Westview Press.

Rockefeller, Nelson A. 1969. *The Rockefeller Report on the Americas: The Official Report of a United States Presidential Mission for the Western Hemisphere.* Chicago, Ill.: Quadrangle Books.

Rondinelli, Dennis A. 1981. "Government Decentralization in Comparative Perspective: Theory and Practice in Developing Countries." *International Review of Administrative Science* 47(2): 133–145.

———. 1983. "Implementing Decentralization Programmes in Asia: A Comparative Analysis." *Public Administration and Development* 3: 181–207.

Rondinelli, Dennis A., and John R. Nellis. 1986. "Assessing Decentralization Policies in Developing Countries: The Case for Cautious Optimism." *Development Policy Review* 4: 3–23. Beverly Hills, Calif.: Sage.

Rondinelli, Dennis A., James S. McCullough, and Ronald W. Johnson. 1987. "Decentralizing Public Services in Developing Countries: A Framework for Policy Analysis and Implementation." Working Paper in Decentralization in Developing Countries Series. Research Triangle Park, N.C.: Research Triangle Institute.

Rosenzweig, Mark R., and Kenneth I. Wolpin. 1985. "Specific Experience, Household Structure and Intergenerational Transfers: Farm Family Land and Labor Arrangements in Developing Countries." *Quarterly Journal of Economics* 100(4): 961–987.

Ross, Stephen A. 1973. "The Economic Theory of Agency: The Principal's Problem." *American Economic Review* 63(2) (May): 134–139.

Rostow, Walt W. 1960. *The Stages of Economic Growth: A Non-Communist Manifesto.* London: Cambridge University Press.

Roth, Gabriel. 1987. *The Private Provision of Public Services in Developing Countries.* Oxford: Oxford University Press.

Sabatier, Paul A. 1991. "Toward Better Theories of the Policy Process." *PS: Political Science and Politics* 24 (June): 144–156.

Sabetti, Filippo. 1984. *Political Authority in a Sicilian Village.* New Brunswick, N.J.: Rutgers University Press.

Sandler, Todd, and J. Tschirhart. 1980. "The Economic Theory of Clubs: An Evaluative Survey." *Journal of Economic Literature* 18(4) (Dec.): 1481–1521.

Savas, E. S. 1987. *Privatization: The Key to Better Government*. Chatham, N.J.: Chatham House.

Sawyer, Amos. 1988. "The Putu Development Association: A Missed Opportunity," in Vincent Ostrom, David Feeny, and Hartmut Picht, eds., *Rethinking Institutional Analysis and Development: Issues, Alternatives, and Choices*. Pp. 247–278. San Francisco, Calif.: Institute for Contemporary Studies Press.

————. 1992. *The Emergence of Autocracy in Liberia: Tragedy and Challenge*. San Francisco, Calif.: Institute for Contemporary Studies Press.

Schaaf, Jeanne. 1989. "Governing a Monopoly Market Under Siege: Using Institutional Analysis to Understand Competitive Entry into Telecommunications Markets, 1944–1982." Ph.D. diss., Indiana University.

Schroeder, Larry. 1987. *Rural Development Grants to Local Governments in Asia*. Monograph no. 19. Syracuse, N.Y.: Syracuse University, Metropolitan Studies Program.

————. 1988. "Intergovernmental Grants in Developing Countries." Policy, Planning and Research Working Paper no. 38. Washington, D.C.: World Bank.

Schultz, Theodore W. 1981. *Investing in People: The Economics of Population Quality*. Berkeley: University of California Press.

Scott, James C. 1976. *The Moral Economy of the Peasant*. New Haven, Conn.: Yale University Press.

Scudder, Thayer. 1972. "Ecological Bottlenecks and the Development of the Kariba Lake Basin," in M. Taghi Farvar and John P. Milton, eds., *The Careless Technology: Ecology and International Development*. Pp. 206–235. Garden City, N.Y.: The Natural History Press.

Sexton, P. C. 1961. *Education and Income*. New York: Viking.

Sharp, Elaine B. 1986. *Citizen Demand-Making in the Urban Context*. Tuscaloosa: University of Alabama Press.

Shepsle, Kenneth A. 1979. "The Role of Institutional Structure in the Creation of Policy Equilibrium," in Douglas Rae and T. J. Eismeier, eds., *Public Policy and Public Choice*, Sage Yearbooks in Politics and Public Policy, vol. 6. Pp. 249–281. Beverly Hills, Calif.: Sage.

Shrestha, Bihari Krishna. 1980. "Nuwakot District (Nepal)," in Bihari Krishna Shrestha, ed., *The Practice of Local-Level Planning: Case Studies in Selected Rural Areas in India, Nepal and Malaysia*. Pp. 35–55. Bangkok: U.N. Economic and Social Commission for Asia and the Pacific.

Simon, Herbert A. 1946. "The Proverbs of Administration." *Public Administration Review* 6(1) (Winter): 53–67.

————. 1965. *Administrative Behavior: A Study of Decision-making Processes in Administrative Organization*. New York: Free Press. (Originally published in 1947.)

————. 1972. "Theories of Bounded Rationality," in C. B. McGuire and Roy Radner, eds., *Decision and Organization: A Volume in Honor of Jacob Marschak*. Pp. 161–176. Amsterdam: North Holland.

Simon, Herbert A., Donald W. Smithburg, and Victor A. Thompson. 1958. *Public Administration*. New York: Alfred A. Knopf.

Siriwardhana, S. 1981. *Emerging Income Inequalities and Forms of Hidden Tenancy in the Mahaweli H Area*. Colombo, Sri Lanka: People's Bank Research Department.

Siy, Robert Y., Jr. 1982. *Community Resource Management: Lessons from the Zanjera*. Quezon City: University of the Philippines Press.

Small, Leslie, Marietta Adriano, and Edward D. Martin. 1986. *Regional Study on Irrigation Service Fees: Final Report*. Kandy, Sri Lanka: International Irrigation Management Institute.

Sommer, John G., Rosemary Aquino, Carlos A. Fernandez II, Frank H. Golay, and Emmy Simmons. 1982. *Philippines: Bicol Integrated Area Development*. Project Impact Evaluation no. 28. Washington, D.C.: U.S. Agency for International Development.

Squire, F. A. 1943. "Notes on Mende Rice Varieties." *Sierra Leone Agricultural Notes* no. 10 (Mimeo).

Steinberg, David I., Robert B. Morrow, Ingrid Palmer, and Kim Dong-il. 1980. *Korean Irrigation*. Project Impact Evaluation no. 12. Washington, D.C.: U.S. Agency for International Development.

Stiglitz, Joseph E. 1986. *Economics of the Public Sector*. New York: Norton.

Stone, Roger D. 1992. *The Nature of Development: A Report from the Rural Tropics on the Quest for Sustainable Economic Growth*. New York: Alfred A. Knopf.

Summers, Lawrence H. 1992. "Summers on Sustainable Growth." *The Economist* 323(7761) (May 30): 65.

Swaminathan, C. B., and N. B. Lal. 1979. "Appropriate Technologies for Rural Road Development." *Road Research Papers* no. 158. Delhi: Central Road Research Institute.

Tait, Alan A. 1988. *Value-Added Tax: International Practice and Problems*. Washington, D.C.: International Monetary Fund.

Tang, Shui Yan. 1992. *Institutions and Collective Action: Self-Governance in Irrigation*. San Francisco, Calif.: Institute for Contemporary Studies Press.

Tendler, Judith. 1975. *Inside Foreign Aid*. Baltimore, Md.: Johns Hopkins University Press.

Theobald, Robin. 1990. *Corruption, Development and Underdevelopment*. Durham, N.C.: Duke University Press.

Thomson, James T. 1991. *Decentralization, Governance and Problem-Solving in the Sahel. Sahel Decentralization Policy Report, Volume 1*. Decentralization: Finance and Management Project. Burlington, Vt.: Associates in Rural Development.

Tiebout, Charles. 1956. "A Pure Theory of Local Expenditures." *Journal of Political Economy* 64(5) (Oct.): 416–424.

Tisdell, Clem. 1988. "Sustainable Development: Differing Perspectives of Ecologists and Economists, and Relevance to LDCs." *World Development* 16(3): 373–384.

Tollison, Robert B. 1982. "Rent Seeking: A Survey." *Kyklos* 35(4): 575–602.

USAID. 1983. *Irrigation and AID's Experience: A Consideration Based on Evaluations*. AID Program Evaluation Report no. 8. PN-AAL-019. Washington, D.C.: U.S. Agency for International Development.

U.S. Government Accounting Office. 1983. *Irrigation Assistance to Developing Countries Should Require Stronger Commitments to Operation and Maintenance*. Washington, D.C.: General Accounting Office.

Uphoff, Norman T., ed. 1982. *Rural Development and Local Organization in Asia*, vols. 1 and 2. Delhi: Macmillan India.

————. 1985a. "Fitting Projects to People," in Michael M. Cernea, ed., *Putting People First: Sociological Variables in Rural Development*. Pp. 359–395. New York: Oxford University Press.

————. 1985b. "Summary of January 1985 Trip Report on Farmer Organization Program in Gal Oya, Sri Lanka." Ithaca, N.Y.: Cornell University.

————. 1985c. "People's Participation in Water Management: Gal Oya, Sri Lanka," in J. C. Garcia-Zamor, ed., *Public Participation in Development Planning and Management: Cases from Africa and Asia*. Pp. 131–178. Boulder, Colo.: Westview Press.

————. 1986a. *Improving International Irrigation Management with Farmer Participation: Getting the Process Right*. Boulder, Colo.: Westview Press.

————., ed. 1986b. *Local Institutional Development: An Analytical Sourcebook with Cases*. West Hartford, Conn.: Kumarian Press.

Uphoff, Norman T., and Milton J. Esman. 1974. "Local Organization for Rural Development: Analysis of Asian Experience." Series on Rural Local Government no. 19. Ithaca, N.Y.: Cornell University, Center for International Studies, Rural Development Committee.

Uphoff, Norman T., and Warren Ilchman, eds. 1972. *The Political Economy of Development*. Berkeley: University of California Press.

Van Voorst, Bruce. 1992. "Why America Has So Many Potholes." *Time*, May 4, 64–65.

von Hayek, Friedrich A. 1945. "The Use of Knowledge in Society." *American Economic Review* 35(4) (Sept.): 519–530.

Wade, Robert. 1984. "The System of Administrative and Political Corruption: Canal Irrigation in South India." *Journal of Development Studies* 18(3): 287–328.

————. 1985. "The Market for Public Office: Why the Indian State Is Not Better at Development." *World Development* 13(4): 467–497.

————. 1988. *Village Republics: Economic Conditions for Collective Action in South India*. Cambridge: Cambridge University Press.

Wall, David. 1973. *The Charity of Nations: The Political Economy of Foreign Aid*. New York: Basic Books.

Walters, A. A. 1968. *The Economics of Road User Charges*. Baltimore, Md.: Johns Hopkins University Press.

Warner, Dennis B., John Briscoe, Craig Hafner, and Bert Zellmer. 1986. *Malawi Self-Help Rural Water Supply Program: Final Evaluation*. WASH Field Report no. 186. Washington, D.C.: U.S. Agency for International Development, Water and Sanitation for Health Project.

Weicher, J. C. 1971. "The Allocation of Police Protection by Income Class." *Urban Studies* 8 (Oct.): 207–220.

Weingast, Barry, Kenneth Shepsle, and Chalmers Johnson. 1981. "The Political Economy of Benefits and Costs: A Neoclassical Approach to Distributive Politics." *Journal of Political Economy* 89(34) (Aug.): 642–664.

Whittington, Dale, John Briscoe, and Xinming Mu. 1987. "Willingness to Pay for Water in Rural Areas: Methodological Approaches and an Application in Haiti." Water and Sanitation for Health Project, Field Report no. 213. Arlington, Va.: Camp Dresser and McKee International.

Williamson, Oliver E. 1975. *Markets and Hierarchies: Analysis and Antitrust Implications.* New York: Free Press.

———. 1979. "Transaction Cost Economics: The Governance of Contractual Relations." *Journal of Law and Economics* 22(2) (Oct.): 233–261.

———. 1985. *The Economic Institutions of Capitalism: Firms, Markets, Relational Contracting.* New York: Free Press.

World Bank, The. 1976. *Village Water Supply: A World Bank Paper.* Washington, D.C.: World Bank.

———. 1988. *Rural Development: World Bank Experience, 1965–86.* Operations Evaluation Study. Washington, D.C.: World Bank.

World Commission on Environment and Development. 1987. *Our Common Future.* New York: Oxford University Press.

Wunsch, James. 1983. "The Provincial Development Assistance Project: Technocratic Strategies and Unintended Consequences." Working Paper. Omaha, Neb.: Creighton University.

———. 1988. "Rural Development, Decentralization and Administrative Reform: Towards a New Analytical Framework." Working Paper no. 18. Washington, D.C.: National Association of Schools of Public Affairs and Administration.

———. 1991. "Sustaining Third World Infrastructure Investments: Decentralization and Alternative Strategies." *Public Administration and Development* 11:5–23.

Wynne, Susan G. 1989. "The Land Boards of Botswana: A Problem in Institutional Design." Ph.D. diss., Indiana University.

Yang, Tai-Shuenn. 1987. "Property Rights and Constitutional Order in Imperial China." Ph.D. diss., Indiana University.

Yoder, Robert. 1992. *Performance of the Chhattis Mauja Irrigation System, a Thirty-Five Hundred Hectare System Built and Managed by Farmers in Nepal.* Colombo, Sri Lanka: International Irrigation Management Institute.

Young, Crawford, and Thomas Turner. 1985. *The Rise and Decline of the Zairian State.* Madison: University of Wisconsin Press.

Yudelman, Montague. 1985. *The World Bank and Agricultural Development—An Insider's View.* Washington, D.C.: World Resources Institute, WRI Paper no. 1.

Other Works of Interest

Bahl, Roy W., and Johannes F. Linn. 1992. *Urban Public Finance in Developing Countries.* New York: Oxford University Press.

Chambers, Robert. 1983. *Rural Development: Putting the Last First.* Harlow, England: Longman Scientific and Technical.

Groenfeldt, David. 1991. "Building on Tradition: Indigenous Irrigation Knowledge and Sustainable Development in Asia." *Agriculture and Human Values* 8 (Winter-Spring): 114–120.

Kaminski, Antoni. 1992. *An Institutional Theory of Communist Regimes: Design, Function, and Breakdown.* San Francisco, Calif.: Institute for Contemporary Studies Press.

Klitgaard, Robert. 1991. *Adjusting to Reality: Beyond "State versus Market" in Economic Development.* San Francisco, Calif.: Institute for Contemporary Studies Press.

Leonard, H. Jeffrey. 1989. *Environment and the Poor: Development Strategies for a Common Agenda.* New Brunswick, N.J.: Transaction Books.

Olowu, Dele. 1985. "Bureaucratic Corruption and Public Accountability in Nigeria: An Assessment of Recent Developments." *International Review of Administrative Sciences* 1(1): 7–12.

Rondinelli, Dennis A. 1987. *Development Administration and U.S. Foreign Aid Policy.* Boulder, Colo.: Lynne Rienner.

Scott, James C. 1969. "Corruption, Machine Politics, and Political Change." *American Political Science Review* 62(4) (Dec.): 1142–1158.

Steinberg, David I., Douglas Caton, Susan Holloran, and Thomas Hobgood. 1980. *Philippine Small Scale Irrigation.* Project Impact Evaluations no. 4. Washington, D.C.: U.S. Agency for International Development.

Task Force on Development Assistance and Economic Growth. 1992. *International Cooperation for Sustainable Economic Growth: The U.S. Interest and Proposals for Revitalization.* Washington, D.C.: Board for International Food and Agricultural Development.

Wunsch, James S. 1992. "Development Administration in Africa: 1960–1990. Themes, Issues and Works," in Mark Delancey, ed., *The Handbook of Political Science Research on Sub-Saharan Africa: (From the 1960s to the 1990s).* Westport, Conn.: Greenwood Press.

Wunsch, James S., and Dele Olowu, eds. 1990. *The Failure of the Centralized State: Institutions and Self-Governance in Africa.* Boulder, Colo.: Westview Press.

Wynne, Susan. 1988. "Institutional Resources for Development among the Kgalagadi of Botswana," in Vincent Ostrom, David Feeny, and Hartmut Picht, eds., *Rethinking Institutional Analysis and Development: Issues, Alternatives, and Choices.* Pp. 213–246. San Francisco, Calif.: Institute for Contemporary Studies Press.

Yudelman, Montague. 1989. "Sustainable and Equitable Development in Irrigation Environments," in H. Jeffrey Leonard, ed., *Environment and the Poor: Development Strategies for a Common Agenda.* Pp. 61–85. New Brunswick, N.J.: Transaction Books.

About the Book and Authors

Integrating recent research in the fields of public administration, public finance, institutional economics, and policy analysis, this book shows how institutional arrangements and the incentives they generate can help or hinder development efforts. The authors present a method for systematically comparing alternative institutional arrangements for developing and maintaining rural infrastructure facilities. Their analysis reveals the special strengths and weaknesses of polycentric as compared to centralized or decentralized institutional arrangements. Descriptions of a variety of infrastructure projects—including roads, bridges, and irrigation systems—in geographical settings as diverse as Africa, Asia, and Latin America are used to illustrate key concepts.

Perfect for courses on policy analysis, development administration, and economic development and for use by professional practitioners, *Institutional Incentives* contributes appreciably and practically to the understanding of sustainable development, infrastructure maintenance, institutional analysis, and the central importance of institutional arrangements.

Elinor Ostrom is Arthur F. Bentley Professor of Political Science at Indiana University and codirector of the Workshop in Political Theory and Policy Analysis there. **Larry Schroeder** is professor of public administration and economics at the Maxwell School of Syracuse University. **Susan Wynne** is a research associate at the Workshop in Political Theory and Policy Analysis at Indiana University.

Index

Abeywickrema, 100–101
Accountability, 67, 111, 112, 115–116, 129, 132, 138, 140(n8), 143, 151, 153–154, 156, 190, 194, 211(n4), 222, 223, 225, 228, 229
Adaptability, 111, 112, 116, 132, 139, 151
Adverse selection, 48, 55, 57–58, 59, 70, 123, 132
Advisory bodies, 168, 170
Africa, 12, 16, 165
  East Africa, 187
  North Africa, 62
African Development Bank, 141
Agriculture, 3, 4, 7, 11, 52, 89. *See also* Irrigation
Ahmed, Raisuddin, 23(n6)
Aid, 4
Akerlof, George A., 58
Alchian, Armen A., 60–61
Amazon region, 109(n12)
Analyses, institutional, xv, 18, 19–20, 127–139, 154–156, 160, 213, 215–218, 231
Anderson, James E., xix
Animals, 58–59, 80, 90
Aschauer, David Alan, 23(n4)
Ascher, William, 152
Asia, 12, 52
  South Asia, 62, 146
Asian Development Bank, 141
Asset specificity, 102–103
Assumptions, 9, 44–46, 143, 197, 204, 215
Authoritarianism, 7, 207
Authority, 164, 166, 177, 178, 190, 193, 207, 208, 209, 219, 227, 231(n1)
  judicial, 186–187

Bangladesh, 11, 23(n6), 31, 95, 110(n19), 159, 201
Banglung project, 69–70
Banks, 109(n12), 141
Barzel, Yoram, 182
Bauer, P. T., 3
Beenhakker, Henri L., 93
Benefits, 13, 15, 77, 114, 117, 118, 132, 160, 217, 221, 225, 226
  estimating, 29, 76, 92–93, 95, 192
  nonexcludability of, 76, 77–84, 113. *See also* Exclusion; Free riding
  See also under Costs
Bicol River Basin program, 171, 175(n2)
Bigelow, Ross E., 83
Biggs, S. D., 52
Bird, Richard, 172
Briscoe, John, 91
Bish, Robert L., 182, 183
Botswana, 187, 204
Brazil, 157, 158
Bretton Woods Conference, 2. *See also* International Monetary Fund; World Bank
Bridges, 25, 69–70, 98, 229
Britain, 152
Brown, James, 12
Brutland Commisssion report, 11
Bryant, Coralie, 66–67
Budgeting, 172, 205, 207
Building codes, 67

Canada, 152
Capital, 3, 4, 98, 150
  capital-intensive projects, 157, 158
  capital markets, 208

capital stock, 85
See also Social capital
Capital cities, 147, 169
Capitalism, 208
CARE/Indonesia, 90, 109(n10)
Cement, 94
Centralization, xxi, 36, 51, 121, 141–
  161, 162(n5), 175, 177, 184, 203, 207.
  See also Decentralization;
  Governments, national
Cernea, Michael, 15–16
Cheung, Steven, 71(nn 4, 8)
Chhattis Mauja irrigation system, 187,
  188–189
Chiles, Lisa, 83
China, 4, 71(n8)
Chubb, John E., xi
CILSS. *See* Comité Inter-état de Lutte
  Contre la Sécheresse au Sahel
Cities. *See* Capital cities; Urban areas
Citizen-consumers, 142–143
Clay, E. J., 52
Clubs, theory of, 211(n6)
Coase, Ronald, 71(n4)
Cohen, S. S., 166–167
Collective action, 18, 77, 78, 79, 199,
  200, 207
Collective choice, 74, 84
Colmey, John, 53
Comité Inter-état de Lutte Contre la
  Sécheresse au Sahel (CILSS), 79,
  199–200
Communication, 86, 228
Community organizers (COs), 171,
  175(n2)
*Community Resource Management:
  Lessons from the Zanjera* (Siy), 191–
  192
Competition, 207, 208–209, 210, 228,
  229–230
Conflict resolution, 223, 226. *See also*
  Disputes
Consumer groups, 125(n8). *See also*
  Institutional arrangements, user
  groups
Consumption, 82, 88. *See also*
  Infrastructure, use of

Contingent valuation method, 91
Contracts, 18, 46–47, 60, 62, 63, 71(n4),
  101–102, 131, 146, 148, 195, 215,
  226, 229, 230
  contracting out, 206, 207
Conyers, Diana, 167
Coproduction, 101
Cornell, Stephen, 232(n1)
Cornes, Richard, 88
Corruption, 48, 65–68, 70, 72(n), 94,
  120, 123, 131, 136, 138, 146–148,
  155, 156, 157, 159, 177, 218, 219,
  228. *See also* Opportunism; Side-
  payments; *under* Incentives
COs. *See* Community organizers
Costs, 5, 27–28, 184, 198, 211(n6), 230
  and benefits, 9, 11, 12, 14, 16, 17, 36,
    37, 40, 44, 81, 85, 93, 95, 109(n11),
    113, 117, 138, 150, 162(n5), 215–216
  collection, 150, 203
  coordination, 119, 120, 123, 131, 136,
    143, 145, 146, 155, 161(n2), 180, 220,
    231
  decisionmaking, 86
  dispute resolution, 194
  environmental, 11, 112
  of errors, 121
  of exclusion, 82, 83
  information, 48–49, 119, 120,
    122(fig.), 123, 131, 143, 145, 149,
    154, 155, 161(n2), 169, 177, 220, 231
  intermediate, 119, 122, 127, 131, 136,
    156
  long-term, 108(n2)
  maintenance, 117, 215. *See also* Costs,
    operation and maintenance;
    Maintenance, financing
  monitoring, 65
  operation and maintenance (O&M),
    27, 30(table), 32, 90, 110(n13), 116,
    117, 143, 151, 155, 170, 232(n2). *See
    also* Maintenance, financing
  opportunity, 14
  paid by users, 30, 70, 109(n10), 219,
    225, 228,

production, 122–123, 124(table), 131, 143, 154–155, 161(n2), 207. *See also* Costs, transformation
provision, 119–122, 124(table), 125(n8), 131, 143
recurrent, 30–31, 215, 229, 232(n2)
sanctioning and governance, 48
strategic, 48, 119, 120, 123, 143, 161(n2), 177, 231
transaction, 18, 47–48, 55, 60, 63, 64, 68, 71(n4), 112, 118–119, 120–121, 123, 160, 175, 183, 231
transformation, 112, 119, 120, 131, 136, 143, 220, 231. *See also* Costs, production
See also Financing; *under* Irrigation
Côte d'Ivoire, 205
Cotton, 64
Credit, 58, 131, 138
Crime, 35, 186–187, 211(n3)
Crosson, P. R., 71(n5)
Currency, 208

Dams, 31, 61, 152, 198, 221
Davey, Ken, 165
Debt, 4, 5, 6, 22(n3), 156
Decentralization, 20, 59, 71(n9), 163–175, 192
administrative, 168–175, 177
centralized, 172
classic, 165, 166
dimensions of, 166–168
meanings, 163–164, 165–166
and privatization, 206–209
public sector, 181
typology, 167
See also Centralization
Decisionmaking, 86, 163, 174, 209, 227, 229
Deconcentration, 166, 168, 219
Demand, 11, 12, 90, 91, 116, 181, 182, 183
consumer demand theory, 92
Democracy, 164, 207
Demsetz, Harold, 60–61
De Soto, Hernando, 186, 221

Development
agencies/ministries, 109(n12), 173–174
institutional approach to, 8–10, 232(n1)
postwar initiatives, 2–7
sustainable, 11, 14, 112, 213–231
theories, 22(n1)
See also Economic growth
Disasters, 116, 233(n9)
Discount rates, 11, 36, 93, 109(n11)
Disease, 11
Dishonesty, 58
Disputes, 180, 186, 194, 195–196, 204, 209, 221, 230. *See also* Conflict resolution
Distribution, 181–182, 199. *See also* Redistribution
Districting, 182–183
Donor agencies, 141–142, 156–159, 199, 215, 222, 227, 232(n5), 233(n9)

Eagle, Eva, 163
Eastern Europe, 4, 21
Economic growth, 12, 23(n4). *See also* Development
Economic theories, 43, 44, 118
Economies of scale, 19, 65, 97–102, 143, 154, 159, 177, 178, 180, 198, 203, 204
Education, 4, 53, 90, 101, 147, 160, 184, 197, 201, 211(n3). *See also* Schools
Efficiency, 14, 17, 54, 65, 91, 98, 102, 103, 111, 112–113, 115, 116–117, 117–118, 122, 138, 146, 151, 157, 158, 182, 183, 184, 185, 197, 208, 210
Ekeh, Peter, 72(n)
Elderly people, 55
Elections, 149, 180. *See also* Voting mechanisms
Electricity, 156
Elites, xxi
Employment. *See* Labor issues
Energy generation, 152
Environmental issues, 6, 10–11, 112, 198

Equity, 111, 112, 113–115, 116–117, 118, 132, 205–206. *See also* Fiscal equivalence
Erosion, 11
Errors, 12, 45, 68, 93, 120, 121, 160, 177
Estimates, 153. *See also* Benefits, estimating
Ethnic issues, 7, 184, 185
European Economic Community, 152
Evaluations, xix, 11, 13, 14, 93, 111–125, 131–132, 156, 197
    criteria, 16–18, 111, 112–123, 124(table), 124–125, 132, 138, 139, 144(table), 233(n5)
    criteria, intermediate, 112, 118–123, 124(table), 125, 144(table)
    of engineers, 57
    impact evaluation studies (IESs), 15–16
    for irrigation, 26, 144(table)
    See also under Institutional arrangements
Exclusion, 81, 82, 83. *See also* Benefits, nonexcludability of
Externalities, 10, 198, 211(n5)

Faiz, Asif, 228
Fallible learners, 45
Familism, 62. *See also* Kinship networks
Federalism, 195
    fiscal, 181
Fees. *See* User fees
Ferris, James M., 71(n9)
Financing, 16, 77, 108(n2), 170, 193, 202–206
    donor financing, 115, 152, 153
    general funds for, 149–150, 220
    recurrent requirements. *See r* coefficients
    See also under Infrastructure; Maintenance
Fiscal equivalence, 112, 114, 125(n2), 205, 206, 210. *See also* Equity
Floods, 14, 116, 145, 159
Foreign exchange, 4
Forests, 6, 23(n3), 109(n12)

Fraud, 123, 132. *See also* Corruption
Free-riding, xx, 48, 80, 96, 120, 125(n8), 131, 136, 138, 139, 151, 154, 159, 177,180, 185, 191, 216, 221. *See also* Benefits, nonexcludability of; *under* Incentives

Germany, 4, 152
GNP. *See* Gross national product
Governance, 48, 193–202. *See also under* Irrigation
Governing the Commons (E. Ostrom), xix–xx
Government Accounting Office. *See under* United States
Governments
    agencies/ministries, 36, 96, 121–122, 144(table), 159, 173–174, 202. *See also* Decentralization, administrative
    local, 168, 182, 183, 190, 194–195, 196, 197, 198, 201, 203, 204–205, 210(n2), 211(n3)
    national, 7, 67, 83, 141–161, 142(fig.), 161, 162(n5), 164, 168–175, 181, 185, 198, 200, 201, 202–203, 216, 217, 227, 229. *See also* Centralization
    officials, 96–97, 121, 143, 146–149, 150, 157, 164, 169–170, 174–175, 175(n2), 180, 185, 190, 194–195, 203, 204, 217, 223, 226, 232(n4)
Grants/loans, 76, 141, 152, 171, 198, 201, 203–204, 229
Gross national product (GNP), 3
Growenewegen, Peter, 202
Guyer, Jane, 151

Haggblade, Steven, 12
Haiti, 91–92
Harral, Clell G., 228
Harvard Project on American Indian Economic Development, 231(n)
Hayek, Friedrich A. von, 51
Hazell, 12
Health care, 4, 83, 147
Heller, Peter, 27
Highways. *See* Roads, trunk

Hirschman, Albert, 211(n4)
His Majesty's Government of Nepal. *See* Nepal
Holland, 2
Hong Kong, 4
Hossain, Mahabub, 23(n6)
Housing, 41(n6), 128, 129–130
Hunt, Robert C., 211(n7)
Hyden, Goran, 184

IESs. *See* Evaluations, impact evaluation studies
IIMI. *See* International Irrigation Management Institute
Illiteracy, 53
IMF. *See* International Monetary Fund
Imperialism, 156, 185
Imports, 4, 152
  duties, 150, 162(n6)
Import substitution, 4
Incentives, xv, 2, 9, 20, 22, 43, 44, 62, 65, 70, 82, 110(n18), 120, 143, 147, 156, 157, 168, 174, 191, 195, 196, 197, 203, 213, 214, 227, 230, 231, 232(n5)
  and allocation rules, 89
  and corruption, 147–148, 159, 160
  and free riding, 77–78, 81, 84, 85, 108(n4)
  and maintenance, 41(n2), 95, 209, 233(n9)
  and monitoring, 111
  and past errors, 45
  predicting, 105
  and rent seeking, 109(n12), 156, 217
  and shirking, 94, 108(n4), 145, 148
  types, 8
  to underestimate/overestimate benefits, 95
Income, 3, 4, 11, 12, 90, 92, 148, 152, 182, 205, 214
India, 10, 172
Individuals, xv, xx, 44–46
Indonesia, 53, 185. *See also* CARE/ Indonesia
Industrialization, 3
Industry concept, 104–105
Inequality, 7. *See also* Equity

Informal economies, 185, 186
Information, 17, 45–46, 91–92, 136, 160, 164
  asymmetries, 49–62, 63, 68, 70, 120, 123, 129, 201
  and budgets, 172
  local. *See* Information, time and place
  loss of, 53, 180, 187
  about preferences, 115–116, 183
  rules of thumb for, 93
  scientific knowledge, 50, 52–53, 131, 132, 121–122, 145, 149, 159, 170, 177, 180, 190, 197
  time and place, 29, 31, 49–55, 56, 67, 81, 98, 100, 121, 132, 145, 149, 160, 168, 169, 177, 180, 197, 218
  See also under Costs
Infrastructure
  adaptability, 17–18
  construction, 32–33, 41(n4), 75, 94, 98, 104, 144(table), 146, 155(table), 157, 162(n9), 220
  definition, 10
  design of, 29, 31, 35, 36, 41(n4), 43, 51, 53, 92, 98, 104, 110(n14), 146, 155(table), 156, 220, 225, 226
  deterioration, 29, 40, 41(n1), 75, 94, 103–104, 107, 112, 117, 160, 219, 220
  development role of, 1–22, 230
  development stages, 29–34
  financing, 32, 41(n4), 75–76, 82–83, 97, 113, 115, 128. *See also* Financing; Maintenance, financing
  importance of physical, 10–13
  inappropriate, 4, 112, 115
  joint use of, 84–90, 154, 224. *See also* Institutional arrangements, user groups
  multiple uses of, 90
  network features, 201
  new vs. existing, xx, 36, 59, 96, 232(n4)
  operation and maintenance, 33, 41(n4), 43, 144(table), 146, 147, 148, 162(n9), 219, 220. *See also* Costs,

operation and maintenance;
Maintenance
private facilities, 128–132, 133(table)
rural, 9, 12
self-governing, 232(n1)
size of, 83, 93, 94, 97, 102, 107, 139,
146, 155, 157, 224–230. *See also*
Irrigation, size of systems
social, 6–7
urban, 2
use of, 33–34, 41(n4), 76, 84–90, 95,
154, 224
See also Maintenance; Production;
Provision; Public facilities;
Sustainability
Inheritance rules, 65
Institutional arrangements, 87, 100,
103, 111, 112, 118, 119, 230–231
analyzing, 127–139
differentiated market, 127, 129–131,
130(fig.), 133(table), 135, 136,
137(table), 138, 227
evaluations, 131–132, 133(table),
135–136, 137(table), 138–139. *See
also* Evaluations
and local beneficiaries, 217
nested, 102, 177. *See also* Institutional
arrangements, polycentric
optimal, 9
polycentric, 20, 21, 161, 177–210,
179(fig.), 231. *See also*
Polycentricity
simple market, 127, 128–129,
129(fig.), 132, 133(table), 136,
137(table), 138, 227
user groups, 125(n8), 127, 134–135,
134(fig.), 136, 137(table), 138, 139,
163, 219, 221
See also Centralization;
Decentralization; Institutions
Institutions, 6, 18
acephalous, 191
analysis, 18, 19–20
changes, 166, 167, 214, 219, 233(n6).
See also Reforms
counteracting, 55, 58, 60–61, 62–65,
76, 132

financial, 129, 130
indigenous, 7, 61, 185, 187, 190, 191–
192, 221, 222–223
institutional rational choice (IRC),
xx–xxi
See also Institutional arrangements
Insurance companies, 55, 57, 59, 230
Interests, 86, 88, 216. *See also*
Preferences
International Irrigation Management
Institute (IIMI), 30–31, 222
International Monetary Fund (IMF), 2,
7
Investments, xv, 1, 4, 8, 11, 12, 13,
23(n4), 34, 37, 40, 138, 163, 197,
214, 225, 228
underinvestments/overinvestments,
84, 138, 151, 160, 213
IRC. *See* Institutions, institutional
rational choice
Irrigation, xx, 10, 11, 12, 25, 26, 33, 52,
53, 61, 64, 89, 95, 98, 100–101, 106,
107, 152–153, 162(n9), 187, 221
associations, 56–57
costs, 30–31, 34, 109(n11), 151
farmer-managed, 172, 188–189,
211(n7), 221
governance, 54–55, 71(n5)
life of systems, 93
ministry officials for, 96–97
Philippine systems, 30–31, 55, 56–57,
87–88, 145–146, 170, 185. *See also*
Zanjera system
size of systems, 134–135, 137(table),
139, 144(table), 147, 185, 188–189,
224
See also Water supply
Italy, 2

Jagannathan, Vijay, 64, 146–147
Jamaica, 5, 35–36, 53
Japan, 2, 7, 152, 185
Jenkins, Jerry, 172
Jones, Charles O., xix
Judicial systems, 186–187, 194, 196,
197, 208, 209, 211(n9), 227. *See also*
Legal issues

Jurisdictions, 179–180, 193, 198, 201, 205, 206, 229

Kalt, Joseph P., 232(n1)
Kenya, 27, 197
Kinship networks, 62–65, 66
Korea, 4, 30, 162(n9)
Krueger, Anne O., 96
Kuwait, 152

Labor issues, 32, 33, 35, 97, 98, 197
    community labor, 61, 69–70, 99–100, 114, 135, 189, 223
    manual labor, 95
    rural nonfarm employment, 11–12
Landau, Martin, 163, 174
Latin America, 16
LDCs. *See* Less-developed countries
Leases, 103
Legal issues, 67–68, 186–187, 193–195, 209. *See also* Judicial systems
Leibenstein, Harvey, 61
Lele, Sharachchandra M., 12
Leonard, David K., 167
Less-developed countries (LDCs), 1, 3, 6, 21
Levi, Margaret, 108(n6)
Levine, Gilbert, 54
Literacy, 193
Loans. *See* Grants/loans
Logrolling, 150–151

Macroeconomic policy, 150, 181
Mahaweli Development Program, 152–153
Maintenance, 14, 16–17, 33, 70, 158, 183, 228, 229
    collective approach to, 86, 95, 104, 107, 110(n18), 136, 219
    by contract, 101–102
    emergency, 33, 36–37
    financing, 25–29, 40, 41(n2), 59, 75, 117, 228. *See also* Costs, operation and maintenance
    hypothetical cases, 37–38, 39
    and investment decision, 37
    levels of, 36, 38–39

and multiple decisionmakers, 40, 43
    routine, 28, 36–37, 101, 233(n9)
    and single owner-users, 34–39, 43, 110(n18)
    See also Infrastructure, operation and maintenance; *under* Incentives; Roads
Malawi, 99–100
Mandates, 198, 201
Marchetti, Peter, 22(n2)
Markets, 19, 83, 118, 155, 183, 207, 208. *See also* Institutional arrangements, differentiated market; Institutional arrangements, simple market
Marshall, Dale Rogers, 167
Marshall Plan, 4
Matrices, 105
Mawhood, Philip, 165, 166
Measuring, 76, 159
    problems, 90–96
Mellor, John W., 12
Methodology, xv. *See also* Analyses
Mexico, 31
Migration, rural-urban, 35
Minorities, 193
Mobility, 183, 184
Modernization, 3
Moe, Terry, xxi, 59
Monitoring, 48, 60–61, 62, 65, 71(n8), 85, 95, 111, 114, 128, 129–130, 145, 146, 157, 159, 183, 221, 223, 225, 230
Monopolies, 98, 208
Moral hazard, 48, 55, 59, 63, 70, 123, 132
Moran, Emilio, 109(n12)
Moynihan, Daniel Patrick, 41(n2)
Mu, Xinming, 91
Multiplier effects, 11
Musgrave, Richard A., 202

National Irrigation Administrations (NIAs), 56–57, 145–146, 162(n9), 171, 175(n2)
Natural resources, 6, 79
Nepal, 11, 31, 69–70, 140(n5), 172, 185, 188–189, 197, 222
Nepotism, 7, 65–68

New institutional economics, 18, 43–44
NGOs. *See* Organizations,
    nongovernmental
NIAs. *See* National Irrigation
    Administrations
Nicaragua, 22(n2)
Nigeria, 22(n3), 64, 200
Niger River, 200
Nonexcludability. *See under* Benefits
Norms, 46, 61

O&M costs. *See* Costs, operation and
    maintenance
Oates, Wallace, 181, 182
Obligations, 66. *See also* Responsibility
Officials. *See under* Governments
Opportunism, 46, 55, 63, 67, 68, 111,
    113, 132, 180
    types of, 48, 70
    See also Corruption
Organizations
    donor, 141–142. *See also* Donor
        agencies
    nongovernmental (NGOs), 190, 191–
        192, 220, 222–223, 229
    relationships among, 190
    voluntary, 79–80
Ostrom, Elinor, xix
Ostrom, V., 183

Pakistan, 10, 31, 101
Parma system, 69–70
Patrons/clients, 170
Paul, Samuel, 211(n4)
PDAP. *See* Philippines, Provincial
    Development Assistance Program
Peru, 186–187, 221
Philippines, 61, 140(n5), 151, 195
    Provincial Development Assistance
        Program (PDAP), 172–174, 196
    See also Irrigation, Philippine
        systems; Zanjera system
Point Four Program, 2–3
Policy issues, 218–230
Policy studies, xix
Polycentricity, 178–184, 208, 220
    concerns about, 192–206

in developing countries, 184–192,
    217, 221
sources of, 185–190
See also Institutional arrangements,
    polycentric
Popkin, Samuel L., xxi, 58
Poverty/poor people, 5, 6, 17, 23(n6),
    114, 138, 153, 182, 193, 196
Power, 68, 70, 97, 164, 172
Pradhan, Naresh C., 69, 70
Preferences, 78, 80–81, 86, 115, 131, 136,
    149, 168, 172, 180, 183, 201, 217,
    228. *See also* Interests
Prices, 4, 57, 89, 113, 117, 132, 183
Principals/agents, 43, 61–62, 71(n9),
    201, 203
Private sector, 19, 57–58, 77, 103, 197,
    199, 227
    and maintenance decisions, 34–39
    privatization, 206–209, 210, 226
    and shirking, 60–61
Problem solving, 44, 45
Production, 133(table), 135, 136,
    137(table), 143–148, 168–169, 197,
    209, 210, 218, 229
    infrastructure attributes affecting,
        97–105
    and provision, 73–76, 102, 106, 156,
        178, 183–184, 208
    See also under Costs
Productivity, 4, 12, 23(n4), 66, 146, 172,
    196–197, 214, 215, 225
    social, 27
Property rights, 128–129, 208, 227
Proprietary funds, 108(n2)
Provision, 133(table), 136, 137(table),
    142–143, 148–151, 175, 177, 182,
    198, 208, 218, 226, 228, 229
    infrastructure attributes affecting,
        76–97, 106
    See also under Costs; Production
Public facilities, 9–10, 43
    beneficiaries of, 14, 16
    See also Infrastructure
Public finance, 181
Publics, 199
Public schools, xxi

Public sector, 19, 27, 39–40, 74, 77, 79–80, 82, 98, 102, 103, 104–105, 106, 119, 120, 161, 181, 197, 209, 210, 221, 229
Public services, 57–58, 67, 101, 102, 103, 104–105, 181

Ramakrishnan, Subramaniam, 27
Ranches, 109(n12)
R&D. *See* Research and development
Rationality, 9
    bounded, 44, 45–46
    See also Institutional rational choice
r coefficients, 27, 28(table)
Redistribution, 17, 111, 112, 114–115, 116, 118, 132, 138, 151, 153, 182, 202–203, 205, 206, 210, 210(n2)
    of authority, 164, 166
    See also Equity
Reforms, 164, 216, 221, 228, 233(n6). *See also* Institutions, changes
Rent seeking, 96–97, 109(n12), 115, 120, 131, 136, 138, 140(n7), 155, 156, 160, 177, 203, 216, 217, 218, 220, 228, 229, 233(n9)
Repairs, 33, 158, 189. *See also* Maintenance
Repetto, Robert, 10, 151
Reputations, 136
Research and development (R&D), 52
Resource mobilization, 70, 116, 118, 220, 225, 227, 228
Responsibility, 81, 85, 86, 90, 131, 138, 193, 198, 201
Revenue instruments, 202–204, 210(n2), 214–215. *See also* Taxation; User fees
Rice, 50, 162(n9), 189
Richards, Paul, 50
Risks, 13, 48, 65, 97, 129, 130
Rivalry, 88, 108(n7)
Roads, 11, 14, 25, 28, 32, 33–34, 82, 83, 88, 93, 95, 98, 106, 139, 159, 201, 230
    feeder, 5, 27, 35–36

    maintenance of, xx, 26, 41(n2), 86, 101–102, 107, 110(n19), 117, 227–228, 229
    trunk, 27, 139, 156, 157, 158
Roell, Peter B.R., 12
Rome, 62
Rules, 20, 44, 46, 54, 79, 86, 89, 95, 113, 123, 128, 131, 135, 138, 140(n5), 177–178, 185, 186, 191, 193, 195, 209, 211(n5), 220, 222, 223

Sahel countries, 79, 199–200
Salaries, 67, 147, 148, 160, 204, 205
Sanctions, 48, 138, 140(n6), 191, 223
Sandler, Todd, 88
Sanitation projects, 90
Savas, E. S., 206
Scaling up/down, 222
Schools, 83, 169. *See also* Education
Science. *See* Information, scientific knowledge
Scott, James, 66
Scudder, Thayer, 10
Second best, theory of, 117–118
Self-interest, xx
Settlers' associations, 186
Sewage treatment, 184, 198, 201, 211(n5)
Shirking, 46, 48, 60–61, 65, 70, 71(n8), 111, 113, 123, 132, 146, 151, 155, 160, 177, 215, 218. *See also under* Incentives
Side-payments, 146–147, 148, 161(n3), 169
Sierra Leone, 50
Singapore, 4
Siy, Robert, 191–192
Social capital, 6, 190, 191, 197, 209, 220, 232(n3)
Social welfare, 14, 113
South Korea. *See* Korea
Soviet Union, 3, 4, 7
Squire, F. A., 50
Sri Lanka, 151, 152–153
Stone, Roger, 22(n3), 190, 222
Structural adjustment, 7, 22(n3)

Subsidies, 41(n2), 47, 109(n12), 114–115,
    118, 153, 162(n9), 205
Subtractability of service flow, 88–90,
    107, 108(n7), 113, 117, 224
Sudan, 63, 64, 164
Summers, Lawrence H., 11
Sustainability, 1–2, 13–18, 21, 106, 111,
    113, 116, 154, 158, 170, 203, 209,
    210, 213, 214, 215, 218, 231
    definitions, 13–14, 15
    See also Development, sustainable
Sweden, 152
Switzerland, 195

Taiwan, 4, 54, 162(n9), 185
Taxation, 81, 84, 96, 108(n6), 109(n12),
    113, 116, 149–150, 151, 154, 160,
    198, 202–203, 205, 212(n10), 216,
    228–229
    avoidance of, 82, 114
    tax farming, 62
    value-added taxes (VATs), 150,
    162(n7)
Technology, 4, 16, 35, 52, 69
Telephone service, 67, 98
Tendler, Judith, 157, 158
Thailand, 30
Third World, 2, 4
Thomson, James, 79
Tiebout, Charles, 183–184
Time issues, 12–13, 77, 85, 93. *See also*
    Information, time and place
Tollbooths, 83
Tourism, 35
Truman, Harry S, 2
Trust, 63
Tunisia, 83

Uncertainties, 43, 46, 47, 49, 94, 130,
    138
Unions, xxi

United States, 5, 7, 41(n2), 108(n2), 195,
    211(n3), 227
    Agency for International
    Development (USAID), 13, 26, 83,
    141, 157, 158, 162(n9), 171, 173,
    232(n2)
    equipment made by, 157
    Government Accounting Office,
    232(n2)
Uphoff, Norman T., 31
Urban areas, 2, 35, 41(n7), 100. *See also*
    Capital cities
USAID. *See* United States, Agency for
    International Development
User fees, 83, 113, 116, 117, 151, 202,
    203, 228

Values, 8
VATs. *See* Taxation, value-added taxes
Voting mechanisms, 78, 80–81, 84, 88,
    135. *See also* Elections

Wade, Robert, 147, 197
Warren, Robert, 183
Water supply, 10, 11, 25, 27, 52, 53, 82–
    83, 89, 90, 91–92, 98, 99–100,
    109(n10). *See also* Irrigation
Weather, 117
Western Europe, 1, 3–4, 7
West Germany, 152
Whittington, Dale, 91
Williamson, Oliver, 47, 103
Willingness to pay (WTP), 90, 91–92,
    151
Winkler, Donald R., 71(n9)
World Bank, 2, 7, 11, 13–14, 15–16,
    23(n3), 26, 92, 94, 141, 152
World Food Program, 153
WTP. *See* Willingness to pay

Zanjera system, 61, 87–88, 140(n8), 185,
    191–192, 195, 197, 209, 221–222, 227
Zimbabwe, 10